D1348259

# CONTENTS

# Introduction

Each time I set out to write an introduction to one of my father's books, I refer first to the transcription of our conversation which formed the basis of my film 'Time and the Priestleys', to glean any useful comments which might give a handy insight into his views. So now I have been looking through the section about the First World War, and found something very telling. I can see, looking back, that I sensed the whole topic of World War I might be difficult, so we didn't plunge into it too deeply.

I asked about his volunteering, and even why he had volunteered, but he didn't hear that question, but said: 'I joined up in September I think, it was long before conscription came; I was a volunteer, and I've forgotten a great deal of all that now I must confess, the early days of being a soldier. I never thought I was a very good soldier, but still I never ran away.'

We then moved on to the question of whether he had continued writing during the war, and though he said he been writing all the time, there is no evidence of this, beyond his letters home.

Later in our conversation we talked about the time leading up to the war and then got to the war itself, and he said 'I spent four or five years of my life being a soldier, which is something entirely different from what I planned. I didn't particularly care for the military life very much, but on the other hand I didn't absolutely rebel against it; I felt I ought to accept it and see what happened.'

I asked about his becoming an officer, and said 'You had been out in France already?'

'Oh sure, yes, yes.'

'In the ranks?.'

'I'd been wounded,' he said. 'I'd been buried alive ... all sorts of stuff. We wore those gilt stripes on our sleeves. There were two kinds - one for service, the other for wounds. I had three ... What's the time? .. I think we'll pack it in for the time being.'

And so we stopped, and that was all he told me about the war.

Looking back I sense that he didn't want to talk about it. He never had.

When I joined the army for my national service, he would sometimes tell army stories, but never about fighting, never about the dreadful experience of the trenches; indeed the only time he wrote about that was when he had rediscovered the box of letters from the Great War, or perhaps decided to face the memories, and wrote about the war in his book of memoirs, 'Margin Released'.

But the letters stand on their own, as the direct experience of his time in the army, or at least that part of it he chose to share with his family. They only cover the first two years, when he was away from home and then away from England, starting with the train journey south on 23 September 1914, and ending in the summer of 1916, when he got his 'Blighty' and was repatriated for a long period of convalescence.

How or why these particular letters survived we will never know. They are written to his small family in Bradford, sometimes addressed to individuals, more often just to 'Dear People'. The people were his father, Jonathan, a school master (and there survives one letter from Jonathan to JB in France); his stepmother, Amy, who effortlessly replaced his real mother after her death when he was only two - he always called Amy 'mother'; his half-sister Winnie, his only sibling; and his paternal grandparents, aunts and uncles.

In the early letters he describes places and activities with occasional comments on the military life; great emphasis on the links with home, especially the important parcels which supplemented the meagre rations and supplied him with his vital tobacco, all of which he paid for from his army pay.

Why did he volunteer so early? He worked at this puzzle himself and concluded he was responding to 'a challenge to what we felt was our untested manhood'. I would put it slightly differently. I believe young men need adventure, and this adventure must take them from their familiar surroundings to a place which will be peculiarly their own, either of their own choosing or supplied by circumstance. We see it today, when entered into in the right spirit, in the gap year.

His adventure was one he shared with too many of his generation, and his experiences were in no way exceptional, but he was a young man who had decided early in his life that he would be a writer and this adds to the immediacy of these letters, even though he was not writing for the public but sharing his feelings with his family, in fact he urges his father at one point not to show his letter to the press. So these are private letters, but to what extent he censored his thoughts and only wrote what he felt would be palatable to his father, readers must judge for themselves. Certainly there was censorship in France, but he found ways to express his views on the army quite forcefully.

We have to imagine him crouched in a muddy trench, damp, cold and filthy, desperately scribbling away with a pencil on such paper as he could find. Sometimes the odd word is completely illegible, too deformed by a fold in the paper, and his writing was never easy to read; perhaps this is why he took to the typewriter, hammering away with his two forefingers.

It is fascinating to compare these early writings by an embryo author communicating directly with his family, with the articles for various papers and journals, and the text of his Second World War broadcasts, the 'Postscripts', a conscious part of the propaganda effort to enhance public morale. He described his writing, and broadcasting, during the second World War as 'what he had to do', in other words his public duty, just as his service as a soldier was his duty in the First World War.

The letters end in summer 1916; no more have survived, beyond two postcards from Devon. The only remaining writing directly about the war before 'Margin Released' is 'The Town Major of Miraucourt' written in 1929. It is a fascinating and unusual story, which develops from the early section based on his actual experience to a world of literary imagination, and in this it echoes his journey from the raw experience of war which lives so vividly in the letters, to his inner thoughts and reflections, his literary life. To quote John Braine's famous remark: 'The human being, John Boynton Priestley, was killed during the 1914 War. He was born again as a writer. He wasn't a man who wrote: He was - and is - all writer, as no one else before or since'.

In 'The Town Major we can almost see the transition'. Returning from the War, he spent three years at Cambridge, before settling in London, where he began to establish a reputation as a new writer with a series of essays, reviews, literary biographies and critical articles, and an impressive number of books, seventeen in eight years to 1930. By that time he had achieved great success with his fiction, allowing him to enter the Theatre with no more financial worries, but no less inner pressure to be endlessly at the typewriter, pouring out the words and the work. Was he trying to allay the ghosts of the war that haunted him throughout his life? He never slept well; perhaps the ghosts were waiting in the dark. In an essay 'The Dark Hours', published in 1928, he described for once an experience from World War 1 when, utterly exhausted, he slept peacefully for eighteen hours, but went on to describe the solitude he often felt when he woke during the night.

'English Journey' marked another turn and he now became a respected social commentator, a role traceable through to the end of this book. A path is detectable, from the interior world of literature, the often cosy world of the light essay, into the more open world of the novel. Remembering his opinion that the central task of the novel is to 'show us Man in the society he has created', it is easy to see a path leading from the fictional account of society to the non-fictional examination of society itself, and on to the position of one society in the world, reflected in an increased interest in world affairs.

If war did not appear inevitable in 1913, it seemed increasingly so after the rise of the Fascists and Nazis, and the excerpts from articles and the letters to his oldest friend, Edward Davison, who had moved to America, trace the evolution of his thought and the path leading to the 'Postscripts'. While galvanising the people to unite and defeat the enemy, the 'Postscripts' also treat the war as an opportunity to change life in a way that had failed after WW1. The answer was not communism, which he held responsible for the rise of fascism, but the kind of socialism he had grown up with in Bradford, where everyone has an equal chance for a decent life and contributes to the community without the bugbears of privilege, elitism and the negative class system.

The Labour landslide in the 1945 election and the social revolution that followed including the introduction of the National Health

Service, perhaps the Labour movement's finest and most enduring monument, arguably owe something to those enormously popular Postscript broadcasts. In the dark days of 1940 and 1941, almost alone among those urging every sacrifice for victory, my father was also demanding a better post-war world for those making those sacrifices.

In the 1950s and 1960s, at a time when most men his age might have settled for the pipe and slippers, my father embarked on a final campaign against nuclear weapons and the arms race which, in his view, the acronym of Mutually Assured Destruction admirably summed up. In this, as in so much else in his life, he spoke for the people who had no public voice of their own.

*Tom Priestley, June 2008.*

# *Editor's note*

My intention in compiling this book has been, wherever possible, to let John Boynton Priestley speak for himself, editing his work only to produce a coherent narrative and limiting the linking sections to the necessary context, so that, as far as is possible, the story is told in Priestley's own words, not mine.

I have drawn on Priestley's letters - primarily from the First World War I, but also including some from the eve of the Second - interwoven with his later autobiographical account Margin Released; the newspaper and magazine articles that this most prolific of authors produced in abundance; the scripts written for radio broadcast to a mass audience; and the polished prose of his literary work.

As Priestley himself was keenly aware, the unpublished First World War letters were often written in haste and are much cruder than his normal majestic prose, but they have been edited only to omit the messages for friends and family members, and some of the requests for tobacco, parcels, etc., and the grumbles about food, conditions and Army 'bull', common to the letters of virtually all serving soldiers in all eras, but which can soon become repetitive and wearisome.

The letters, scripts, books and articles may be disparate but they form a coherent whole, tracing the personal odyssey of one of the Twentieth Century's greatest literary figures from the callow youth who went willingly to war, to the seventy year-old man who waged a very different campaign in an attempt to outlaw the nuclear weapons he abhorred.

Much had changed in the course of that life's journey, but Priestley's humanity, compassion, sense of fair play and justice, and the love for all the people of his island nation shine through in almost every piece he ever wrote. He was a literary giant, but unlike some of his peers and modern successors, he never patronised or ignored those who lived and worked in less rarified atmospheres, and in him, ordinary Britons never had a more gifted nor more committed champion, in peace or war.

*Neil Hanson, June 2008.*

# PART I
# The Great War

# Chapter 1
# The canyon smoking between them

*On 7 September 1914, just six days short of his twentieth birthday, John Boynton Priestley volunteered to go to war. On the face of it, this was an extraordinary decision for a young man of liberal-socialist views, who little more than a year earlier had written a firmly anti-war piece in a left wing periodical,* The Bradford Pioneer.

War appears to be in the air at present; it is quite impossible to get away from the topic. Our newspapers are hammering at the question in their usual eloquent manner and all our reviews are thirsting for the blood, not of minor poets, but of continental enemies. I am being told daily that a great war is inevitable, and I always emphatically state that I don't believe it. Nor do I!

Those who believe in war can be divided into two classes: the first are the people who gain a great deal by the advent of a war - the professional war-makers. The other individuals are worse: they are weak in the head — war-scarers. In every European country there are war-scarers who feel sure that their country is about to be invaded. And at last, along with the war-makers, these war-scarers succeed in making a war, and then they turn to their sensible neighbours and triumphantly cry "Didn't I tell you so." So all the Great Powers are building huge fleets and equipping and training large armies: why? – for protection. All for purposes of protection. Who is going to do the attacking or invading? And if armies and navies grow much more, there will be nothing left for them to protect. It reminds me of the story of an Irish servant, who, on being told by his master to build a wall round a very valuable old ruin, built the wall with the stones of the ruin...

If I had my way, war would be abolished tomorrow. But I am not hard-hearted. To those who think that war is necessary for the advancement of the human race, I would give a scythe – individuals of this type would be gathered from all the various nations and herded together in a an enclosure. I would then ask them to mow each other down with their scythes and feel proud that they were doing it in the cause of human progress. For those who like the picturesque side of war, I would organise a series of fancy dress balls and cycling carnivals, always ending with a display of fireworks.[1]

*Born in Bradford in 1894, JB Priestley – christened 'John' but always known as 'Jack' – had left school at sixteen and was persuaded by his schoolmaster father to start work as a clerk at a wool firm in the city's beautiful, wrought iron and glass, Swan Arcade. In his spare time Priestley wrote, because already his real ambition was to be a writer. He sent short articles to various publications, and took an unpaid position writing articles for* The Bradford Pioneer. *His column, 'Round the Hearth', carried a health warning: 'It must be distinctly understood that "Round the Hearth" is pre-eminently a personal feature, so that the opinions expressed therein are not necessarily those of the paper itself. Letters dealing with subjects treated in "Round the Hearth" are invited, and should be addressed to: "J.B.P. c/o Bradford Pioneer".' What response his anti-war article drew from the readers has not been recorded*

*The wool textile 'capital' of Britain, Bradford was a cultured and cosmopolitan city in those days, with a large German-Jewish community, and Priestley's German contacts may have influenced his choice of destination when he went travelling in Europe in the spring and early summer of 1914.*

I chose June for my fortnight's holiday, 'wangling' – a term I did not know then, but it was rushing to meet me – another free pass, this time from Hull to Holland. I stayed in Amsterdam a day or two, staring at the Rembrandts and Vermeers. My luggage on my back, I set out from Cologne on a walking tour of the Rhine, not the river I have often seen since but another one, lost, gone.

I bought and smoked one of those yard-long pipes, still in common use then, not manufactured for the tourist trade; I stayed in tiny inns, buried among leaves, swimming in green air; I strummed on pianos in low-ceilinged back rooms for peasant tenors and basses who put down pipes even larger than mine, calling for more rounds of wine and beer. I had a roaring good time, not in this world, perhaps not even in that other which was ending; I suspect now I was having a walking tour in picaresque and romantic literature.

I came back by way of Belgium, staying in Brussels for one-franc-fifty in a rather sinister decaying hotel, where I slept uneasily in that enormous bed, itself uneasy on the creaking floor, which looms in so many old travellers' tales, Uppsala to Granada. The city itself, though, was still leafy and comparatively small then, an operetta kind of capital, where I could exchange the few gold coins I had left for superb food and drink, and where, most suitably, I saw and heard for the first time Der Rosenkavalier.

When I sailed for Hull, late at night, late in June, later still in an epoch, I watched the lights of Europe retreat to a glimmer and then vanish from sight for ever. I ought to have heard a vast muted orchestra and Ewig, ewig – but I knew no Mahler then. Those lights, that shore, really were gone for ever. The Europe I left that night sank into history, banishing itself from immediate experience as my Atlantis had done when the sea sucked it down.[2]

During the first eight months of 1914, one might say, I was running round at a standstill. I was cramming the hours with experience, tasting this and gulping down that, widening my acquaintance, making a few new friends; but in the centre of all this nothing much was happening. My life was like a roundabout with the gilded cars and cockerels flashing by, the bray of the organ, the drums and cymbals, never silent, while the man in the middle wipes his hands on an oily rag and yawns.

I have never been much of a planner, but at this time I was not visited by even the ghost of a plan. Not only did I not know which way I was going, I never even looked to see if there were any signposts, any paths. I had not the least notion what I was going to do, and now – or so it seems, if memory is not cheating – at last nobody, not even my father, asked me... What did I think I was doing anyhow, in this spring and summer of 1914? But the self that survived the War, putting such questions almost angrily, twenty-five-year-old to nineteen-year-old, could not supply the answers himself; and he was out of touch with that Bradford youth; the canyon smoking between them was too wide, too deep, also too new.

Now, so far removed that twenty-five and nineteen seem to be joined, the gap bridged, I can bring to each question the same answer: I believe I know now what was happening that summer. I believe I did nothing but enjoy what could be enjoyed because we were soon to be at war. Consciously of course we never entertained a thought of it; but deep in the unconscious, which has its own time and a wider now than consciousness knows, already the war was on, a world ending.[3]

*War with Germany was declared on 4 August 1914, 'when the newsboys were running and shouting every day and all day'* [4]

Oddly enough, I can remember nothing about this day, which was a Tuesday, although I have a sharp recollection of the evening before, that of Bank Holiday Monday. That part of Bradford where I lived then, had its annual fair at that season – it was called Manningham Tide. And I remember going to this fair with a friend, a young artist, and explaining the international situation to him on our way home. It was the last time I ever knew the glitter and jangle of Manningham Tide – it vanished, and with it vanished a whole world. I remember, too, how hot it was during those first days of August 1914. My feet used to swell and ache in my stiff Brogue shoes – it never seems to be as hot as that now.

A queer chap I knew had insisted, that summer, on telling my fortune, by cards, and had told me, earnestly, that I was about to change my whole way of living; that often I would be in great danger, that my life would never be the same again after all this strange, desperate journey. And I didn't believe a word of it. But it was all true. On August 4th war was declared, on the 5th Kitchener became Secretary of State for War, and on the 7th he appealed for the first hundred thousand men.

Already, as I went whirling round the switchbacks to the tune of "Hitchy Koo" the three blind Fates were cutting the threads of a million destinies. Half my generation was doomed, and at the fair I was seeing for the last time many a face I had known since I was a child. Well, there it was, this change in my whole way of living, as the fortune-teller said, a change indeed, from one world to another.[5]

*Priestley at once decided to answer Kitchener's call and volunteer, but his family were on holiday at the seaside, and he waited for them to return before doing so. He did not record their reaction, but it is hardly likely that his father and his stepmother (his natural mother had died when her son was just two years old) would have been pleased by their son's determination to go to war. A fiery character and a lifelong socialist 'in the looser and warmer tradition of English socialism'[6] as his son described it many years later - in the city that had been the birthplace of the Independent Labour Party, Priestley's father, Jonathan, must have been aghast at his son's eagerness to fight.*

*No record remains of what Jonathan Priestley said in a vain attempt to dissuade his son from enlisting; it is tempting to search for echoes in the views expressed by 'Uncle Nick' in Priestley's* Lost Empires, *a novel about a theatre company on the brink of the First World War, but Priestley himself never acknowledged any parallels between the fictional character and his father.*

As soon as we were in the war – though we didn't know how far in we were or what was really happening, Uncle Nick ended the act with what he called 'children's party conjuring', pulling out of a tube of paper a lot of flags – the 'big flag finish', he called it, jeering at himself – and always concluding with a gigantic Union Jack, which brought more applause than all the clever illusions put together. 'We'll find ourselves in a madhouse soon, lad,' he muttered to me as we came off, one night. 'I can feel it coming. Bloody idiots!'

I think he damned the war, there right at the very beginning, because he saw it as another, bigger, more impressive and demanding performer, a rival top of the bill. When the newsboys came running and shouting along the streets – a sight and sound I'd almost forgotten until I made myself remember those August weeks – I would sometimes buy a paper, but Uncle Nick never did, though, if we were together, he'd always contrive to learn the latest news from me while still appearing to be aloof or contemptuous. Never an admirer of ordinary people at any time, he was now savage in his scorn.

'Just notice the way they're taking it, lad. Like a free trip to Blackpool or Margate. It's a brand-new bit of excitement at last. They lead such dreary lives in their Land of Hope and Glory... that they think a war, so long as it's somewhere, is a treat. And they'll display their patriotism by throwing stones at German bands and looting pork-butchers' for free sausages: It's a nasty excitement too, lad. I can feel it in the audiences. They don't want to settle down, look and listen properly, enjoy themselves like civilised people. If one of us broke our bloody neck, they'd be delighted, the mood they're in...

There came through the open window the sound of confused cheering, probably from the pub down the road. 'There they go,' said Uncle Nick. 'All cheering and beering. Hurray for the Navy! Hurray for Kitchener – who only knows how to beat fuzzy-wuzzies and Boer farmers! Three cheers for the red, white and blue!'...

One afternoon, when Doris Tingley was with us, we had to stop the car at a crossroads to let a battalion of territorials, headed by a band, march past us. Doris cried, and was furious. 'Every dam' time I hear one of those bands and see all these boys marching, I can't stop myself crying. I ought to put my head in a bag. Crying!'

'You've hardly started yet, Doris,' said Uncle Nick. 'There's going to be plenty of crying before we're out of this. God's truth-look at all the dust they've kicked up.'

When we were out of the dust and had come to streets again, we stopped near a hoarding. 'See that poster, Richard. Kitchener wants you. What d'you say to that, lad?'

I didn't say anything. Not then.[7]

*Whatever his family and his peers may have thought, Jack Priestley had inherited something of his father's stubbornness, and his resolve to enlist was unshakeable, even though, in his haste, he left his friends behind. None of them were quite so eager for the fray then, though almost to a man, they enlisted in the 'Bradford Pals' when it was formed the following year. Priestley, the man who had written an anti-war article only twelve months before, now could not wait to volunteer. Almost half a century later, in 1962, he offered an explanation for that unexpected and apparently impulsive decision, when he made his first real attempt to write about his war experiences in his autobiography,* Margin Released.

Early in September I joined, like a chump, the infantry – to be precise, the Duke of Wellington's West Riding Regiment, known in some circles as 'The Havercake Lads', in others as 'The Dirty Duke's'... I often asked myself why I had joined the Army. The usual explanations were no good. I was not hot with patriotic feeling; I did not believe that Britain was in any real danger. I was sorry for 'gallant little Belgium' but did not feel she was waiting for me to rescue her. The legend of Kitchener, who pointed at us from every hoarding, had never captured me. I was not under any pressure from public opinion, which had not got to work on young men as early as that; the white feathers came later. I was not carried to the recruiting office in a herd rush of chums, nobody thinking, everybody half-plastered; I went alone. (Most of my friends joined elsewhere and later, when the local 'Pals' Battalion' was formed – and in July 1916, on the Somme, that battalion might have been dry moorland grass to which somebody put a match.) I was not simply swapping jobs; though the office bored me, life in the Army certainly did not attract me, and for some years I had regarded with contempt those lads who wanted to wear a uniform and be marched about. This was no escape to freedom and independence; I may not have known much about military life, but I was not so green. And I certainly did not see myself as a hero, whose true stature would be revealed by war; that had never been one of my illusions. What is left then to supply a motive? Nothing, I believe now, that was rational and conscious.

Remember that for months before, as I have already suggested, though enjoying myself, perhaps almost feverishly, I had come to a standstill, refusing to make any plan, even to consider the future, really because in that other time scale of the unconscious my world had already ended. I was kept from making any move by some mysterious prompting from the dark of my mind. And now, prompted again, there was a move I had to make. I went at a signal from the unknown... There came, out of the unclouded blue of that summer, a challenge that was almost like a conscription of the spirit, little to do really with King and Country and flag-waving and hip-hip-hurrah, a challenge to what we felt was our untested manhood. Other men, who had not lived as easily as we had, had drilled and marched and borne arms – couldn't we? Yes, we too could leave home and soft beds and the girls to soldier for a spell, if there was some excuse for it, something at least to be defended. And here it was.[8]

*Despite his explanation, it is possible that the almost seventy year-old Priestley was embarrassed by the youthful naiveté of his younger self and was seeking to put a gloss on his motives for enlisting. Perhaps, like so many others, he was more caught up in the excitement and patriotic fervour of the time than he later cared to admit, even to himself, a state of mind scathingly dismissed by 'Uncle Nick' in* Lost Empires.

'You're what?'

'Enlisting. Joining Kitchener's New Army.'

He put his cigar down. 'Lad, you must be out of your bloody mind. Army? Why should you go and join any army? I'll give you a dozen good reasons why you shouldn't. Now just give me one good reason why you should.'

'It's hard to explain,' I began slowly.

'It's impossible to explain, unless you're going up the pole-barmy... What you really believe, even if you don't say so, is what all these other silly buggers believe - that it's going to be a kind of picnic, a few months of marching and cheering and flag-waving, then Germany'll be done for and you'll be all back home, heroes with medals to show.'

'No, I don't think –'

'Just listen to me,' he shouted. 'And get this into your head, lad. I'm not like all these people. I've been to Germany. I've played Berlin, Hamburg, Munich, Frankfort – and I've kept my eyes and ears open. I know the Germans. They've built up a military machine that'll make you lot look like so many tin soldiers. They may take Paris – I don't know – but what I do know is that they're going to take a hell of a lot of beating.

All over in a few months! They're all talking like school kids. This war isn't going to last months, it's going to last years and years – and every year it'll get worse. You're asking to be put into a bloody mincing machine, lad... We're in for the biggest bloody massacre of all time. And you can't even wait for them to fetch you.'[9]

*Whatever his motives, Priestley enlisted on 7 September 1914, and the next morning, he reported to the regimental depot in Halifax, a few miles from his home town.*

A regular sergeant, noting sardonically the newish sports coat and flannel trousers that, like a fool, I was wearing, set me to work at once removing the congealed fat from immense cooking pots. For a week or so I was free to return home at night, so long as I was back in barracks before eight in the morning... The last regular tram-rides I ever made – it is the last clear memory I have of this time – were those early morning journeys back to barracks, when I sat yawning and shivering a little, my new Army boots weighing a ton, on the empty tram top as it climbed and groaned up to Queensbury, on the Pennine roof and cold already, and then dropped me among the thickets of mill chimneys in Halifax.

I can still put myself on that tram, still feel those boots and the puttees that were too tight or too slack; though I have forgotten most of what happened at the end of the ride. I think I tried to walk smartly, though I was still more of a Swan Arcadian[10] than a soldier, past the guard at the barracks entrance...[11] I clomped in boots that seemed to weigh a ton to and from those barracks in Gibbet Lane. That was a fine start for my war: Gibbet Lane!'...[12]

From Hull, Hell and Halifax, our great-grandfathers declared, God must defend us. I had sailed to Hull from a Europe I never knew again. I had arrived at Halifax to begin my soldiering. Hell, no doubt was on its way...[13]

We slept for a week in a disused skating rink, along with various old tramps slipping in late, looking for a free doss, so that after a few nights there were lice about. This was my first but by no means my last acquaintance with the louse, whose pasture we were in the trenches.[14]

*On Wednesday 23 September 1914, Private Priestley, of Number 8 Platoon, B Company, 10th Duke of Wellington's Regiment, and a thousand of his fellows were sent by rail to a tented camp in Farnham, Surrey. That night he wrote the first of a stream of letters home to his family.*

Dear People, We only left Halifax this morning. We had to get up at 3.00 a.m. in the darkness and caught a train at 4.30 a.m. for Farnham near Aldershot. We landed about 2.00 pm. It was an enormous corridor train entirely filled with recruits. All the way people cheered and waved at us. The camp we are staying at is at Frensham about four miles from Farnham. There must be at least 10,000 men here, of various regiments. The rules are very strict: up in the morning at 5.30, drilling all day, in bed before nine. We sleep in tents, 12 in every one. I am writing this in my hut by the feeble light of a candle; it is a very difficult business; we are all huddled together and then we shall be shifted to a winter camp; after that our next move will be to Belgium and Germany. We wash in a lake about quarter of a mile distant. I am sorry to say that there have been a few deaths here. However, I never felt better in my life. There is only one canteen for all the camp and consequently the place is packed out and everything is sold. They do not take money in the canbteen, we have to pay with tickets. Up tothe preent there has been no pay given out, but if things do not alter, there will be serious trouble...

It is very beautfiul country around here, wooded and hilly. The camp is on a heath. When I arrived here, I was surprised to find the weather very hot, and no trace of autumn in the landscape. I understand, however, that it is frighfully cold at night.... It is all work, eat and sleep here, but I am enjoying myself all the same... I am writing this in the early morning light. It is very cold and misty, quite a contrast to the heat of the day. We are on active service and all the laws apply here.[15]

*In his next letter, Priestley was feeling the effects of the intensive training they were undergoing..*

I am dog-tired. We have had a very hard day indeed; judge for yourself: we had breakfast at 7; from 8 to 9.45 - physical exercises; from 9.45 to 12.15 squad drill; from 1.0 to 4.15 skirmishing drill; from 5 to 6.30 route march; and now I am tired out, but not unhappy. [illegible] had a shave, we have to [sleep?] on a heap of blankets in the tent. After I have posted this letter I shall "make my bed", get in and smoke a last pipe, and sleep soundly until morning. We were inspected by the King and Queen the other day. Also we went through another medical inspection; I got through alright, but some chaps from our company have been discharged as medically unfit.

Today we have been given 10/-, 5/- of which I enclose. I am keeping the other 5/- as I have no money left. Lyons are doing the catering here and the food is scarcely satisfactory. Breakfast is alright – tea, bread and butter, and a slab of brawn or ham. Dinner is far from good and we have to fight for the grub. Tea consists of the eternal bread, butter and jam. We spend something every day on buns, or fruit and chocolate, to fill up. I take very good care of my feet, because the strain put on them is enormous, and an infantryman with bad feet is useless. I wash them constantly, and rub any sore places with Vaseline every night.

As for the future, the captain of our company has been giving us some definite information. We shall move into winter quarters at a place in this district called Whitley, in about six weeks. Towards the end of February or the beginning of March our battalion is due for special service at the front... I am getting used to this life in a city of tents with all its strange sights and sounds... PS. Tell Winnie [his sister] I have had a "regimental crop"...[16]

Until the rains of winter finally washed us out of this camp altogether, we slept twelve in a bell-tent, kneeling after Lights Out to piss in our boots and then emptying them under the flap. The old soldiers told us that this was good for our boots, making them easier for route marches. Unlike battalions formed later, we had plenty of old soldiers, many of who had served in India and carried little tins of curry powder to sprinkle over any meat that came their way. Some of them of course were already wearing crowns or stripes, but many others, dour or wily types, refused promotion. They would do what they considered their essential duty, and in all circumstances as time proved, but they were, so to speak, against the military Establishment, would not be associated with it, and remained suspicious and grumbling privates to the end. (Though genuinely anxious, during the first year or so, to get into some fighting, I soon discovered that I belonged by temperament to this type myself.)

We were almost all West Riding [of Yorkshire] men. In my company there were a few suburban junior clerks and the like, of my sort, with whom I soon made friends. And the closer of these, those whose names I still remember, were all killed, even before the Somme battles in 1916. Most of the others were mill workers of various kinds. In my own platoon, by an odd chance, were some men, with names like Grady, Murphy, O'Neill, who came from the local 'back o't mill',[17] where my mother, whose name was Hoult, had grown up; they were almost cousins of mine. Perhaps it was the Irish in them that lifted their grumbling, which never stopped, to an Elizabethan height. The only remarks I have ever heard that Shakespeare might have borrowed all came from private soldiers in that war.[18]

*In his letters home, Priestley often joined in the traditional Army chorus of grumbles about food and facilities, but in the early months at least, he revelled in the training, He worked ten hours a day but felt 'as strong as a bull',[19] and even the route marches, agony for many, were much less taxing for him. Like many of his Bradford peers, Priestley had been used to regular long-distance walks over the moors that surrounded his home city.*

I thought nothing of twenty miles or more; and later, marching in the Army, never once failed to stay in the column when man after man was dropping out and others were staggering on blindly, unable to shoulder the rifles the remainder of us had to carry for them...[20]

As the weeks pass by and our training advances, the work becomes more interesting. We have musket drill and are becoming quite accustomed to handling a rifle. We have manoeuvres of various kinds, especially at night, when we practise moving about silently in the darkness. Sometimes when we are lying on the ground with our rifles in hand, at night, it seems almost like the real thing.[21]

*Priestley's letters also give the lie to later claims that, unlike the regular soldiers of the British Expeditionary Force, the volunteer troops of 'Kitchener's Army' were nothing but 'brave but half-trained amateurs, so much pitiful cannon fodder'.[22]*

In the earlier divisions like ours, the troops had months and months of severe intensive training. Our average programme was ten hours a day, and nobody grumbled more than the old regulars, who had never been compelled before to do so much for so long. It was only in musketry that we were far behind the Regular Army, simply because we had to wait for months for the rifles we would eventually use. We began without any equipment at all. There was not enough khaki cloth for regulation uniforms, and I remember my own mortification – I had been one of the few who were wearing khaki a day after enlistment – when I had to turn in my uniform and wear instead a doleful convict-style blue outfit, together with a ridiculous little forage cap...[23]

We have all got our "Kitchener's Army Uniform" on now; it is made of fine, blue serge, and is absolutely without any decoration whatever; not even a stripe down the trousers! Also we wear the old-style service caps. We look like convicts. It is a great blow to our vanity!...[24]

We never felt ourselves to be soldiers again, hardly wanted to go out, until, as excited as girls, we tore off that dismal blue, somebody's bad idea, and put on real khaki uniforms. When we stood for hours in rain and sleet, waiting to be inspected by Kitchener and Millerand, the blue dye ran out of our forage caps; I do not know if we looked like clowns or murderous Indian braves; we felt like both.

For my Christmas leave, I remember that somewhere or other I picked up an old, much larger and dead-black forage cap, which gave me – or so I fancied – a half-raffish, half-sinister look; and when I wore this and a long black overcoat, part of a swap, and the oddest of the scarves I had been sent, I looked a long way from Kitchener's Army, somebody who had enlisted in some dark bloodthirsty legion in Tashkent; or so, forgetting my innocent pudding face and guileless Bradford accent, I hoped. Certainly the girls I knew at home stared at me in bewilderment lit with fascination. 'Ah knew you'd joined up, Jack - but - Ah mean to say - what are you in?...[25]

Tent life wasn't too bad during the warm and dry September, but when we were into the second half of October, and it rained and it rained, we led a miserable existence... They drilled us and yelled at us from early morning until dusk, after which we limped to the canteen and argued noisily about nothing and stupefied ourselves with pint after pint of beer. I had braced myself for heroism; I was ready, I felt, to face shot and shell and possible cavalry charges; what I hadn't bargained for was this convict uniform, beer and backache existence under dripping canvas in Surrey.[26]

*As autumn turned to winter, the tented camp at Frensham became a morass of mud and standing water. Their only time off was on Sunday afternoon and early evening.*

Sunday afternoon, accompanied by a tent-mate, I went for a walk. When we were several miles from camp, we found that it was tea-time, and so we turned to the nearest farmhouse and asked if we could have tea. We were led into an old-fashioned kitchen, where a cheerful wood fire was burning, and very soon tea was ready. There was new bread and butter, boiled ham, and sweet cake. All good. We could have as much as we wanted, and I may tell you, that is no small amount. It was glorious to sit down on chairs at a table covered with a cloth and drink real tea in cups and saucers. And they charged us 6d each! Sixpence!

And it was worth 1/6 at least to us...[27] It is odd to remember now how rural and remote that Surrey countryside seemed in 1914; the farmhouses, their enormous kitchen fireplaces hung with hams, looked in my eyes then to be out of Thomas Hardy.[28]

*Rumours of a move to winter quarters in Aldershot came and went throughout a 'dreadfully wet' October and November, and still Priestley and his companions – perpetually cold, damp and prey to illness – endured the miserable conditions.*

2 November... Last week the general came round the camp before we got up, and seeing the soaking tents, the large pools, and masses of mud, said "Poor lads", and condemned the camp. So the story goes, and I believe it is true... We shan't be here long now.... All sorts of rumours are going about, but they are not worth detailing. You may be sure we shan't stop here; we spend half [the] day trying to drain the place. Still wilder rumours circulate as to our ultimate destination: India, Egypt, South Africa, France, but it just depends on how things progress with our troops at the Front. No one knows anything definite. I hope to be home for a few days at Christmas, but more of that anon.[29]

11 November... I have been unwell this last few days, since Saturday, but am feeling alright now except for a sore throat. I saw the Doctor on Sunday and Monday; the first time he gave me two black pills, the next time I had to swallow a powder. Our Doctor is no good, though, all his medicine is "working" medicine for the bowels, whether you want it or not. I didn't, for my bowels were in good order, and his pills and "muck" only made me run to the latrines frequently, and did me no good. You will be wondering what was the matter with me; I can't give it a name, but here are the symptoms – head aching and dizzy; limbs weak; no appetite, but constant thirst; body very cold and head very hot; spirits below zero! That is the formidable list.

It is awful being sick in camp, no fires and nowhere to sit. Mind you, within the last week, half the chaps in my tent have been just the same. I hate to grumble, but I feel wild with the authorities for keeping us here so long; it seems that we don't leave until the 22nd of this month and then we go to live in Barracks at Aldershot. It's so miserable in camp during the evening; the Y.M.C.A. tents are good in their way for reading and writing, but they are vastly overcrowded. So on these cold drizzling nights, we sit huddled in our tents, and often the prospect is so dreary that we lie down in our blankets about 7 o'clock and try to sleep.

If you are well you can put up with all this, but when you are out of sorts it is very depressing. They have no right to keep us here so long, I don't think there's a camp in England treated so badly. Some days ago I read, in the "Daily News", an article complaining, in no measured terms, about keeping recruits in camp.[30]

15 November... I am feeling alright again now. I take the quinine regularly. Though it is so cold now at night, I do not need another blanket, as I have three and a paliasse, and these are ample, along with my overcoat.

The doctor is an ass. Last Monday, when I went to him, he gave me "Medicine and Duty" which meant that I had to go back to drill. I felt very dizzy and weak, as I told you, but I went back thinking I should be able to stick ordinary drill. But it wasn't drill, it was a ten mile route march, in which our company had to try to break another company's record for speed. Well, I set my teeth and stuck it all the way through, but it's an experience I don't want to undergo again. When I'm well I enjoy route marches and can march with anybody in camp. But talking about the doctor: – a day or two after I had seen him, a young chap went and received some medicine and was told to go back to work. He went and an hour later he had to be carried off the parade ground. The next day he was dead! So much for the doctor!

I have heard today from reliable sources that we are leaving here on Wednesday for Oudenarde Barracks, North Camp, Aldershot. But don't let it intervene with you sending anything, I shall get it alright if you send it here and I have left. Still, I will let you know as soon as we have shifted. I feel sure we shall get leave at Xmas or New Year, and I shall come home, of course.[31]

23 November... Orders for going to Aldershot have been cancelled and we are still at Frensham and may be here all winter. It is very cold but frosty weather is better than wet.[32]

27 November... It is pouring down and has been practically all day. Indeed we have had a lot of rain this last few days, and now the camp is a sight for the gods. Mud, mud everywhere - nearly knee-deep in some places. Pools all over the place! It is a mess! Everything is wet and crowded.

We are going to Aldershot on Tuesday - half the battalion in barracks, the rest billeted out – and then, after a week or so, the two halves will change quarters. I think there is no doubt about it this time, and I certainly hope not. These last two or three weeks have knocked a lot of enthusiasm out of the men. Still we keep fairly cheerful on the whole and have our jokes and songs. It takes a great deal to dampen youthful spirits. If it is very cold at night, we light a great number of candles and make the tents look a bit more cheerful.

There is no doubt that the Y.M.C.A. has done magnificent work in the camps. There are two Y.M.C.A. tents in the camp; one for each Brigade, you can imagine that the tents are crowded. Attached to each large Y.M.C.A. tent is a smaller one, in which buns, coffee etc. are sold at night. The ladies who preside at the counters are mostly wealthy ladies who live in this district and give their services. It would strike some people as very strange if they saw titled ladies (this is an aristocratic district) waiting on labourers from Bradford, rough-tongued miners from Barnsley and Rotherham, clerks, shop-assistants, – a motley Yorkshire crowd. Yet such is the case, as you would see for yourself if you visited the Y.M.C.A. tonight. But we are [not] clerks, labourers, etc., we are soldiers! These are strange times, and Democracy rules.

Last Saturday night I had a great treat! A red-letter night! I had a hot bath – a real hot bath! I, along with two tent-mates, went by invitation to the house of Lady Napier, (who serves buns to us in the Y.M.C.A.) and there had a hot bath in a beautiful bathroom, and then had the delirious pleasure of sitting in an armchair in front of a fire! An armchair and a fire! - rarities indeed... We are all expecting a furlough at Xmas, and building castles in the air as we lie in our blankets smoking the dear old briars...[33]

It was not until late November, after the whole camp had been sinking into mud for weeks, that we were finally washed out of Frensham. I had come to loathe those dripping and steaming bell-tents. Some objects are to my mind symbols of that half of England I detest, and one of them, mean and cramping and a miserable idea, is the bell-tent.

Aldershot, where we moved into barracks at last, was no Victorian inspiration, a whole town given up to button-polishing and saluting, bugle calls and guards turning out, but after Frensham its brick huts were a Ritz.[34]

*Even though they were now notionally based at Oudenarde Barracks in Aldershot, Priestley and his comrades regularly found themselves decamping to other places for specialised training that lasted one or two weeks. On 7 December 1914, they went to Camberley for 'field work' including musketry and night trench-digging.*

We left our barracks at Aldershot this morning and marched to a place called Camberley, some miles away, where we are staying for a week for field work. There is only half the Battalion here, the other half will come next week, when we return to Aldershot. We are billeted in large, empty semi-detached villas, about fifty men to each house, and as we have our usual blankets and mattresses, we should be quite comfortable. We shall have our lunch, which we take in haversacks, and have our dinners at night... With regard to Xmas furlough, a wave of pessimism has swept over our chaps and everywhere one hears grave doubts as to the possibility of a holiday [at] home. We are getting very advanced in our training now, and when we have fired our course of musketry, we shall be nearly ready for the front...[35]

*The following week they were sent to the remote village of Eversley for a fortnight's 'Brigade Training'. Meanwhile, the everlasting rumour mill filled the gaps left by the absence of any real news.*

I am told [Eversley] is a very desolate spot, and as the work is very hard, we look like "going through it". I don't think we shall go to France as early as was anticipated, but one never knows. There is a definite rumour going about that we are going to Ireland in a few weeks' time to finish our training. I certainly hope we do. The work we do now, though hard, is interesting, and, indeed, it is my spare time, welcome as it is, that I find somewhat dull... By the way, will you please send me my Palgrave's 'Golden Treasury'... it will not take up much room, and I always read that with pleasure. You can send some of Baylet & Holdsworth's tobacco, too, to take with me into the wilds? If possible will you send these things to reach me before Wednesday, as we leave here that day. Of course, things will be sent on, but it is slow and somewhat precarious...

I suppose you have seen an account of the division of the New Armies; we are in the Third under Sir Archibald Hunter; the 'Pals", I see, are in the Fifth. We were doing Battalion drill, this morning, in the famous Long Valley (Laffan's Plain), the great ground for Field Days and Reviews, and a general who watched us for some time, complimented us very highly and said we were superior to any battalion in the First Army!

The hardest work I have done for some time was on last Wednesday night at Camberley. We were marched out at night, and had to dig trenches, within a certain time, in the darkness. We succeeded, but you ought to have seen and felt our hands! Talk about piano-playing! – it will be a long time before I can do any.

*In January or early February 1915, (Priestley's letter is undated and the envelope is lost), his battalion changed quarters again.*

The whole battalion has come, this time, and we are living all over the place. Finchamstead (in Berkshire) and Cressley (in Hampshire) are adjoining hamlets; one can hardly call them villages, for there are houses merely scattered here and there, and only a couple of shops for both places. We [are] living as we can; some in stables and haylofts, barns, coach houses, etc., some in a school, and others, including myself, are in empty houses. But we are not all together, as at Camberley, but scattered all over the place. God knows how we are going to get anything to eat! They gave us breakfast this morning in barracks, then we walked the 12 to 14 miles here, and since then what food I've had, I've bought...

The reason why we stayed in Aldershot was the visit of Lord Kitchener and the French Minister of War last Friday. And what a day it was! All the morning it snowed heavily, and then after dinner changed to a veritable tornado of sleet. Well over twenty thousand of us lined up on our parade-ground and then we had to wait over two hours in the most awful deluge of sleet, cold and pitiless, that I have ever known. After the first ten minutes we were soaked through, and the rest was a matter of sheer endurance. And the review consisted of six motor-cars driving past us on the road! It is pretty certain that we are going to Ireland next month.[36]

*After months of training and rumours about impending deployments, in late February 1915 the 'Dirty Dukes' departure for the front line seemed imminent when they began the 'great march' from Aldershot to the Kent port of Folkestone, the main departure point for troops deploying to the Western Front.*

This is a test march, and Kitchener inspects us (23rd Division) en route. We travel with full pack and a weight it is, I assure you. We carry: rifle, ammunition pouches, great-coat – folded, bayonet, water-bottle, shirt, drawers, socks, towel and soap razor, etc., etc., mess-tin – a sort of combination frying-pan, pot and plate, etc., etc. It is no joke marching with that lot... There is a sign of Spring in the air here, and also there are signs of movement in the great masses of troops here. The Great New Armies have started moving, slowly, but surely, and the end of the war is in sight, though afar.[37]

*The week-long, 'great march' followed a circuitous route of over 130 miles from Aldershot to Folkestone by way of Guildford, Dorking, Tonbridge and Maidstone - 'only towns of some size could provide the schools and public halls'* [38] *where the men were billeted en route. They eventually arrived in Folkestone on 1 March 1915.*

The great march has ended at last... We have gone through three counties, slept in six towns, and passed through innumerable villages. We have not [taken] the shortest way from place to place, but in many cases, have gone a roundabout way. And what a reception we have had in the villages we have passed through and the towns we have stayed in! This march has been firstly a test of efficiency and endurance – for we have done nearly twenty miles every day and one day over twenty six, and we have all had very sore feet and many have dropped out – secondly, I fancy it was intended as a recruiting parade. Imagine, if you can, a column of men a mile and a quarter long, with four bands. For food we have had bully-beef and any odds and ends (I've bought a lot of mine myself), and at night we slept anyhow in schools and various public halls. [39]

This was my idea of soldiering – constant movement, unknown destinations, fluttering handkerchiefs and cheers – and I enjoyed it hugely, sore feet and bully-beef and kips on hard floors and all. [40]

Yesterday (Sunday) we were inspected by Lord Kitchener. It was kept very quiet, and took place five miles from anywhere. We marched past him, and I was only about two yards from the great man, and so got a very good view of him, not much like the portraits of him - older and greyer, with huge staring eyes... [41]

The image I retained was of a rather bloated purplish face and glaring but somehow jellied eyes, an image not of an ageing man, already bewildered by, reeling under, the load of responsibility he refused to share, but of some larger-than-life, yet now less than-life figure, huge but turning into painted lead. It was a frightening and not pleasing image, and a year later, when we heard he had been drowned, I felt no grief, for it did not seem to me that a man had lost his life: I saw only a heavy shape, its face now an idol's, going down and down into that northern sea.

Yet it was he – and he alone – who had raised us new soldiers out of the ground. This, not anything he did in Egypt and the Sudan and India, was a stroke of genius; he created armies when all the others, mischievous clowns like Henry Wilson or the huntin'-and-shootin' cavalry captains pretending to be generals, said he was an obstinate old fool and laughed at him. Here I was, I still am, on his side. But the image that remained after that inspection, of something immensely massive and formidable but already hardening and petrifying, nearer to death than to life, haunted me to my disquiet for a long time. Even when at last we... straightened our shoulders for the final miles... that image was there, the eyes glaring out of death not life...[42]

We started off this morning from Ashford with clenched teeth, and had the finest march of all. We passed through miles of Kentish hop-fields, and then through a cleft in the Downs we caught a glimpse of the sea – the sea! – and a huge cheer went up from the long weary ranks. We walked five miles on the edge of the sea, and it was glorious, for it is Spring here. We passed through Hythe, then Sandgate, and finally reached Folkestone, a beautiful town, full of large hotels and boarding houses.

I am billeted at the house of some French people, where I shall live entirely while we are here. Think of it! – I shall sleep in a bed, and have real meals! It is like having a holiday at the seaside. It is a grand experience, and I have seen places that I probably never would have seen...[43]

But of course I added this holiday bit to cheer them up at home. Actually at this time, bored with drill and exercises, physical and military, I began to look out for odd jobs that would keep me off parade. Earlier I had refused to become an orderly-room clerk; I had not joined the Army to exchange one office for another. On the other hand, though not lazy, still with energy to burn, I now found the sheer repetitiveness of parades and exercises hard to endure.

Moreover, most of us felt it was time we were sent out to the Front, now that we had had seven months' hard training. Indeed, three of us decided that if the battalion were still in England in eight or ten weeks

– I forget the date we agreed upon – then we would desert, to join up again at some depot where men were being sent out almost at once. This could happen even early in 1915; if a regular battalion had been heavily punished in the line and there was a shortage of regular reserves at the depot, then some recruits might be drafted to the Front. This explains why some untrained men did find themselves in the trenches even then; but of course it does not justify the statement that whole New Army divisions had had no proper training and were a kind of brave rabble.[44]

*While at Folkestone, Priestley was 'rescued from boredom'* [45] *by being put on 'Officers' Mess Fatigue' with another soldier to act as 'washers-up and kitchen dog's-bodies'.* [46] *To Priestley's delight, they were given the same food as the officers.*

I'm not going into details as to what I get, because I should only set your mouths watering. We're all having a delightful time here, and the weather's quite summery. I was on the Leas (the fashionable prom) this morning, and sat listening to the good orchestra and watching the sea. A seaside holiday for nothing, eh?[47]

*The first day of April 1915 found him 'still in Folkestone, and likely to be for another week or two, I think.'. While there he had received several parcels from his family and friends. Parcels from home were welcomed by all soldiers boosting morale and providing much-valued supplement to Army food, clothing and equipment, but Priestley could sometimes be curmudgeonly about the gifts he received.*

It is very good of these people to knit scarves, etc, but I've no earthly use for a scarf (I have one already, which I've never used), and I haven't the room to spare for one. I don't wish to be unkind or ungrateful, but people might have a little thought. All my socks need darning, so you can send as many pairs of socks as you wish; also the 'housewife' [a sort of household repair kit, including needles, thread, darning-wool, etc,] and my watch. Before we came on the big march, I gave one or two pairs of socks away to some poor chaps who hadn't a decent pair to put on.

I will have my photograph taken before we leave here and send one to Lidget Green [in Bradford]. I could get a pass for the weekend, that is for four days, but the journey is so long that I should have little more than two days at home and the fare would be over a sovereign. But I may put a pass in yet; anyhow I will let you know. Do you think it is worthwhile?... I am still working at the "Officers' Mess", and living in the lap of luxury. There are two of us and we are the "Kitchen Porters". I am quite an authority on house-work and will be a useful appendage to any kitchen...[48]

This was not a cushy job in terms of work and hours, but I enjoyed it... The Mess, in a detached villa, was being run by a catering firm – I think, though I could not swear to it, the Junior Army and Navy Stores. The staff were all civilians. The chef was a Frenchman, fattish and untidy, always angry because the kitchen range was inadequate for his needs and he had to perform miracles of improvisation and sharp timing. I never saw him sit down to a meal; he drank a good deal and nearly always had a ragged cigarette smouldering and drooping; he would droop and smoulder too, then go blazing into action. The waiters were middle-aged professionals with a code and jargon all their own. One of them, melancholy, blue-chinned, with those beaten spaniel's eyes that seem to encourage women to misbehave, was having trouble with his wife, who was unfaithful and might leave him for ever at any moment; and she kept rushing in to make a scene and provide drama that we all enjoyed.

The wine waiter, a suave young man, beautifully dressed, had been the valet of a well-known aristocratic type, who afterwards became even better-known and must be nameless here. Milord had gone to the front, but this valet could not follow him because he had been rejected on medical grounds; so here he was. When neither of us was busy he told me stories of dissolute high life as strange and fascinating to me as passages from the Arabian Nights; one of them, describing how milord and his mistress used anchovy paste in their sexual play, makes me marvel even now.

My fatigue mate, a dour man from Huddersfield who smoked thick twist in a short curved pipe, just did what he had to do, devoured the excellent food we were given, lit his pipe and vanished; but I loved to explore and savour this backstairs world so new to me, this behind-the-scenes of catering, and so did not resent the long hours, which left me just sufficient time to smoke a pipe or two on the Leas [the cliff-top area with panoramic views over the Channel] in the late morning, when the band played, and to take a walk after the lunch dishes, an immense pile, had been washed, dried, cleared, and before the evening chores began. To this day, if need be, I can wash up and dry as fast as anybody I know; but other skills I learnt then – for example, I could toast eight slices of bread at the same time, using four toasting-forks – have decayed for lack of use.

We lived well in the kitchen, the staff looking after its own; many a time I saw a fine portion of some specially good dish set aside for me when I could hear in the distance the waiters telling belated officers in the dining-room that that dish was 'off'.[49]

*In early April Priestley was promoted: 'please address me as Lance-Corporal in future instead of Private'.[50] His hopes of a home leave before he went to France had now been dashed. 'I can't get a pass now, even if I want one, for there have been so many men who have overstayed their time that the Major has stopped all passes except for urgent cases'. Like the other men in his battalion he was vaccinated and was 'suffering considerably from a bad head and arm',[51] but despite the vaccinations, the arrival of new equipment and the usual flood of rumours – a 'very widespread' one had them 'destined for the Dardanelles or Egypt, and there seems some foundation for it too',[52] – the prospect of deployment to France or anywhere else still remained a distant one.*

As for going to France, Kitchener's First Army goes out next week, and we, in the Third Army, shan't go out for a month or two, unless something happens over there, rather disastrously, and then we should go straight away. The "Pals", who are in the Fifth Army, will be a long time yet before they go out.[53]

From what I can see, I believe that the general situation is much worse that the Government cares to admit... I have heard that the Bradford "Terriers", the crush [unit] that Foster, Parcey and Lacey are in, have gone to the Front. I wish I'd joined them now, and then I should have been out with them... I am well in health and spirits, but am getting more and more impatient and disgusted as time goes by, and we are still fooling about here... Please keep anything you may have gathered from this letter confidential.[54]

*In late April, Priestley's battalion made a temporary move to Maidstone, 'where on the first night we all got drunk on the uncommonly strong local ale'.[55] There they were to assist in work on the outer ring of London's defences; even though the rapid 'war of movement' of the opening months of the war had now ossified into a trench-bound war of attrition, fear of invasion remained strong.*

We left Folkestone last Friday afternoon, and came along here by train. Every morning the Battalion are journeying by train to a certain spot (I cannot name the place) there to construct some elaborate trenches which are part of the great London Defence Scheme. I think we shall be going back to Folkestone district in about a fortnight...[56]

I detested digging, in which the few navvies among us made us all look silly by setting to work slowly and methodically and shifting about three times as much soil as we did; so I was delighted when I was given a stripe and put in charge of the company's billeting arrangements. Each householder was paid a fixed sum per day – let us say, as a near guess, 3s. 7 1/2d. [c19 pence] – for providing board and lodging. I had to allot these billets, for which the supply far exceeded the demand, pay for them, and deal with complaints from either side. It was tricky, and I learnt much about the private life of Maidstone.

Some of the senior N.C.O.s wanted to change their billets not necessarily because of any lack of food and comfort but because they were lured away by housewives more comely, amiable and compliant than others. I myself changed my billet, after the second day, because an extremely pretty girl called Dorothy, a cool and sharp wench, sought me out to tell me that her mother, a widow, had room for one soldier and couldn't I send them one, please, please? So I sent them myself. They seemed to be a family that had come down in the world, living sparely in a ramshackle house; the whole set-up was like a play, though not the kind of play that was being produced in 1915.

There was this sharp and bright-eyed Dorothy, who really ran the show although she was only about eighteen and who, unless she had the worst of luck, probably restored the family fortunes later; there was her rather bewildered, defeated and gentle mother; and sleeping among the lumber in the attic was a kind of vague gnome, with a suggestion of the holy fool about him, called Tommy, who was no relation but earned enough to give them a few shillings a week. Nor was that all, for Dorothy's older sister was a film actress – a fantastic profession then – and once when she was filming not too far away she came dashing home, astonishing me by her mask of yellow makeup, her chain-smoking, her drinks and nervous uninhibited talk. She seemed to me as exotic, as remote from any young woman I had ever seen before, as a mandarin's concubine...

I had already felt something like this – even though they did not look as strange as Dorothy's sister, and I was not observing them so closely – about several actresses who had come to entertain us earlier. The one I remember best, from a Sunday night show at Frensham given by some musical-comedy players, was Nellie Taylor, a favourite at that time.... she can have been no more than twenty when I stared at her, that Sunday night in 1914, over the rows of officers' smooth heads. It was not any particular talent she showed that excited me then and made me remember her; now in fact I cannot recall what she did. No, it was the way she looked and sounded, her undisguised enjoyment of the situation in which she found herself that night, the dancing light of her high spirits, her quintessential young femininity, to which my heart went out. All this brought me joy in this vast snarling clutter of men; but mixed with this joy was a painful feeling of being altogether outside her world, not Shaftesbury Avenue and the Savoy Grill but some shining mysterious region of unattainable girls. I felt a sense of exile and loss, a wound that still ached long after that evening. When she blew us her last kisses and vanished, the lights went down for weeks, my Army boots felt heavier and clumsier than ever.[57]

*On 17 May, Priestley's entire Division received orders that they were to decamp once more, transferring to 'what was really a new wooden town, hutments for all the division'. His parents had been planning to visit him in Folkestone and he had to write to them at once, putting them off.*

Just received your letter, but am sorry that it will be impossible for you to come here, as the whole division leaves this district for Borden Camp next weekend. we have received definite orders, and the advance parties go this morning. We should be out [in France] in less than six weeks, but in the meantime I will try very hard to get a few days at home.

*A week later, on 24 May 1915, the Division transferred to Bramshott Camp in Hampshire.*

It is a gigantic camp (how big I cannot say, as I have not explored it yet), and looks like a small town (a sort of Dawson City or some other Klondyke mushroom town) with its rows and rows of huts all exactly alike. Though it is in the wilds of Hampshire, and far from a town, the camp is lit throughout with electricity. There are Dry and Wet Canteens, Regimental Institutes and YMCA's galore. But a word about the weather! I suppose you are nice and cool at Keswick, but here it is absolutely stifling. Day after day, cloudless skies and a blazing sun. And dust everywhere! The roof of each hut is lined outside with gas-tar; and during this exceptionally hot weather it has melted, and constantly drips through, with deplorable results.

The camp was last occupied by a number of Scotch regiments, which left here for the Front about a fortnight ago. Many of the men are lying wounded in the Aldershot Hospitals. I believe we shall mobilise here and go straitway. The sooner the better, I am heartily sickened of waiting.[58]

Now we no longer talked of deserting to get to the Front; every day brought rumours, usually picked up in the latrines, about where and when we should be going. In the cool of the evening my friends and I would solemnly discuss these rumours as we walked, rather stiffly, the two miles or so to Haslemere.[59]

*Still the weeks dragged by without definite news of a deployment, as the Division continued its endless round of weapons-training, exercises, digging and drill. Priestley was also given the 'poison chalice' of temporary replacement for the battalion post corporal, whose job was to deliver the men's mail and who became the unwitting recipient of all their pent-up anger when parcels from home or letters from wives and sweethearts failed to appear.*

Something, I have forgotten what, happened to the battalion post corporal, and I was commanded to take over his duties, which left me little leisure and no social life at all. I was now identified with missing letters, parcels that ought to have turned up a week before; all ranks stopped me and eyed me suspiciously – 'Now, look here, are you sure there was nothing for me today? Because if so there's something bloody queer going on'; I was no longer a man and a brother...[60]

20 June 1915

Our Colonel was back at the Front the other weekend, but has returned. It seems that things are almost at a standstill on the British Front, and our men can do nothing without large quantities of high-explosive shells. Tomorrow our Brigade is going to spend the night in some trenches we have dug in the neighbourhood, and later in the week, the whole division is going to bivouac. I don't think we shall go out just yet for a while, though we are ready, and some of the regiments here have already blackened their buttons and cap-badges. I have got a new uniform, a green colour – with green buttons instead of brass ones.

We were glad to get back from Langmoor and Whitehill camps; they were wretched places, and the food was very bad. We were on the big ranges day long there – Saturday and Sunday as well. The heat was terrific, and on the last Sunday and Monday – that is a week ago – large numbers of our men had to be taken to hospital suffering from sunstroke. I felt queer – indeed everyone did – but not as bad as most.

They are certainly trying to make us as comfortable as possible here at Branshott. The food is very good. First thing in the morning – at 6am – we have what is called 'gunfire' – tea and sweet biscuits. Then at eight comes breakfast, when we have bacon, or a couple of boiled eggs. For dinner we have roasts and stews – sometimes meat and potato pie – and also jam or currant puddings or stewed rhubarb. For tea we have jam or cake or tinned fruits. Our battalion has a recreation room with the day's papers, illustrated weeklies and every kind of game. In fact I am sat in the recreation room now, writing this letter on paper provided free by the regiment.

Of course there is the usual crop of rumours, but one can't listen to them with any degree of faith; in any case there are many things I cannot speak of.

I can't get any decent tobacco here, so will you plesae send me some 'Idle Hour Cut Plug' or some other really good tobacco for a nicotine-soaked epicure; also some Cope's 'Courts'. Blow the expense, I'll pay you later.[61]

3 July 1915

Many thanks for the tobacco and cheroots. The promptness with which my wishes were fulfilled does not fail to exact my gratitude. What an Early Victorian sentence! I received your letter yesterday after I had posted mine. Is that lucky or unlucky or just nothing at all?

There is a chance for us to see some fighting, after all, for 'Old Moore' says that the war will not end until 1932! Or so it is rumoured here. How the time flies! (I am not the creator of this profound remark). I have been in the Army nearly 10 months, and the war has been on nearly a year...

We are going to sleep in the trenches next week. They are teaching us all the new methods of warfare now, bomb-throwing, sniping, etc. Our 8th Battalion went out to the Front the other day. They were stationed at Whitley, a few miles from Bramshott. This country for miles around is devoted to military use. Within a six-mile of our camp are the following camps: Bordon (a very big camp, used in peacetime for the Cavalry), Whitehill, Longmoor, Whitley, Frensham, and probably some I don't know.

There is a cinema show connected with the camp. Two of my chums persuaded me to go with them last night, and I was entertained vastly. The management evidently buy, or hire, old films at a very cheap rate, consequently they are always breaking, the result being that last night we never saw the end of the single picture. Personally, this amused me, but it must have proved very tantalising to those who take 'pictures' seriously.[62]

*It was now the eve of the anniversary of the declaration of war and almost as long since Priestley had enlisted. Now released from his post duties, but still awaiting word of when and where his division would be deployed, he noted the deaths of a steady stream of friends who had already been serving in the front lines.*

2 August 1915

I chanced to see a copy of the "Weekly Tele" and therein found an account of Day's death in the firing line. Through Foster, I knew him quite well; he was one of our Lyons cafe habitués and a frequent visitor to the "Camp". Intellectually, he was not so brilliant as the appreciation in the "Tele" made out he was, but, nevertheless he was a fine fellow, an upright and clean-minded Englishman. He was the idol of his parents and sisters; it must be a fearful shock to them!

Aug. 2nd! and still in England! How the time passes on. It strikes me that they will need a great many more men in France shortly, so perhaps we shall go there. I hope so. The men here are getting thoroughly dissatisfied at being kept so long – training and training month after month, and there are many slight signs of disturbance, so much so that the discipline is much stricter, heavy pack drill being given to defaulters. Of course we are being trained to do things that were not dreamed of in modern warfare a year ago, and when we do go, we shall not go to our slaughter as the Regulars did, but properly equipped with machine-guns, machine rifles (the new invention) and bombs of every description.[63]

August 14 1915

We have not gone out yet, as you see, but we have [heard?] rumours – thousands upon thousands of them. We have received strict orders that when the time comes, we have not to mention the port of embarkation to anyone. The latest rumours assert that we're for the Dardanelles, not France, but nobody knows definitely... If you don't hear from me for a long time, you'll know we're on our way to the Dardanelles.[64]

*In late August, the 23rd Division finally received their orders to depart for France.*

Our old colonel, too old for service at the front, had watched us march past for the last time, not hiding his tears, suddenly ancient and done with now... Then after a brief last leave, spent mostly in crowded trains which, as they moved along the platforms, as if pulling a horrible string, jerked away smiles and then crumpled so many women's faces, we waited about until it was very late and dark one night, and sailed for France.[65]

# Chapter 2
# A strange exultation

*Priestley's last letter home containing the news that he was embarking for France brought a rapid reply from his father, Jonathan, written at the Bradford school where he was headmaster. 'Your mother and Winnie are in Grassington [in the Yorkshire Dales] and I have had to tell a mild untruth about you as I thought it would spoil the little holiday to let mother know. I shall catch it when she gets back... Take care of yourself. Do your duty but don't go into needless risks.'* [66]

*Having sailed from Folkestone to Boulogne, the 23rd Division were now marching towards the Western Front, with the endless rumble of the guns already sounding in their ears. Priestley's first letters home were now subject to even more rigourous censorship and even the heading 'Somewhere in France' proved too much for the censor, who amended it to 'Somewhere in [censored]'* [67]

I am writing this in a very dilapidated barn, where we eat, sleep and generally exist. Our food – bully beef and biscuits. It's all like a dream: – the cheering crowds as we left England; the marches on fearful roads with ton-weights on our backs; the long rides in cattle trucks - it's all like a dream. [68]

8 September 1915.
We have moved since I last wrote to you, and we have been living in a deserted, partly ruined farmhouse – all huddled together on the stone floor. We are moving again tonight... It has been all mud and rain lately here. You have doubtless heard a lot about YMCAs, canteens, and concerts for the troops, but I have never seen anything of them yet. I have never had my trousers off since I left England, but there are no signs of vermin yet, which is surprising, considering the places I have slept in. The fellows across the way are in pigsties.

If anyone wants to send me anything, the following would be very welcome: Tobacco, chocolate of any kind, a tin of vermin-killer, a writing-pad suitable for the pocket, a stick of shaving powder, a good razor. I don't want you to send all these things and I don't want people to send clothing of any kind for the present.[69]

I was hotter than I had ever been in my life before, just as in a few months' time I was to be wetter and colder. Humping along those cobbled roads in full marching order, choked by the dust of military transport, was murderous, and even the rat-infested barns we slept in every night never seemed to have known cool fresh air. Yet while aware of unpleasant physical sensations, I felt at heart detached from them, moving – as I wrote in my first letter home – almost floating, in a long dream. I suspect that this feeling, that here was no reality, never from this time entirely left me, out at the Front or back at home, until the day I was demobilised, nearly four years later.[70]

18 September 1915

Since I wrote to you last, many things have happened. We have marched till we dropped, slept in fields, marched again and so forth. This is our third day in the Fire-trench, or first line trench. My home, at the moment, is just off Watson Avenue, which branches off Shaftesbury Avenue. I've seen a few Germans, but only through the periscope.

Every now and then, bullets and shells come whizzing over our heads. At night, it is very weird; we are all on the alert, and star shells – like rockets – are sent up now and again – making the place look as light as day. The nights seem to stretch out to eternity. Rats and mice, wasps and gigantic bluebottles abound in the dugouts. Taking it all round, we are all in good spirits, but dreadfully filthy...[71]

Unlike some later divisions, who found themselves entangled in German barbed wire and slaughtered by machine-gun fire before they knew where they were, we were lucky, being initiated by degrees. We relieved the long-service Regulars of the 8th Division in what was then a quiet sector, Bois Grenier - Laventie - Fleurbaix, where in many places the two front lines were wide apart, so that we had listening posts out in no man's land.

I spent two or three hours alone in one of these, I think on my second or third night in the line, staring so hard at black nothing that it stopped being black or nothing and began to crawl with greyish shapes; I would then shut my eyes for a few moments, and when I opened them again the shapes had vanished. I do not think I am flattering my twenty-year-old self if I say that I was less apprehensive in that listening post than I am now on all manner of comparatively safe occasions. Youth, hard training, a genuine desire to get into the war at some point, had turned me temporarily into a brave soldier. I was less and less brave, in that sense, the more and more I saw of this war.

The truth is, as anybody can discover from the behaviour of very young children, terror arrives first through the ear. Turn off the sound on a television set, when old newsreels of war, later of course than the 1914-18 War, are on the screen, and the menace goes; we stare unmoved at a shadow play. Turn the sound on again, even though it has been cut down and muffled, and the scenes are alive and terrible again. Now the First War, with its massed artillery, was the noisiest of all time; the sound hit you harder and harder as the months passed. Some things you got used to – sniping and machine-gun fire if you were not entangled in the open and a sitting duck, hand-bombs and rifle grenades if you had sandbags and room to dodge – but as time went on, the vast cannonading, drumming hell into your ears, no matter whether it was their guns or yours, began to wear you down, making you feel that flesh and blood had no place in this factory of destruction. So in that war it was not the recruit but the veteran who began to feel he was being hammered into the ground.

Every time I went back into the line, especially after being out of it long enough for my ears to be open to civilisation again, I felt more and more apprehension. In that listening post I was the gallant Tommy of the home-front legends; but as time wore on I was more and more a chap who wondered what the hell he was doing there and how the hell he could get out of it - a mouse in a giant mincing machine.

In that sector, where in places we were not in real trenches at all but between breastworks of sandbags, there were still, of all things, catapults here and there, big ones, the kind the Romans had used. We were in fact still short of guns and ammunition, but when we moved over to the right, nearer Neuve Chapelle, we knew that guns and ammunition were piling up behind us.

On 25 September 1915, when the disastrous Battle of Loos was fought, we were in the front line, wearing full kit and so weighed down with extra cartridges and bombs we could hardly move, waiting to climb the scaling ladders all along the fire trench, Over our heads, where the ladders would take us, invisible express trains seemed to be passing both ways, there was such an unceasing exchange of shells. Once up the ladders and out of the trench, I felt a cat would not live five minutes. But the luck was in – I had a lucky war – and because the attack on our right had not gained sufficient ground we were never thrown into the assault, stayed where we were, and saw the scaling ladders taken away.[72]

*Two nights later, they were relieved from the trenches and withdrew to 'little wooden huts about two miles from the firing-line.'*

27 September 15
We were in the fire-trenches 12 consecutive days before being relieved. The latter part of our stay was spent in wretched weather – cold and wet. We were up to the knees in water and covered with mud from head to foot. Our boots, puttees and trousers – which we have never been able to take off – were firmly fastened together with a thick layer of mud.

Things are getting very exciting round this quarter now, and in the last four days in the trenches, I don't think I'd eight hours sleep altogether. It is frightfully difficult to walk in the trenches owing to the slippery nature of things, the most appalling thing is to see the stretcher bearers trying to get the wounded men to the field dressing station.

On Saturday morning we were subjected to a fearful bombardment by the German Heavy Artillery – they simply rained shells and our artillery rained them back – and there were we, the poor, long suffering infantry, crouched in our trenches, expecting each moment to be our last. One shell burst right in our trench – and it was a miracle that so few – only four – were injured. The man next to me had his finger broken, but I escaped with a little piece of flesh torn out of my thumb. Nothing serious at all – I bandaged it up myself when I attended to my neighbour. But poor Murphy – your Murphy you know – got a shrapnel wound in the head, a horrible great hole, and the other two were the same. They were removed soon after and I don't know how they are going on.

I have seen some terrible sights, and endured some hardships, but believe me, I never lost my nerve, and strange to say, I felt a strange exultation of the soul at the expense of the body. Do not be afraid for me; I am not afraid.

I suppose I am a man now, and am certainly going through an ordeal. Perhaps it would be as well if everybody went through some test of manhood.[73]

19 October 15

We came into the trenches again, a week yesterday (Sunday) and at the present moment we are in the fire-trenches, but not the same as last time, in fact quite a distance away. It is quiet here (though the snipers are particularly deadly), monotonous and bitterly cold. The night with its long, weary vigils commences at 5pm and lasts till 5am next day; I do no sleeping at night, and the result is that these 12 hours seem like a lifetime – spent near the Pole too, by the weather. I am feeling a little off colour these days, nothing serious, and the result is, nothing seems worth doing and everything a failure.

Speaking seriously, I am disgusted with my company officers as a whole, and the way in which our men are badgered and hampered by silly little rules and regulations which other regiments have not to submit to. In fact I am so "fed up" of being compelled to bully men to obey this or that ridiculous little order that I have been thinking of reverting to the ranks, so don't be surprised if you have to address me as 'private'. The 'rest' which we are supposed to get when relieved from the trenches is a ghastly fraud; I never grafted and sweated so much in all my life. We were "supernavvies" for a week. And that's the rest.[74]

*A week later, writing from 'The Usual Place' Priestley was at pains to allay the concerns he'd aroused in his previous letter to his parents.*

October 26

You have taken my last letter too seriously; I was out of sorts and was indulging in the 'luxury of a grouse'. You must remember that it is supposed to be the privilege of a British soldier. This endless trench fighting and trench making is very wearisome – we should very much prefer to jump over the parapet and drive the cowards out with the bayonet. We were just on the left of the great advance, and were expecting to have to charge ourselves, but we were apparently not needed.

At the present time we are billeted in a fair-sized town, three companies of us in an old and very rickety flour-mill. In order to get to the spot where I sleep, I have to go up three flights of rickety stairs, dodge under a quantity of beams and I'm 'home'. This place is full of all sorts of troops including large numbers of Ghurkas, Sikhs, and other Indian troops.

It is a grievance with our fellows and the infantry generally, the number of men out here with well paid, soft jobs; these bases are full of them – tradesmen of the ASC, AOC and APC men, and many of the RAMC and RE men. However we get the 'glory' out here, and these fellows acknowledge their indebtedness to the Infantry.

We have been digging trenches for the RE's since we have been here; it is very hard work, as the soil is extremely heavy clay, the heaviest clay I have ever dug, and I've as much experience in digging as most navvies. You may gather the speed we work when a man has to do a 'task' – 6ft long, 4 ft broad and 2ft 6ins deep in an afternoon. Yesterday afternoon I had got right down to the bottom of the trench, and consequently every blooming shovelful of clay I got I had to throw a height of 12 ft. to get it out of the trench and over the parapet You try it and see!...

What I was grumbling about last letter was the extra-super-officiousness of most of the officers; I'm not grumbling about the ordinary work of the soldier out here. I take that as it comes, naturally. But when it comes to flagrant acts of injustice, my blood boils!...[75]

In the months that followed, after the rains came, then sleet and snow, there were no more full-scale attacks, only occasional raids. These could be very unpleasant, and I was on one when the barbed wire entanglements, which the artillery said had been cut there, proved to be still intact; and there we were, trapped, no longer in darkness but in the sinister illumination of star shells and pistol lights, asking to be machine-gunned out of this world, as many were. I never knew how many, but I know that another man and I, untouched, somehow contrived to crawl back, half-carrying and half-dragging between us a third man, badly wounded.[76]

8 November 1915

We have been in the trenches this last five days and shall stop for some few more, these trenches are in quite a different part of the line to the others we have been in; and it's a part we don't want to see again. Talk about a hole! The communication trenches are simply canals, up to the waist in some parts, the rest up to the knees (one of the chaps was enquiring about the fishing rights); there are only a few dug-outs and those are full of water or falling in (three killed this week with falling dug-outs), and the parapets are tumbling down.

O! it's some place I can assure you. And Fritz (our name for the gentle Hun) keeps things pretty exciting here with snipers, trench-mortars, aerial torpedoes, etc. Good old Fritz, he does relieve the monotony. And the jobs they give us here. The other night, a crowd of us had to go over the parapet with shovels, crawl through deep water and under barbed wire for about a hundred yards and then start digging about fifty yards from the German lines. But it's little digging we could do; for they must have heard us, and then sent up six flare-lights right above our heads – we of course being as still as statues. But they spotted us, and then the bullets came and we had to get back as best we could. Two were killed outright just near me. And mind you this isn't a V.C. business, it's just a 'Working Party' in this part of the line. We're attached to another division here, and it's said that they've brought us down here to these exciting jobs, as the regiments here are too nervy and won't do 'em.

Anyhow the Battn is getting something of a name. I should say that there are – or were – at the very least 300 Bradford men in our Battalion. Of course since we came out here, we have had two drafts from the Reserve Battn to make up the strength, but we're not at full strength by a long way, owing to continual casualties.

I haven't had a wash since we came into these trenches, and we're all mud from head to foot. I believe the hazardous nature of this place has bucked me up considerably, for I feel more cheerful than I have done for some time. We're supposed to start leaves on he 26th of this month, but it takes a long time to get everybody through.[77]

*In late November 1915, Priestley missed one rotation into the front lines when he was sent to 3rd Corps Headquarters as a temporary replacement for a clerk who had been hospitalised.*

We worked and slept in a wooden hut, receiving, decoding, distributing or filing telegrams, starting fairly early in the morning and finishing between ten and eleven at night. The only break I had was during the afternoon, when I would walk in the grounds of the chateau with a little London clerk, who had a wife and children and dreaded any possibility of going up into the line. We had little to say to each other on these melancholy walks; the chateau grounds were almost without colour and form, deep in wintry weather that had no ice and glitter; we were like two empty sad characters in one of those avantgarde films or novels in which nothing happens.

Though safe and dry for once, I hated this job and this place, and longed to get back to the men I knew, trenches and shellfire and all. The staff warrant officer in charge of us was one of those sadistic types often found far behind the line; he bullied and tormented men like my London acquaintance who were in terror of being sent into action; there was a smell of fear in that hut; and he disliked me from the first, and after he threatened to return me to my battalion and I told him that was what I wanted, nothing I did was right.

It was like being a low-grade civil servant, working double shifts, being sworn at all the time, not getting enough to eat, and still feeling dirty and lice-itchy. And all the telegrams, many of them unnecessary and making no sense, all the filing and fuss, together created a Kafka atmosphere, though of course it was years before I found this name for it. But after that hut, trapped in the middle of what seemed a huge idiotic system, I have never rid myself of the feeling that we British – perhaps the whole Western world – both in war and peace are now committed to wasting men and time and money collecting and receiving and distributing and filing unnecessary information, and that before we go broke and barmy we should hire a team of bold haters of clerical work to cut nine-tenths of it out. Let them empty floor after floor of those ministerial buildings, rising higher every year, burn or pulp those acres of filing systems, cart away tons of in-trays and out-trays, then start again, without Kafka.[78]

*Priestley returned to his Battalion on 1 December to discover that yet more of his friends had been killed in action. The incessant toll of deaths, the futile trench raids and the gruelling, often pointless activities when rotated out of the front lines fuelled a growing disenchantment with the war. As he later confided, 'I spent the first year trying to be a hero and the rest of the time trying to stay alive'.[79] For the first time Priestley's letters begin to refer to his hope of 'a Blighty' – a wound that, though not bad enough to kill or permanently disable, was sufficiently serious to see a man discharged from service and returned to 'Blighty': Britain.*

When I got here on Wednesday, I suffered an enormous shock in learning that Irvine Ellis, my best chum in the Battalion, had been killed while I was away. A shell landed in the middle of a group, wounding fifteen and killing two. Ellis was not killed on the spot, but died a few hours later. Poor Irvine! – he enlisted at the same time that I did, and we were together all the time; his cheery companionship helped to lighten many a dark hour. I had a very pathetic letter from his sister last night – there is only his mother and sister at home –

saying that they had received no official statement but had heard
rumours that he had been killed. They couldn't believe it though and
she asked me to give them some news. I have written to her this
morning... I have just seen the news of Varley's death in the 'Weekly
Telegraph'. Poor Varley – another promising life cut short![80]

## 12 December 1915

We came into the trenches last Monday and went straight into the
firing line... last night we left the firing line and are now in the reserves,
but are going back in a day or two. I fancy I shall be spending Xmas in
the trenches.

Winter has set in very thoroughly, and the trenches are in a frightful
state: mud and water everywhere. A great part of the country around
here is under water, for it is always raining here. I thought Bradford
was a bad place for rain, but it is a Sahara desert compared with this
miserable country. There is very little fighting now, because both sides
are suffering from the awful conditions. Yesterday though, the German
artillery gave us a terrible bombardment, in return for one that our
artillery gave them the day before.

Of course, you know, we do not look at all like the soldiers you see
at home. We have khaki caps with flaps on, very much like the caps
civilians wear. Then we have rubber boots that reach up to our thighs,
and fur jackets that we call our 'Teddy Bear' coats. Then, besides our
overcoats, we have very long mackintosh capes. We have to keep
rubbing our feet and legs with whale-oil and anti-frostbite grease. Yet
with all these things, we cannot keep ourselves either warm or dry. I
had three pairs of thick socks under my rubber boots, yet my feet were
both wet and cold.[81]

## 17 December 1915

We are still in the trenches, and it is very miserable. I hope you will
contrive to spend a merry Xmas, and don't make yourselves miserable
on my account. I should be far happier myself if I thought you were
having a jolly time. I should have a good time, if I were at home. My
chances of seeing Saltburn Place are very remote for a long while,

unless I happen to get a 'blighty'... Things are very quiet here now, and rather monotonous, save for an occasional bombardment by the artillery.[82]

1 January 1916

We came into the trenches (an emergency call) the day before yesterday, but we are in the reserve trenches, not the firing line. I am writing this in my dugout (about two feet high and five feet long) by the miserable light of a guttering, little bit of candle. Soon it will go out, and then (for its only 5.30 and a wild night) come the long, long dark hours until 'stand to' in the morning.

Last night, old year's night, was a nightmare evening. At 1 o'clock, the troops in the front line made two bomb attacks on the German front line, and we'd to support them. For an hour, it was literally hell upon earth. I had to spend most of the time crouched in the mud by the side of a machine gun. It was going nearly all the time, and the noise nearly stunned me, then the sickly smell of cordite, and the dense masses of steam from the Water Cooler didn't improve matters. Both our artillery and theirs were going for all they were worth, and they lit up the sky. You could see some of the shells going through the air, swift, red streaks. Then an incessant stream of bullets from both sides, bombs, trench mortars, making a hellish din, and the sky lit up with a mad medley of shells, searchlights, star lights, the green and red rockets (used for signalling purposes); just about an hour of hell, and that was our introduction to the year of 1916!

This morning I learned that we lost about 80 men and several officers, so that it cost us pretty dearly... I'm afraid that you would hardly recognise me if you saw me now. It is three days since I had a shave, and two since I had a wash. I'm a mask of mud. My hair is matted, and I resemble an Australian beachcomber.[83]

Worse than the raids, worse than the German heavy batteries that occasionally got our range and dropped 'Jack Johnsons' among us, were the mere conditions of existence in the front line and communication trenches, now with winter upon us, that were mud and water. For days and days on end, wearing six pairs of socks and high gum-boots and a sheepskin jacket that was either wet or caked in mud, I slithered around, trying to sleep on the trench firestep or crawling into some hole in the wet clay, filthy and maddeningly lousy, never seeing anything that looked like hot food. (I was fortunate, more than most, in two respects: I could cheerfully chew away at Army biscuits and bully-beef, which was all we had many days; I was rarely out of tobacco, and if I could smoke my pipe I could often forget I was hungry and short of sleep.) That dugout we have all seen in productions of Journey's End would have looked to me then like a suite in some Grand Hotel: I never did find myself within miles of anything so dry and commodious.

Some of the worst nights, in that winter of 1915, were spent carrying heavy coils of barbed wire up communication trenches, knee-deep in water and sometimes under shellfire, continually slipping and then being pinned down by the coils of wire. I saw men, no weaklings but powerful fellows, break down and weep. It was not the danger, which might easily have been worse – though at that, I lost every close friend I had in the company that winter – but the conditions in which the lower ranks of the infantry were condemned to exist month after month, worse conditions than the Germans and French ever knew except briefly in battle, that drained away health, energy, spirit, and with them any real confidence in those cavalry captains, back in the chateaux, who saw themselves as generals fit for high command.

They tell me Passchendaele in '17 was worse still – I was never there, thank God – and now I believe the Army ought to have turned on Haig and his friends and sent them home. Even without the negotiated peace we ought to have had in 1916, we could have saved half a million British lives if we had handed the whole mess over to a few men from Imperial Chemicals, Lever Brothers or Lyons and Co...[84]

After a few more weeks in the line I was wounded in the hand by a rifle grenade, no great matter, not the 'blighty' that sent you to England. I was dispatched to a hospital and then a convalescent camp at Le Treport on the coast. I did not like either of them, especially the convalescent camp, where we never had enough to eat, were always being rounded up for fatigue duties (detested by all front-line soldiers), and, being cut off, had no money, no letters, no parcels, no anything. I was glad to get back to the battalion, a kind of home, however dangerous and uncomfortable. I was not the keen, fit warrior I had been months before, but I still felt that if I had to wear a uniform, obey orders, serve in France, then I wanted to be with the battalion wherever it was.

By this time I might have had a commission but I refused to apply; I still wanted to be with the men who had gone up Gibbet Lane, Halifax, when I did, even though one friend after another was vanishing. Later I was sorry I had not applied; it was a rough war for junior officers but an even rougher one for men in the ranks. It is true that in attack the subalterns had to move around more than their men, and so were more likely to get killed or wounded, but they were not so badgered and sworn at, underfed and overworked, and escaped the very worst conditions. They were all right, our own junior officers; my quarrel, which still continues, was with their superiors, especially the red-tabbed kind, who seemed to me then, so far as I could judge in my raw youth and innocence, mostly a lot of jackasses. And now I am no longer young and have lost all innocence, I see it was a good guess.[85]

*Like many of his fellows, Priestley sometimes self-censored his letters or summoned a cheerful tone that did not reflect his true feelings, but the privations and fears, and the deaths of an endless succession of comrades could not always be ignored.*

22 January 1916

Just returned from hospital this morning... We go into the trenches tomorrow night for 16 days. By some strange irony of Fate, each time I have been away from the Battalion, I have lost a very dear friend. First it was Ellis, and now it seems that Waddington, (whom you met at the station) is either dead or wounded in the hands of the Germans. I am feeling rather lonely these days, and the loss of these chums has a greater effect on me than the experiences I go through personally...

Sorry about Foster, and strange to say, while I was in hospital I wrote to him for the first time for months, to his Battalion of course. My illness had nothing whatever to do with my kidneys or my bowels; it was a common complaint out here – a sort of debility, due to overwork, lack of sleep, and general rotten conditions. The hospitals are so crammed full of sick men now. I enclose a very dilapidated 10s note, which has been gnawed by rats or mice in the trenches. They gnawed through the back of my pocketbook. Ask Players to send me some White Label Navy Mixture – duty free. Get some of my money to pay for it. I'm tired of the tobacco they issue here.[86]

*Priestley's Battalion sometimes found themselves 'in situations impossible to imagine, far stranger than bad dreams'.[87] On 1 February 1916 they were in an 'Edgar Allan Poe setting', occupying a support trench that ran through a French village cemetery.*

Just about in the centre of the British line there is a village, which must, in the far-off happy days of peace, have been the home of a prosperous and happy little community. Now – alas! – the civil population have long since [gone] and the village is a ruin. Some of the houses are almost intact, while others – the majority – are battered indescribably. The beautiful old church in the centre of the village is a ruin, roofless, with only about a quarter of its steeple left.

Now, if you turned down to the right of this same church; and walked about five hundred yards you would come across a cemetery – in fact the village cemetery. And at the present moment, among the tombs of this same cemetery lives – or rather exists – your humble servant, for a line of reserve trenches runs right through the cemetery, and our platoon is occupying these trenches. The French graves have all large stone or wooden crosses on them – mostly 8 to 12 feet in height, and we are entirely surrounded by these dismal things. Crowded here and there between these are little wooden crosses that mark what must be the most pathetic graves in the world – those of British soldiers. On some of them, little French memorials have been placed – how and by whom I do not know. At night, our surroundings look very weird – to put it mildly. But we are veterans now and we take everything as it comes...[88]

We had great crosses and monuments of marble and granite all round us, unbelievable at night when the darkness was split by the white glare of Very lights and the shadows were gigantically grotesque, though often we had not time to notice them, having to duck down as machine-gun bullets ricocheted off the funeral stones.[89]

*In March 1916 the 23rd Division came out of the line, preparing to move south to relieve the 17th French Division on the Carency-Souchez front.*

The rest I wrote to you about is 'off', decidedly 'off'. Only a few days after I wrote to you last, we had to pack up hurriedly and march back to the line. At the time, the weather conditions were absolutely arctic – blizzards and terrible frosts. The first night, we slept, or rather, tried to sleep, in a ramshackle old shed, huddled together without blankets or anything. We messed about several days but evidently weren't needed there, so returned wearily to our 'rest' camp – in six inches of snow. We were there exactly one day, and then we had to pack up again! This time they shoved us onto a train – in cattle trucks of course – and after several hours travelling we landed in a town somewhere in the French lines! From there we marched and marched, and are now in a place just within the British lines. For two days we had no proper rations and had to depend on what we could buy.[90]

It happened that I was one of a tiny advance party. A glance at the map today suggests we made the kind of move that would take about forty minutes in a car. But in this war, in another world, another time, it seemed an immense and complicated journey, like going to Afghanistan now. (Much later, it took me three days, never at any point abandoning the journey, to move some men from Rouen to Calais.) We might have been explorers creeping into some blank space on the map. I remember how four or five of us in this advance party, now utterly lost (we had a genius for getting lost) and completely out of touch with the British Expeditionary Force, found ourselves in some unknown French town with nobody to report to, no food, no money to buy any food, so that to bring ourselves out of destitution we had to sell – we called it 'flog' – all but the most essential parts of our kit and equipment.[91]

[Date uncertain - March 1916]
We were inspected this morning by some big general – I don't know his name. What's going to happen to us I don't know, but all our Division is down here, so perhaps we are going to take over part of this line. However, we take everything as it comes. The weather is bright now, though we are rather further south, which may account for the change. The French Army, from what I have seen of it, is rather of the ragtime order. There is neither the organisation nor the cleanliness of the British Army. There are many factories and collieries around here, which make the place look more like home to our fellows...[92]

When finally we reached the French lines we made some discoveries that heightened our prejudice against the British higher command. The poilu, a bloke supposedly so low in morale that he was near mutiny, enjoyed substantial and tasty hot meals where we would have been opening another tin of bully. Unshaven, untidy and at ease, he sat in deep dugouts passing the wine and talking about women when we would have been – and shortly would be – shoved into forward fire trenches, however bad they were, and then ordered on a raid or given some hopeless task just because it was assumed by chateau types that muck, jeopardy and misery were good for us...[93]

I have now had some good opportunities of observing the Poilus and I have no hesitation in saying that the French soldiers are better fed and better treated than we are, and the British public can put that in their pipe and smoke it! (Don't send this letter to the paper, by the way. There are enough A.S.C and R.A.M.C. men at the various bases to keep the Press supplied with exciting news.)...[94]

These same French now taking it easy were, however, a remnant of the divisions that had stormed these ridges, from Lorette to Vimy, in 1915. The Germans had dug themselves in on the higher ground, from which their artillery, heavy and closely massed, dominated the valuable industrial region still held by the French, who were working coal-pits not ten miles in some places from the front line.

This was a very sinister sector into which we crept now, half-blinded by the last snowstorms of the winter. Names there enjoyed a grim notoriety – Notre Dame de Lorette, Souchez, Vimy Ridge, and the Labyrinth. Into the Labyrinth we went, relieving poilus who obviously looked relieved. These were old trenches that had simply been wired off, and when we explored them we found them filled with bloodstained clothing, abandoned equipment, heads, legs and arms.

Further on, in a trench still open, several of us late at night, bitterly cold, crawled into the nearest dugout, and soon went to sleep although the straw in there hardly protected us from some uncomfortable objects: in the morning we left that dugout in a hurry, for we had been sleeping with enormous aerial torpedoes. Gone were any communication trenches labelled with the names of London streets; there were no clearly marked fire and support trenches; you crawled through the dark and a belated blizzard and found a hole somewhere.[95]

13 March 1916.
We are 'soldiering' (as the Tommies phrase it) in earnest now. We have just been in the ghastliest part of the whole Western Front. There is nothing like it. We relieved the French there, and they looked relieved too. You must have heard of the famous 'labyrinth'; well that's it. Great hills half blown away with enormous shells; villages absolutely raised to the ground; old trenches full of heads, legs and arms, bloodstained clothing and old equipment. Talk about 'souvenirs'! The place is one vast morgue, it has been taken and retaken so many times. The front line trench is a ditch about three feet deep; there are no communication trenches, you simply crawl up in the dark, and lie in the trench until relieved, which is often 24 hours...[96]

It had been quiet recently around there until we British arrived, but of course we had to hot it up for the sake of our morale, to keep our fellas on their toes, in spite of the fact, not hard to discover on the map and all too obvious to any staff officer who went to see for himself, that if we did start anything the Germans, higher up, well dug in, and in places not more than twenty yards away, would have the better of it. So very soon, having asked for it, God knows why, we caught a packet.

Outside any plan of campaign, without any battle being fought, any honours being won, we went through the mincer. It was not long before our own B Company, with a nominal fighting strength of 270, had been reduced to a grim and weary seventy. Two hundred men had gone somehow and somewhere, with nothing to show for it. The German trenches are very close, in some places only 20 yards away, and there is great execution with bombs and aerial torpedoes. Luckily my company only went into the Reserves, for those who went in the front line, lost very heavily...[97]

And there was snow, sleet, blizzards and about a slice of bread a day to eat. We've marched and marched, slept in cellars (a few inches under water) while all around the great shells were roaring and blasting.

There are a number of huge military burial places, both French and German, round about and when the big shells ploughed their way into these, the result was gruesome in the extreme. There is nothing in the British line to equal this little lot. However we are now back some way from the line, billeted in a town. Also there has been a sudden dramatic change in the weather, for behold! old sol has come, the snow has disappeared like magic, and it is Spring!...[98]

Spring came suddenly and between the pounded and bloody chalk of the front lines and the mining area in the rear there would be glimpses, good enough for Pissaro and Sisley, of fields bright with poppies and lanes beginning to smell of honeysuckle. When we were given a few days' rest, we went back to a mining village that had an enormous slag-heap. Far away, behind the ridge they held, the Germans had a great naval gun that had the range of this village. The shell it fired was of such a monstrous calibre that you could easily hear it coming, like an aerial express.

We would be hanging about, smoking and talking, enjoying the sunshine and the quiet, when suddenly we would hear this monster coming. There was only one safe place, behind the slag-heap, and everybody would run for it pellmell. Shirrr-brirrr-bump! There it went, and we would come from behind the slag-heap and see the smoke clearing and another six houses gone. Fortunately that gun did no night-work, and we did not really mind it during the day.

Up in the line, what we did mind, what soon began to get us down, were the Minenwerfers, the big trench-mortars; and at Souchez we always appeared to have the Minenwerfer specialists against us. Often we asked for their attention; not us, the ordinary infantry who had to stay in the front line, but the Brigade, the Division, the Corps, the Army.

What happened all too often was that our own specialists would rush their Stokes guns up into the support trenches, blast away for quarter of an hour, and then hurry off with their infernal things to where their transport was waiting. Pampered and heartless fellows – this is how we regarded them – lunatic experts who had to interfere, off they went to some back area, to roofs and beds and estaminets, beer and wine, chips and eggs; while we poor devils, left behind in holes in the ground, now had to face the anger of the Boches they had been strafing.

The Minenwerfer teams got to work on us. Up and then down came those monstrous canisters of high explosive, making hell's own din when they landed, blasting or burying us. If there was any infantryman who was not afraid of these things, who was not made uneasy by any rumours they would shortly be arriving, I never met him. Perhaps because they were such short-range affairs, perhaps because if you were on the alert, looking and listening hard, you could just dodge them, perhaps because they made such a hellish row, they frightened us more than bullets, bombs, shells of all calibres. And in and around Souchez we crouched below a nest of them.[99]

*In late March, Priestley was hospitalised after falling ill.*

Though I've not said anything to you, I've been unwell for some time; I've kept going to see the doctor, & he's kept giving me odd pills & excusing me from duty. Finally last week, he sent me to hospital. I was at the Field Ambulance for 4 days, in bed all the time, pulse and temperature taken twice a day etc. etc. Then they moved me on to the Divisional Rest Station, a large Hospital-cum-Convalescent Home, where I am at the present moment. This is the first day I've been allowed to get up, & I'm feeling much better. I've had no letters or parcels forwarded from my regiment yet, so if you've sent anything, you'll know why I haven't replied.[100]

*On 16 April he wrote to his father again, complaining about shortages both of letters from home and of money in his pocket.*

I wrote to you a fortnight ago last Thursday from No.3 Convalescent Depot, to send me, at once, some money & an old pipe. Well, if you have written or sent anything, I haven't received it, & in the meanwhile I have changed my address & am now at the Base. I [have] been in front of a Medical Board & am passed fit for the Line. I shall be going up there with the next draft, which may be a week or two. I have waited impatiently for the mail every day, hoping to hear something from you, & putting off writing until I did. We don't get any pay apart from our Battalion, & it is miserable to be without money for weeks & weeks, & there are plenty of Y.M.C.A's etc here. If you have sent it I can't make out what has become of the letter, because, though I have changed my address, the people at Con.[Convalescent] Camp send letters on here. Better make some enquiries. If you didn't receive my letter, please send off a 10s [shilling] or £1 note & an old pipe (not a new one)... I am hundreds of francs in credit & yet I have had no money for weeks – very ironical. This place is one enormous camp - huts & bell tents, for it is the Infantry Base for most of the Divisions out here.[101]

4 May 1916[102]

Just received your letter with 10s [ten shillings – 50p] enclosed. The money will be very useful here – we are in a town – to augment the slender and not over palatable fare provided by His Majesty. It is summer now and as hot – or possibly hotter than it is at any time in Bradford... If you have read my previous letters carefully, and read the newspapers you will know the district we are in. Remember, we took it over from the French troops. You see the names of these trenches in the paper every day.[103]

18 May 1916

We came out of the trenches last night after spending five days in the firing line, and we shall be going in again in a day or night. Our trenches around here are very close to the Germans, and in consequence, every form of death and destruction abounds. Rifle grenades, trench mortars (minnen werfers or "sausages" – bombs bigger than a Rugby football), aerial torpedoes, are sent over into our trenches at regular intervals, and underneath there are mines ready to be blown at any moment.

A rifle grenade caused my wound; it dropped right into the bay of the trench I was in, and killed one and wounded four. I've had some very narrow escapes from them this last day or two, and since I got wounded, they've made me rather nervy. The part of the line we hold now is absolute 'hell'; the French said it was the worst part of their line, not counting Verdun at the present time.

As I told you, the battalion had been about fifteen to twenty miles back for a fortnight's 'rest"', and then we came back in the train to a little town about six miles from the firing line. Our train was just steaming into the station when the Germans started shelling it, because it is the railhead - the furthest point the railway reaches. Enormous 12 inch shells dropped all about us - the engine driver bolted, so we were left about twenty minutes in the train, every minute expecting a shell to hit it. But not one did, though the carriages were well battered with shrapnel, and eventually we backed out the station and were landed a couple of miles back.

One night, while I was at the base, a Zeppelin dropped four bombs on the camp, killing and wounding a few. The Zepp bombs make a nice hole and a tidy noise, but as an experience it's small beer. I've given over thinking about passes. Never mind, I shall be home with a 'blighty' soon...

We were near the first aid Dressing Station, this morning, and there, I saw the body of a young lad of 18, who came into the trenches last night for the first time, and was shot through the head. Fate seems to have a grim and gruesome humour of her own, and out here she sometimes exercises it. There were two Derby men with the battalion on our left in the trenches – I mean two amongst others – of course – and these two, not used to the hard conditions out here, complained bitterly of cold feet. The same day, a shell came and whipped both feet off one man and one off the other.[104]

### 1 June 1916

We spent 5 days in a village just behind the trenches, went in again for four days, and are now in the reserve trenches until tomorrow. Curious you should mention loss of trenches at [censored, but probably the Labyrinth], as that is the terrible place we took over from the French three months ago, and we are only just on the left of it now. I have seen all the battles for the crest (when we were there the Germans had it and we were crouched in shell holes about 25 yards away – and 6 inches of snow on the ground).

The village we were in last Sunday was shelled with armour-piercing Jack Johnsons, but we had only one man killed, though there were many civilians killed and wounded. It was a ghastly day. All the roads leading to the trenches were shelled too, and there were mules and limbers going up in the air. They sent every kind of shell over – gas shells (it was quaint to see the French children with gas helmets on), tear shells (everybody's eyes were watering and sore), incendiary shells, shrapnel, and last but not least – the enormous Johnsons.

I tried to imagine Saltburn Place being shelled in a similar manner, but it was too horrible to think about. They crash through houses and roads and steel girders like going through paper. And the concussion! Our heavy batteries, just near, were thundering in response, and our stretcher bearers had to keep dashing down to the gun pits to bring out the wounded, poor maimed creatures – burnt, twisted torn and many of them dazed beyond immediate recovery with the sheer noise. I've had some narrow escapes from rifle grenades and trench mortars this time in, but I'm all right and carrying on.

Ten months out here and no signs of a leave; it's a shame! Some of the officers have been three times. We are expecting large drafts of

Derby men this time out, for notwithstanding regular drafts mainly of men who have been out before, we have only a handful of men left. My company is not the weakest in the Batt. and we have only a fighting strength of about 70 men instead of 260. People get the impression that we've ample men out here but that's wrong. We've taken over such a lot of new frontage that the actual number of men per mile of trench seems less than ever. It's at the bases where you 'can't stir for men' - not in the firing line. As for food, when we were in the firing line this last time, we had a loaf for every 4 men for a day's ration, and no fresh meat or even Maconochie, but just bully beef.

Now that you know where we are, you'll be able to follow the events in our part of the line with interest. It's the star turn on the British Front and second to none in hellishness. They say we go to [censored] the next time we go to the trenches. Send me another parcel soon, but it's no good sending stuff to mix with water as there's very little water. Some of mother's homemade tuck would be very acceptable. There seem to be quite a lot of heroes around Toller Lane [Priestley's home district in Bradford]. Love to all, Jack. NB Enclosed are flowers plucked from the parapet, probably growing out of dead men; there are plenty in these parapets, it's no uncommon sight to see a hand or a foot sticking out.[105]

*Although Priestley must have written many other letters during the remainder of the war, none of them have survived, but his later war experiences are described in his autobiography,* Margin Released. *As Priestley well knew, despite a couple of minor wounds, he had been lucky so far, but in June of 1916, his luck ran out.*

One day it had to happen. It was June now, hot again, thirsty weather, a lot of chalk dust about, and we were in the front line on a beautiful morning. The platoon rations had just come up. I sent Private O'Neill down the communication trench to bring up some water – and sixteen years went by before we saw each other again. I helped a young soldier, who had only just joined us out there, to take the rations into a dugout, not a deep dugout but a small one hollowed out of the parapet.

In this dugout I began sorting out the bread, meat, tea, sugar, tinned milk, and so on, to give each section its proper share, a tricky little job. I had done it many times before, hardly ever to anybody's complete satisfaction; but on this morning I suspect that it saved my life. After the explosion when everything had caved in, nobody was certain I was there, but several fellows knew the platoon rations were in there somewhere: that stuff would have to be dug out.

There I was then, deciding on each section's share, when I heard a rushing sound, and I knew what it meant and knew, though everything had gone into slow motion, I had no hope of getting away before the thing arrived. Just as on earlier and later occasions when I have thought all was up, the first shrinking in terror was followed, as I went into the new slow time, by a sense of detachment. I believe from what I learnt long afterwards that the Minenwerfer landed slap in the trench, two or three yards away. All I knew at the time was that the world blew up.

# Chapter 3
# Hanging on the old barbed wire

I do not remember how and by what route I travelled from the front line at Souchez to the military hospital at North Evington, a suburb of Leicester. Any man who was ever around, not as close as I was but, let us say, about three times the distance, when a big German trench-mortar went off, will agree that I was lucky to be carted away in one piece. Had I been as near as that and out in the trench, I would have been blown to bits. As it was, though I had some minor injuries from the dugout caving in, was partly deaf, and ran a high temperature that kept me in bed for some weeks, no parts of me were missing and there was nothing wrong with me that prolonged treatment and rest would not cure. I was lucky in that war and have never ceased to be aware of the fact.[106]

*The experience of being buried alive left Priestley with a lifelong claustrophobia. He never conquered his subsequent fear of travelling on the Underground – even the word must have summoned memories and fears - – avoided it whenever possible, and even used it as the setting for a horror story 'Underground', written in 1974.[107] His convalescence was a long and slow one.*

The first clear recollection I have of the North Evington hospital shows me my parents, arriving out of a haze, staring at me mistily across the bed. Day by day for ten months or so, they had probably had a worse time than I had had, wondering what was happening, waiting for those letters that now I realise said too little, never really tried to grasp their hands. Speak now and I will answer .... But too often we don't speak in this sense, certainly not in my family. We are affectionate and have plenty to say on general topics, but never have we spoken from heart to heart, not I to my father, not my children to me, and so far perhaps not their children to them. With us the Lord our God is an inhibited God, visiting the awkward silences and unspoken endearments of the fathers upon the children unto the third and fourth generation.

There may be people who enjoy a hospital life, but at no time have I been one of them. Once my temperature began to come down and I was no longer wandering in the land of delirium, 1 longed to be out of that bed, that ward. Opposite my bed was a table on which there was a gramophone, and on the turntable of this gramophone was a record of a baritone singing 'Sussex, Sussex by the Sea!' Everybody who went past halted a moment or two to start the gramophone going, but nobody ever changed the record. Lying there, forbidden to move, indeed in no condition to take action, 1 had to endure hours of that cursed instrument grinding out 'Sussex, Sussex by the Sea!' Now and again a small piano arrived and with it some well-meaning but not brilliant local talent, mostly wobbly sopranos. One of them, not remarking how we glared from our beds, nearly always sang that drivelling refrain:

> We don't want to lose you
> But we think you ought to go,
> For your King and your Country
> Both need you so.

The First War, unlike the Second, produced two distinct crops of songs: one for patriotic civilians, like that drivel above; the other, not composed and copyrighted by anybody, genuine folk song, for the sardonic front-line troops. Of these some were bawdy, like the famous 'Mademoiselle from Armentieres' and 'The Ballad of Bollocky Bill the Sailor and the Fair Young Maiden'; some were lugubrious and homesick, without patriotic sentiment of any kind, like 'I Want To Go Home'; others were sharply concerned with military life from the standpoint of the disillusioned private. The best of these, with its rousing chorus of 'I know where he is', asked in one lilting verse after another if you wanted the officer, the sergeant-major, the quartermaster-sergeant, and so on, and then told you what these nuisances were up to. The last verse and chorus, however, changed the form and the mood, for here the battalion was the subject, and after 'I know where it is', was repeated quietly there came the final reply:

> It's hanging on the old barbed wire.
> I've seen 'em, I've seen 'em
> Hanging on the old barbed wire.

And to this day I cannot listen to it unmoved. There is a flash of pure genius, entirely English, in that 'old,' for it means that even that devilish enemy, that death-trap, the wire, has somehow been accepted, recognised and acknowledged almost with affection, by the deep rueful charity of this verse. I have looked through whole anthologies that said less to me.

From the hospital at North Evington, before the summer was over, I was sent to convalesce to a country house in Rutland. It was an unbelievable move. After all, the hospital was like the one I had known at Le Treport; it was, so to speak, only a clean white extension of the war world I had lived in for the past year; it might almost have been an immense hygienic dugout. The country house in Rutland was in another world, outside the war, but it was not at all the one I had known before I enlisted. It belonged to light comedy and those trifling novels, not without charm and an appealing absurdity, that were one of the literary fashions before 1914. Even Rutland itself was as near to being an imaginary county as the map of England would allow. A country house there did not seem to be anything that could appear on an Army Order. It was as if one end of the vast military machine dissolved into fantasy. I travelled to Rutland, no distance from Leicester of course, wearing the sky-blue coat and pants, the white shirt and scarlet tie of the wounded and convalescent in the First War, sensible enough, nevertheless the gaudiest outfit I have ever worn in a public conveyance.[108]

*The Rutland country house, Hambleton Hall, was supervised by a bumbling, elderly doctor and a motherly nurse who led a team of volunteer auxiliaries – naive young girls who were 'all County', with pretty faces straight out of the pages of* Tatler *and* Bystander.[109] *The convalescents were an exotic cast of characters who Priestley soon marshalled into a concert party. This idyllic, near-miraculous interlude in the midst of bloody war, was marred only by one example of what Priestley had now come to term 'The Enemy': stiff, upper-lipped 'brass hats' and rule-bound NCOs, who used the power and authority that Army rank gave them to belittle and make miserable their subordinates.*

Rutland had tried to entertain us; we would now entertain Rutland. No doubt we were terrible, but we amused ourselves and a great many other people during a bad hour, when the slaughter-house of the Somme was working overtime. The only person who did not like us, and indeed hated me, was a dark and savage-looking sergeant – he had been in the police at Penang – who joined us for convalescence about then, felt out of it, wanted to claim authority he did not have, and anyhow was obviously one of The Enemy. He was a type I rarely failed to encounter wherever I went in the army, nearly always enjoying some sort of authority; the mutual dislike was immediate and never changed except for the worse; it was The Enemy. But though this Sergeant blustered and sneered, he could do us no harm, and soon he vanished.[110]

In autumn rain I left Rutland and its cast of unlikely characters, its summer day's dream, to report at the depot in Halifax, wedged firmly in reality. From there I was dispatched for further treatment to a convalescent camp at Ripon. There I was miserable, like everybody else I knew.

It was a bad camp, so bad that not long afterwards, I believe, the men mutinied. There was too much mud, too many unnecessary restrictions, too many P.T. instructors swelling their chests, which had never known a front-line parapet, in their red-and-black-striped jerseys, and bellowing at better men, as we thought, to look alive and jump to it. We realised that we ought to attempt some physical training, but we resented being treated like recruits by these swaggerers who had never been further than the P.T. School at Aldershot. To hell with them and their jumping to it! Confined to camp, because of some recent rumpus, we muttered and growled in corners, making plans to get out of this hole by hook or crook, though we had all heard rumours of what happened in the terrible 'glasshouse', the military prison where they systematically wore down your resistance, broke your spirit.

One of our most notable pieces of self-deception is that we English on all levels, at all times and places, are an easygoing people, kindly disposed whatever the situation, unlike callous and cruel foreigners. This may be true of our ordinary relationships, though even there we have a bad record in our treatment of children; it is certainly not true of official England, which often turns on us a very harsh visage. We still hang men when most other countries have abolished capital punishment. There are demands that we should start flogging again, even restoring the terrible 'cat' (cat o' nine tails, a sadistic inspiration) that in a few strokes tears a man's back to red ribbons.

Until recently many of our prisons were far more inhumane than most prisons abroad. And in the earlier part of the First War, when the Services were crowded with eager volunteers, decent young men who had not been brought out of gaols or collared by the press gang, those Services retained brutal forms of punishment discontinued by those inferior and cruel foreigners. One of them I remember was Field Punishment Number One, in which a man was tied to a gun-carriage, out in the open and unable to move for hour after hour. It was dropped later in the war, together with some other savage anachronisms, but not before much damage had been done to English bodies and spirit.

We have in English society a large number of men on a certain level, not at the top but a long way from the bottom, usually in authority somewhere, who have been insensitive and brutalised from boyhood, who are psychological misfits and haters of life. Drop out of a clean-collar-and-bank-balance style of living, even if only by enlisting as we did, and these types come looming up. Take the wobbling lid off, give them a free hand, and even now they would show us a nasty thing or two.

After a few sullen weeks, perhaps in less time than that, a trainload of us was removed from Ripon to a larger and better convalescent camp just outside Alnwick in Northumberland. I forget how many months I was up there; it seems like years, an exile in some cosier Siberia. I needed no more treatment of any sort but was not yet passed fit, and anyhow I had now applied for a commission...[111]

Being large and heterogeneous, it was a good camp for dodging such parades and fatigues as there might be. Every morning for weeks, I attended the full parade with a group of fellow dodgers, and at the sergeant-major's cry of 'Fatigue parties, dismiss!' I marched off my little party, back to the hut to do nothing. A corporal of the West Yorks, needing some leave and having been refused it, bluffed his way home by sheer magnificent impudence. He collected about a dozen West Riding men who also wanted a spell at home, though they had not a single leave pass and railway warrant between them, and marched them smartly to the station and barked at them to board the train.

At Newcastle and York they had to change trains to reach the West Riding, and both these stations swarmed with 'redcaps' (the military police) ready to pounce upon any soldier on his own and looking a bit shifty, demanding to see his leave pass and railway warrant. But each time this corporal marched his party on to the right platform, stood them at ease while waiting for the train, and looked so regimental and important that he was never challenged, so took them all home.

They may have had a few bits of paper to show if necessary. In the back room of a pub in Alnwick, two or three artful characters, soldiers not civilians, did a fine trade in forged leave passes and railway warrants. I knew a corporal who, having been once given a warrant for some obscure place in Cornwall or Cumberland, never gave it up, and used it for going by train anywhere he pleased, nobody knowing or caring if he was on the way to this mysterious place or not. I was sent, with two men, to bring a man, absent without leave, from Wakefield, and we took the best part of a week over the job. They were having a party at his house when we arrived there. 'Nay, yer won't want him for a day or two, will yer?' they cried. 'What about comin' on Thursday?'

We were now well into 1917, the only full year of the war I was never near the front, never out of England. It was a sort of dead time for me. I was neither dodging the war nor anxious any longer to be a good soldier in it. I did a little writing, but my heart was not in it, because my heart was not in anything...[112]

When I had left Alnwick, having been passed fit at last, and was temporarily attached to the Third Battalion on Tyneside, waiting to be sent as a cadet to an O.T.C., I seemed to be in an ugly army, on the edge of a rotten war. The Enemy was there, with hate at first sight, with attempts almost every day to trap me into making some mistake that would finish me for a commission. If I made a single friend, then I have forgotten him, and this is not likely.

Drafts of officers, noncoms and men were being sent to the Front. I do not know what happened with the officers; I was out of touch with the men, all strangers; but I saw what went on among the noncoms, especially those who were rather older than I was, many of them married, more or less settled in the town. To be threatened with being put on the next draft, to some of these men, was like being rung up by Murder Inc. Their only chance of escape was to persuade, let us say, The Enemy, to leave their names off the list. Sometimes it took money; sometimes a pretty young wife had to be obliging. I loathed what I saw and heard inside the regiment; and if there was anything happening just then outside it, anywhere in the neighbourhood, to uplift the heart of man, then I missed it.

Even so, I was lucky. I might have been at Passchendaele, where Haig, who ought to have gone up there himself or gone home, was slicing my whole generation into sausage meat held above a swill bucket. Once in New York in the Thirties I saw a musical sourly entitled Hurray for What? We ought to have thought of it earlier and used it for Victory Parades.

The 16th Officer Cadet Battalion – I think that was its name – to which I was posted, much to my relief, was at Kimmel Park Camp in North Wales. We were worked hard there, but I enjoyed it all. I was jerked out of my apathy, my slack habits of mind and body. I made no close friends among my fellow cadets – there was hardly time – but they were pleasant to work and live with. The Enemy did not show up among the officers and instructors...

A great deal of what we were taught I could not take seriously, not simply because I was not really a military type, though of course I was not, but also because I believed much of it to be out of date, merely an attempt to improve on what we did in the Boer War. All that musketry, for example, in which one of our chief instructors was a major in Orders, perhaps a parson-schoolmaster before the war, a cheerful pagan who was fond of referring to 'we old Bisley bullpunchers', hardly an ecclesiastical Order. It seemed to me that the rifle was all very well in frontier skirmishes, but the war we were in was chiefly an affair of machine-guns, bombs, mortars, shellfire. And I had a sharp dislike, together with much mistrust, of all that he-man guff about 'the spirit of the bayonet'. We might have saved about half a million lives if we had forgotten all those campaigns against Fuzzy-wuzzies and Boer commandos and had given some thought to the German General Staff.

Not that our platoon commander, though an oldish regular, was so limited in his outlook. His name was Tredennick, and he was an odd fish, conscientious but probably a bit cracked, and when he got going on strategy, his eyes glittering and the words pouring out, whole continents, not yet fully involved, rose and took to arms, Asia rushed to meet Africa, and soon, while we lit our pipes and stayed out of the rain, the globe was on fire. We were back at school, dangling the bait we knew the master could not resist, triumphantly wasting time.

We dined in turn at the officers' mess, to prove we did not always eat peas with a knife. We sat for an examination. All but an unfortunate few were passed out and duly commissioned. Out of the allowance we were given we bought greatcoats and British warms, tunics and Sam Browne belts. We were officers free for ever from cookhouse fatigues and carrying coils of barbed wire. I was commissioned to the Devon Regiment, and after a few days' swagger at home I arrived at its headquarters and barracks at Devonport, as new and shy and glossy as a bridegroom.

Except for a few courses at camps in Cornwall, I was there at the barracks in Devonport for months and months, until almost the end of that summer of 1918. Although it seemed to me, after what I had known so far, the life of Reilly, I made no attempt to avoid being drafted out to the Front. I was ready to go if I was wanted. Perhaps because all but one of the Devon battalions were not in France then, were serving without any great loss of men in distant theatres of war, I was not wanted. After tents, barns, trenches and wooden huts, and the greasy stew and congealing bacon that went with them, those barracks were four-star quarters. We lived well, dined with the regimental silver and with the regimental band playing outside. I got to know that band very well. We junior officers were supposed to turn out and be drilled, in a highly elaborate and quite useless fashion as if we might have to join one of Marlborough's armies, by a mad old Marine sergeant, who had drilled himself out of his mind.

The adjutant, discovering that I was dodging these insane parades, came roaring up in one of those scarlet-faced professional fits of bad temper that must have ruined the blood pressure of many regular officers, and told me that from now on I would be in charge of funeral parties. Why he thought this some form of punishment I cannot imagine. There was a large military hospital in Plymouth and hardly a day passed without a death there; and the bodies were sometimes buried in the local cemetery, but more often than not they had to be taken to the station and ceremonially entrained. It was our duty to supply a firing party for the cemetery or a guard to present arms at the station; with it went the regimental band, a sergeant who knew all the drill and gave the commands, and an officer who really did nothing. I was that officer.

Morning after morning we slow-marched to the station, where often there were weeping relatives on the platform; we gave the coffin a last salute; then off we went, marching briskly, the band playing a lively tune. After taking part in this ironical piece, I considered myself free – without reporting back to the adjutant – for the remainder of the day. If it were a fine afternoon I might stroll along the Hoe and wonder if the bright-eyed girls were married to naval officers. After dinner I rarely stayed boozing in the mess; usually I went into Devonport or Plymouth, perhaps to a cinema, rich then in new Chaplin and custard-pie short films, or to a music-hall, where variety was then in its Indian summer, brilliant and dying.[113]

It was three years after I had first gone to France that a little batch of us subalterns were given our orders and crossed to Boulogne. We sailed by day in a fantastic American ship that might have been fetched from the Mississippi. We were the only British aboard among thousands of American troops, new, raw and hearty, with nothing in their mode of address to distinguish their rank. A vast bunch of Kiwanis or Shriners might have been off on a river picnic. Way up on the top deck – it was a tall, narrow sort of ship with a lot of decks – a big band, with more than its share of those gleaming sousaphones, blared and clashed out ragtime. It seemed a hell of a way to sail to a war but not completely ridiculous, not without a suggestion of something more generous and heart-warming, much closer to the democracy we boasted about on our side, than anything we had known before. On that daft but not altogether inglorious troopship, I realised afterwards, I was for the first time in America.

Where all those 'doughboys' went I do not know, but our little group had to join what was left of a battalion of dismounted yeomanry. It was somewhere beyond Peronne, and took some finding in the dust and heat, on roads jammed with transport. There were about six of us, I think, mostly going out for the first time; and I never knew what happened to three of them, but the two I knew best, friends I made at Devonport, were killed within a few days. Again I was lucky, or perhaps by this time unconsciously artful. The battalion, which I never really took in as a unit, was far below strength but still up in front, attacking. We were in a narrow railway cutting one evening – at least the only troops I knew anything about were there – and into it the Germans dropped a lot of gas shells.

Gas-masked myself, I ran about to make sure the men were wearing their masks, a thing they hated to do. No doubt some gas seeped through my mask, as the doctors said afterwards; but I must add here that later that night, when we crept out of the cutting, ready to move forward just after dawn, I drank a good many tots of rum, which now, unlike 1915 and 1916, was in generous supply.

We went to the attack in the early morning, on a front much too wide for us, and there was one of those very thick mists, dense as fog, common in September. After ten minutes – and you may put it down to gas, rum or carelessness, just as you please – I had lost the whole battle, which I could hear all round me but could not see. I was wandering about, befogged inside and out, entirely alone. But I must have been more or less advancing, not retreating, for a figure came looming up through the whiteness, and I saw it was a German and waved my revolver at him. After all, he was not to know that I had been on two revolver courses and never could hit anything.

He was a lad about sixteen, who ought to have been several hundred miles away, putting his school books into a satchel. He raised his arms, poor lad, and made gibbering noises. I tried to look a little less idiotic than I felt, and pointed sternly in what I hoped was the direction of the British and not the German Army, and off he trotted, leaving me alone once more in the mist, wondering where to find the battle. I never did catch up with it. My head going round, too short of breath to move any further, I took a rest in a shellhole, where I was found by a couple of stretcher-bearers. So much for my last glimpse of action in the Great War.[114]

From the base hospital... I was forwarded, a wheezy parcel, to the Medical Board Base Depot in Rouen. There were worse places than the MBBD, Rouen. You waited there until the medical board, yawing and in despair, decided to see you, and perhaps after that until it decided, now yawning harder than ever and deeper in despair, to see you again. We officers earned our keep there by censoring vast piles of letters or going to distant huts and paying out troops who always seemed to come from the Hebrides or the West Indies: you sat there hour after hour, while some purple quartermaster-sergeant called out the most outlandish names.

The mess was like a railway refreshment room towards the end of an hysterical Bank Holiday; even at breakfast-time the likeness was still there; but it had an unlimited supply of those small export bottles of Guinness Stout at one franc the bottle, and you spent most of your leisure ordering more and more of these bottles and conducting long and idiotic arguments with men you had never seen before and never wanted to see again. Towards midnight, the infantry and the engineers began to swear at one another...

There were other amusements. Round the corner was the best soccer team in the world, twenty-two International legs too precious, too beautiful. to be exposed to red-hot fragments of shell. There was also ... camp music-hall where a whole series of R.A.M.C. orderlies pretended to be George Robey or Leslie Henson. It was not a bad life: the pile of letters, the heap of franc notes to be paid out, then back to the bottle-strewn smoky mess, the stout, and the idiotic arguments; but it was not quite real. I could not place it on the map.[115]

The medical board decided that I was B2, unfit for active service but fit for something.[116] The M.B.B.D. bad no further use for me. I was told to report at the other side of the town. There I found a very neat little colonel in a depressing little house in a back street. The house came straight out of realistic French fiction of the later Eighties, but the colonel was fighting it – tooth and nailbrush. This explained his responsible air, his solemnity: he was an English gentleman keeping his end up in the remote waste places. He spoke to me gravely about dinner and dress, (perhaps I could find him, even now, somewhere behind those wire-screened windows in Saville Row, disdainfully turning over the newest range of Gents' fancy suitings.)

The depot itself was a large factory building, which swarmed with men who never seemed quite real, unlike the men one knew in the trenches, who had been real people to a hair. There was something ghostly about these fellows, perhaps because they were very tired, very bored. Only the sergeants, spick and span, terrific saluters and callers to attention, were familiar figures. You met them, keeping the old flag flying, the brass buttons polished, at every base; real professional soldiers, waiting for this unwieldy amateur affair, this blood-thirsty melodrama of bombing bank clerks and machine-gunning gardeners, to blow itself to pieces.

This factory had been turned into a sort of lunatic labour exchange. You had only to make out, in correct triplicate, the proper indent for any kind of labour, and we would supply it. Entertainers were our favourite commodity. If the Fourth Army wanted two comedians, three conjurers, a couple of female impersonators, and a few baritones, it sent us a wire saying so, and we paraded the most likely specimens, tried one or two on the stage (we had an excellent stage on the third floor), and packed them off by the next train. Fresh relays of comedians and female impersonators arrived every day or so, had their kits and paybooks inspected, their claims to histrionic talent investigated, and. were handed over to the beery and brilliantined sergeants...[117]

I began to feel like a variety agent in uniform, or a man dreaming he was one...[118] There are times when I do not believe any longer in that fantastic depot and tell myself that all vague memories of it must be packed up and huddled away with the scenery of old dreams...[119]

During dinner, with the little colonel at the head of the table, correct but at ease, we talked a good deal about the war, which was beginning to wobble. A report came of an armistice, and the little colonel bought us all champagne on the strength of it, and was furious when the report was denied...

One day, taking the afternoon off, I went walking along a wide straight track through a wood; there came towards me, like a figure in an old-fashioned painting, sad and with too much brown in it, a hobbling crone, who when we met and I gave her good-day, stopped, grinned toothlessly, and produced a small document for me to read: it was a licence entitling her to ply her trade as a prostitute in Rouen and district. I told her, in the fluent bad French I spoke then and can no longer command, that I was not in the mood...[120]

A new arrival came to share my room, a tall thin youth with a slight squint, and he could talk of nothing but Miss Nellie Taylor, the musical comedy actress, whom he had once met in Birmingham. The streets smelled of autumn, and dead leaves drifted down to the canal. A smokiness came in the morning and returned early in. the evening; the little house was besieged by dank air; and the men were more ghostly than ever as they limped up and down the stairs of the mad factory. I ate and drank heartily, smoked my pipe, sat in the orderly room or inspected kits, sent for conjurers, and talked about the War or Miss Nellie Taylor; but I did these things mechanically, without inner conviction. I had lost my bearings.

I had lost one set at the beginning of September, 1914, when I walked into a dismantled picture palace with a dirty blanket over my arm and tried to sleep on the same floor with about five hundred other recruits and fifty old tramps who had sneaked in for shelter. Perhaps I had never exactly found my bearings during the four years that followed, when every horizon spat and belched and erupted and rockets of death went hooting and flaring every night; but I had come to some sort of terms with the shattering idiocy, like a man sharing a house, year after year, with a lunatic.

Nothing that had happened before, however, neither in the mysterious golden war before August, 1914, nor in the War itself, had prepared me for these antics in Rouen. And there was perhaps always a suspicion in one's mind that the whole thing might be slipping out of any kind of control, even that of roaring death. Sanity, one concluded, might easily be bombed away for good and all, and the portion of this world from now on might be fantasy with broad interludes of slapstick. Already, perhaps, generals were beginning to whiten their cheeks and put vermilion on their noses, and there were telephone inquiries to the docks at Havre about the first consignments of paper hoops. When I was off duty, wandering down the side-streets or by the darkening canal, I was faintly plagued by such suspicions. On duty, there was no time: I was in the ring with the rest, waiting for my turn to be rolled in the carpet and poulticed with custard pies.

There came a morning when the adjutant took me aside after breakfast. This adjutant was an enormous. plump pink fellow who wore most unconvincing curly little bits of ginger whisker and moustache... He took me aside and suggested that I might like to see an unusually large draft of men to its destination at a Corps headquarters. This is how I came to discover Miraucourt. The men were not going there. Nobody was going there. The destination of the draft was a very different place, and there is no reason why I should mention its name.

In the middle of the afternoon we boarded a train at Rouen, and this train, after innumerable whistles and groans and wheezings, pulled out and ran nearly half a mile, after which it stopped for four hours, and then returned, with many a whimsical shrug, to a siding at Rouen, where its engine was used as a hot-water urn for tea by the men. After that, for two days, I sat in my windowless compartment and stared at the autumn, which was moving nearly as fast as we were. When the train could do no more for us, we climbed into some lorries and went rattling down roads given over to dust and Chinese coolies.

We limped up to Corps Headquarters, and my duty was done. I did not linger there. I had to get back to Rouen, and I was determined to try a different route, for otherwise I might find myself on that train again. Nobody at Corps Headquarters cared what I did: they did not know what they were doing themselves. So I claimed a seat in a lorry that appeared to be going more or less in the right direction, and, after a few more hours of dust and Chinese coolies, it landed me in a little valley composed of two chalky hillsides, vast mounds of props and rusted barbed wire, and an ancient Irish Colonel who was living in the smallest and chalkiest Nissen hut I have ever seen. He appeared to have been there for a long time, and may have been left over from some other war. We crouched in the hut, like two leprechauns, and he gave me some warm Maconochie and Jameson and chalky water in an aluminium cup, and then we sat at the door, under the mild stars, and he pulled his long drooping moustache and crooned at me. His subject was fly-fishing. Somewhere behind us, beyond those mild stars it seemed, the air thudded.

The lorry I boarded next morning – I suppose it carried the colonel's Maconochie and Jameson – was not going to Miraucourt. Nobody, nothing, I repeat, was going there. I had never heard of it then and I have never heard of it since. Miraucourt was never mentioned. This lorry was bound for Custincourt, but I never arrived there. A dashing corporal on a motor-cycle stopped us, produced his orders, and the lorry had to turn round. It was wanted elsewhere, and not the way I wished to go, so there was nothing for it but to get out and – as they liked to say in those days – proceed independently.

The corporal, who had arrived out of the blue, returned there. The lorry driver and his mate had no suggestions to offer; they knew the road to Custincourt, and that was all; and they did not advise me to try it on foot. While I was still hesitating, there came a wreck of a cart on which were perched a bearded peasant and one of those little French boys who are all bones and eyes. Their destination was the hamlet, the mere speck, of Bovincourt – not any Bovincourt you ever knew – and they would take me there, for beyond Bovincourt, a few kilometres, was a great village, a town one might say, a considerable place, where there were soldiers English and an officer of the first importance, as all the world knew, since this long time.

In this fashion then, among the jolting potatoes, I came to Bovincourt, where they pointed out the track that would lead me to the great village and the officer of the first importance. It was called Miraucourt. Clearly, the officer was a Town Major. So down the narrow lane I went to report myself to the Town Major of Miraucourt. They had, as usual, underestimated the distance, and that track went spinning out kilometres long after it ought to have stopped. I only passed two people on the way. The first was an old woman who gave my uniform a surly look, I thought, and mumbled something unpleasant as I went by. The second was a cheerful slut of a girl, driving two cows, a girl who seemed almost too favourably disposed towards my uniform, for she giggled and made round eyes at it. I gathered from these two encounters that the English at Miraucourt were on certain terms with their hostesses, living in a mixed atmosphere of approval and disapproval.

Then I arrived, dusty, a little footsore, and parched, at the village itself, which showed me its red roofs among the plane trees just as I had decided that it could not possibly exist. It was one of those villages and little towns that are hidden from you until the last moment, when they spring out, like a waggish uncle, and give you a pleasant surprise. The War had not touched it. Not a tile was missing. It was built snugly about a square and had an air of cosiness you rarely find in France. A few women and old men were hanging about, but there were no signs of the military, not a single glimpse of khaki. The long shadows of late afternoon were creeping across the square, and all the noises of the world were crumbling away. Somewhere, beyond the darkening bosom of those hills, there was a war, but it seemed incredibly remote, the wildest rumour of violence and sudden death.

The first thing I had to do was to find the Town Major's office, and that did not take me long. I found it on the ground floor of a fat little house in the square. The door was open, so I marched in. That absurd office ought to have given me the first hint of what was happening to me, but I do not think it did. The room was an incredible jumble of bottles of every size and shape, mostly empty, cigar and cheroot boxes, broken gramophone records, dubious literature, and the more opulent illustrations from La Vie Parisienne and similar periodicals. There were military papers there too, of course, stacks of them, but they were lying about in a hopeless confusion, and many of them seemed to have been torn across, presumably to make spills.

Hanging behind the door was the most voluminous officer's tunic I have ever seen, a major's, and decorated with a number of mysterious medal ribbons. Evidently the Town Major of Miraucourt was an enormous fellow. Facing the table was a very large armchair that was leaning, as if in despair, to one side, where its hind leg was propped up with two or three volumes of official regulations. And on the table, flung down carelessly upon the litter of bottles and papers, was a gigantic Sam Browne belt, monstrous in its girth. But there was no sign of the major himself nor of any orderly or batman. Nothing stirred but a reek of onions.

I was by this time badly in need of food and drink, so I crossed the square to the Estaminet of the Little Calf. The proprietress was a very different creature from the usual sallow and harassed vendor of fried eggs and grenadine. She was a ripe and bustling female, blue-eyed and moist. She seemed glad to see me but rather surprised, as if stray English officers were a rarity. When I told her I could not find the Town Major, she stuck out her lower lip, wagged her head drolly, then laughed, as if the very thought of him was entertaining. He had, it seemed, his affairs, and would doubtless return before the night, though he did not always so return, oh no. Meanwhile, I could have something to eat, something to drink.

She left me sitting by the window, with a silent, pipe-sucking old peasant for company. And then I saw two figures in khaki crossing the square. When they drew nearer, I could see they were a couple of hard-bitten corporals. They had that curious wooden swagger of the 'old sweat'. One of them was distinguished by a great beak of nose, so red, so inflamed, that it was a conflagration in flesh. The other had one of those flat, almost pushed-in faces; he was the kind of man who always talks out of a corner of his mouth, as if everything he has to say is a bitter secret. They were both wearing an incredible number of wound stripes and blue chevrons. Just before they reached the door of the estaminet, the flat-faced one halted; the other pulled up too, and their voices reached me through the open window.

'...E'll gie! me something, an' 'andy, too,' the flat-faced one was saying. 'That's my ruddy style. 'E gets me my leaf or 'e gives me the eighty francs 'e's dropped on the mudhook, one or the other. An' I'll tell 'im so, sergeant-major or no flamin' sergeant-major. I'll give 'im the office. That's my ruddy style.'

'Take it easy, chum, take it easy,' replied the other, the one with the nose. 'You'll get it in time. You'll get it.'

'I want it now, an' I'll get it or I'll know the flamin' reason. That's my ruddy style,'

'Where's the queer feller gone this afternoon?'

'Ask me! Promenad avec vous with Mar-ee, that'll be 'is ticket.'

'No, 'e isn't. Saw 'er meself a bit back. 'E must be lookin' over the rookies.'

'E can start lookin' for my eighty francs. All right then. Lead on for the pig's ear. That's my ruddy style.'

The next moment, they were inside, gaping at me. They were even more surprised to see a strange officer than the proprietress was. Evidently very few people found their way to Miraucourt. This did not astonish me. I do not think anything would have astonished me. That was the way things were going.

They saluted smartly enough, but then promptly retired before I had a chance to say anything to them. 'Cor lumme!' I heard one of them cry, and then the other began, '... 'Ere,' in what seemed to be an aggrieved tone, as if I had no right to be there. But then, I do not know if I had any right to be there.

Madame returned, a trifle flustered, with some soup and bread, and said that if I went back there, later in the evening, I could have an entrecote, some salad, some fruit, a little bottle of wine, in short, quite a dinner. Meanwhile, this snack would ease the pangs. After the soup and bread, perhaps a little drink, to give me comfort? She had the excellent liqueur of Martinique, perhaps I would try that? I rather wearily assented, and actually had three glasses of the dark and mysterious spirit. That was not very much, but it was enough to blur the fine edges of sight and hearing, to conjure forth the oddest fancies and give them the colour of reality, to introduce that fatal subjective element into things. There was something very curious about that liqueur of Martinique. But it suited Miraucourt. It might have been distilled for the place. Perhaps it was.

Nevertheless, I am sure that I saw and heard that sergeant-major and his little squad in the square outside. They came before daylight had faded and while all was quiet. Oh, they were there all right! There were six of them in the squad, and even in the motley army of the last desperate year, in the flotsam and jetsam of soldiery I had noticed in the labour depot at Rouen, I had never seen half a dozen such awkward and forlorn creatures gathered together on parade. They all appeared to be wearing one another's uniforms; they were not the right shape; they were all heads, feet, elbows, and hands; they were anything but soldiers. This could not be said of the sergeant-major, who was soldierly enough, too soldierly, in fact, in the antique style.

He was a thinnish fellow, who strutted and pranced in the absurdest fashion. I could not see his face very clearly, but it was of a purplish hue and was decorated with one of those long waxed moustaches that brought little tubes of Hungarian Pomade into the barbers' shops of yesterday. Like the corporals, he was wearing ribbons, gold stripes, and chevrons enough to suggest that he had been soldiering not merely since this Mons but since the Mons before that, had been swaggering on and off Parade, mostly off, since the Fifth Harry's time.

He brought his six misfits quite close to the estaminet and then, with a fearful bellow, halted them. I went to the door. Evidently their movements had displeased him, as well they might. He set them going again, like rusted clockwork figures, and then went through the whole repertoire of familiar barrack-square jeers. 'Yer might break yer mother's 'eart but yet won't break mine – Errboutt Turrn!' and 'Don't forget while your tea's getting colder, mine's getting 'otter, an' I can stay 'ere all day.' There were others too, about wooden soldiers; in fact, all the old jibes.

When he had brought them back again, one of them must have protested, said he was sick or something of that kind, for immediately this sergeant-major plunged into the most fantastic and passionate speech. 'What, you bag of rotten dumplings, you flea-bitten turnip-eater?' he roared. 'Are we soldiers or are we bloody scarecrows? Are there no Huns to fight? Do King and Country call? Is Belgium Kaiser Bill's? Who's for the peg? Speak up, you Derby rats!'

'Please, 'zur,' quavered one of them.

'Silence, you suet,' he continued, working himself up into an astonishing rage. 'God let me live, are we conchies? Do we object while Empire falls? Has Hindenburg the laugh? Soldiers yet, if we 'ave to skin you! The 'eathen in his blindness bows down to wood and stone. Two-an' -thirty sergeants an' corporals forty-one. You put some juldee in it. or I'll marrow you this minute. Are we not White Men? Mons, Wipers, Nerve Chapelle, Vimy, an' Martinpush, that's me, an' before yer number was dry. Women an' children first an' keep the old flag flying. Dis-miss.' And he turned away, purple, magnificent, leaving the six gaping and scratching their heads. I will swear that is exactly what I saw and heard. Martinique or no Martinique.

Moreover, before I could return to my chair, I saw the Town Major himself. He was crossing the square at the other side, going towards his office, an enormous fellow, quite old but still fairly sprightly, and he was wearing the twin of that tunic I had seen hanging behind the door, and a colossal pair of slacks. He moved across that square like a brown galleon with the fires of sunset in his topsails. And behind him, trying to catch him up, was the giggling damsel I had passed in the lane, a little cleaner now, better dressed, and carrying a basket. He disappeared into the little villa, unaware of her. She followed him, and. after a moment's hesitation, I slipped across the square and followed her.

I waited a few minutes, then knocked at his office door, through which was coming the sound of tittering expostulations in the patois of the neighbourhood. A sonorous voice told me to go away; I saw no sound military reason why I should go away, so I knocked again. This time the door was flung open. I was confronted by the major, whose vast bulk quite obscured the girl behind him.

'What's this?' he cried. 'A soldier? Will they never end, these wars?'

I reported myself to him, as solemnly as I could. He was old and amazingly fat, immense, ruinous and unbuttoned, but his eyes, creased round though they were until sometimes they nearly disappeared altogether, blazed with intelligence and humour. I can see them shining yet through the mist of intervening years and the time's lunacies and the fumes of Martinique.

'Come in,' he cried, and stepped back, at the same time looking with a droll assumption of surprise and severity at the girl, who seemed to be removing certain traces of disorder. He waved a hand at her and then dismissed her in fluent but queer French, telling her to be a little earlier next time and to find larger eggs and fatter chickens. 'A good girl,' he remarked when she had gone, 'but the child of dishonest parents. They bleed us, these French peasants. They take advantage of our innocence. We are anybody's mark, we old soldiers. We go away to the wars and whether we are ever seen again, nobody cares, as somebody said to me years ago, before your time. Here I am – who might have had a brigade – Town Major of a place so small there's not a man can go on leave for fear he'll never find it again. I shall take it home with me as a keepsake.

'I've a sergeant-major who can't write, two corporals who can't read, and now six men who can't walk. But they can all eat and drink. And we're so far away from anybody, they won't send us proper rations. What we get now is what there happens to be a glut of. The week before last, nothing arrived here but a load of socks and puttees, not a tin of anything you could eat. Last week, it was worse; they sent up a load of wire and sandbags, devil a thing else. I've had sun-helmets, diving-boots, sailors' hammocks and tins of paint for armoured cars in desert warfare, all dumped on me in place of ration issue. We're expecting half an observation balloon next or seven gross of snow spectacles, or five carrier-pigeon outfits, without the pigeons, for fear we should be remembering the taste of food in our mouths and be eating them.

'And what with that and the press of business,' he added, pouring himself out a drink, then pushing the bottle towards me, 'I'm so villainous low. I've half a mind to take to drinking and looking at the women, and let the war rot. Fill up, my lad, don't stint it. Madame across the way there's got another bottle of the same handy, and it won't take you a minute to slip out and get it when we've finished this. And what do you want me to do for you?'

I explained where I was going, where I had been, and all about it, to all of which he paid very little attention. He had now lit a cheroot, and was sprawling, monstrously at his ease, in his lopsided armchair.

'There's a bunk and a blanket or two you can have tonight up there,' and he jerked a thumb at the ceiling. 'Tell one of the corporals or the sergeant-major, any of them. Just call 'Smith' when you're going out. It's the damnedest and oddest thing in the world, but we're all Smiths here, every man jack of us. I'm Major F. Smith. There's Sergeant-Major P. Smith. There's two Corporal Smiths, B. Smith and N. Smith.'

I had hardly time to digest this – though indeed I never did digest it because I never succeeded in swallowing it – before there came a knock at the door and there entered two little elderly Frenchmen, dressed neatly in black and obviously two local officials. They were furiously angry and began pouring out a torrent of remonstrance even at the very threshold. This and that, it seemed, were abominable, and could not be endured another day, another hour, another moment.

The major rose from his chair and patted them each on the shoulder. Then he turned to me. 'If I don't fetch off these two little black shavings of Monseers, there'll be no peace for the British Amy, and this one on my right will scream himself into hysterics. He's lathering now and smells of goat. Go find your bunk, my boy, and make it early to bed. Leave it to us old soldiers, we're hard-wearing. Kitchener never meant to use you so hard. He told me himself. I knew him well. Go to Madame of the Little Calf - though she's not that, either - and tell her from me to treat you well. Give her fifty francs for me; eat a little, take water with your wine, write to your mother, your sister, say your prayers and then sleep sound.'

It was the corporal with the great red nose who showed me my bunk and found some blankets for me. We hardly exchanged a word because we were both too busy listening to the other corporal and the sergeant-major who, in defiance of all military discipline, were quarrelling furiously and at the top of their voices: I do not know where they were, but I could hear them plainly enough.

'That's my ruddy style,' the flat-faced kept shouting, over and over again; while the sergeant-major, in his turn, retorted wildly with 'Base cur,' and 'Filthy mudhook wangler,' and other, more fantastic terms.

This did not astonish me. It is hard to say exactly now, but I think that by this time I had guessed who they all were. The corporal and his nose vanished; I descended the shadowy stairs; and as I passed the major's door, I heard no voices raised in anger but roars of laughter, which followed me out into the square. I knew by this time he was sitting at ease with the two little officials, who would not remember their grievances, which no doubt were real enough, until they had left the room and his tropical presence.

The dinner that Madame had promised was ready, and I lingered over it, dreamily finishing the wine. A few old men drifted in and out, but I saw none of the English, not a glimpse of the two corporals, the sergeant-major, and the great major himself. Twice, however, Madame, very buxom, very gay, hurried through, carrying a smoking tray and a bottle or two and I knew she was taking it all across to the major. Nor did she return in a hurry. She was there, though to tell me what I owed her, to bid me good night, and tell me I was a brave boy.

When I turned out at last into the square, now a pool of purple with sable banks and a faintly spangled canopy above, the little house across the way was dark, and, though I was sleepy now and hazy with dream, I did not return there but wandered with my pipe along the shadows of the village. It must have been an hour later when I came back, saw that the major's window was bright gold in the dark, and crept up to it.

Yes, they were there, major and men together, toping it in

unbuttoned ease while the seven stars paled, as they had so often done before. They had not changed to the sight; the moustachios, the cut of the hair, the uniforms and badges were ours; but now they had dropped all pretence of being contemporaries of mine, mortal men, and I caught the old rich phrases, dripping with sherris-sack, rolling out into the night while they bickered and jested and roared. And now I knew I could not join them, that if I opened the door, or even merely tapped on the window, some magic would be broken; they would be huddled back into Smiths again, the Smiths I might find round any corner; or perhaps they would not be there at all. So I did nothing but stare, out of the dark, until at last I felt too cold, too sleepy, too hazy, to stand there any longer, and tiptoed past the door, up the stair, to my blankets.

The sergeant I saw next morning was a good fellow, who understood the art of lorry-jumping, knew the roads, and was at some pains to show me exactly how I could find my way from Miraucourt back to Rouen. He was a talkative soul too, and explained how he came to be there and why he had been absent the day before. I could have asked him anything in reason. But I could not ask him what had become of Falstaff, Pistol, Bardolph, and Nym, not even when I was in the act of boarding the lorry, because that would not have seemed to him in reason. He was obviously a man who knew where to draw a line, even in 1918. I have always found that difficult at times, and then it was impossible.

I returned to the factory at Rouen, to find the stairs more ghostly than ever with dim men, conjurers in brisk demand, the little colonel more exquisitely turned out, the curly red adjutant still sweating over the gramophone handle, and talk of Peace added to the talk of War and Miss Nellie Taylor. And if I had started drawing lines, I might have had to draw one clean through the middle of that factory, through Rouen itself, and then where would we be?

Why, we should never know.[121]

The genuine Armistice took us by surprise after so many false reports, and we had to hurry to get drunk enough to go shouting and reeling round the town. I can remember trying to work myself up into the right Bacchanalian mood, trying to ignore the creeping shadows, the mysterious rising tide of regret and sadness, which I think all but the simplest men suffer from on these occasions.

Two or three mornings later, I was told to report for duty at a prisoner-of-war camp near Calais, and to take a party of men with me... During my first evening in the P.O.W. camp mess, I decided I had run out of luck, for here was a collection of fellows I disliked on sight. Later, when I had retired to my thin-walled cubicle, I overheard, not being able to help it, two of them discussing me in the next cubicle, making it clear they did not like the look and sound of me either. This did not upset me because I had never considered myself a charmer, and most of these types, who had dug themselves in here long ago, looked to me like artful base wallahs.

The company to which I was attached was commanded by a red-faced major, not himself a regular soldier – he had done some easy job 'out East' – but closely related to the red-tabbed Top. From the first he obviously considered me an opinionated young North Country cad, and I thought him a pompous ass who did not even try to do properly the soft job he had been given. And on these terms, living in close quarters, we were to be associated for the next three-and-a-half months, though fortunately he gave himself a lot of leave.

This big camp supplied prison labour, working in shifts round the clock, for the largest quarries I had ever seen, greyish-white canyons, from which had come the road metal used by the Chinese coolies. I rather enjoyed my turn at the late-night shift in these quarries, where I had little to do but marvel at the eerie effects of the brilliant artificial lighting down there, the dazzling cliffs and battlements, the dead-black shadows, the glimpses of distant groups who looked like ants at work. The German prisoners were not driven hard; their living conditions were not bad; they were fed better than they would have been in their own army, far better than their folks at home, whose parcels, which we had to open and inspect, were pathetic offerings of ersatz sausage and all manner of crumbling muck. Yet just because they were prisoners, because the psychological effect of their status was so strong, most of them had the drawn and large-eyed look of men overworked, beaten and half-starved.

In point of fact they were far more frightened of their own sergeant-major characters – iron men with Iron Crosses, Kaiser moustaches, terrible rasping words of command – than they were of us, the unmilitary amateur British. Though these iron characters showed me tremendous respect, as if I were a general, I went a little in awe of them myself. Later, when our company was on its own, far from these quarries, and it was Christmas, I remember how astonished I was, paying an official visit to the German warrant officers' tiny mess, to discover these four military monsters sitting round a very small illuminated Christmas tree, deep in a sentimental reverie before they caught sight of me and jumped quivering to attention, banging their heels. There was all Germany in that little scene.

Long before Christmas, however, our company received orders to move up to the Lille-Roubaix- Tourcoing area, to do salvage work. By chance, the major and the lieutenant senior to me being away, I was in charge of the company when these orders arrived, and I had to be responsible for the move. We had between six and seven hundred prisoners, and about eighty British troops, all men no longer fit for active service. Though the fighting was over, conditions were no easier, perhaps rather more chaotic, so that problems of transport, rationing, supplies, medical services, were no joke, especially with such an odd mixture involving seven to eight hundred men. This was easily the most responsible job that had come my way in the Army, and it lasted for a couple of weeks or so and I enjoyed every moment of it, planning and working hard with several decent and conscientious senior noncoms. I cannot believe there was in me somewhere a master of logistics, a first-class staff officer; I make no claim to any peculiar merit; but I must set on record the fact that I did the job and for once, in my four-and-a-half years of army knockabout, really enjoyed doing it.

We had to march the company through Tourcoing, which had had years of German occupation, and its citizens lined the streets to curse and scream at our columns of prisoners, whom we had to guard not against possible escape but lynching. We ended up in the country outside, packed into a few big barns. It was then, after a few days, I ran into trouble, finally picking a quarrel, a most enjoyable shemozzle, with the Fifth Army: A Four-round Contest between Subaltern One, in the blue corner, and Army H.Q., in the red-and-gilt corner.

After more than forty years it is easy to oversimplify or to exaggerate, but this brief report of the contest is as true as I can make it. Round one: still temporarily in charge of the company, I receive an Army order telling me to move it to a given map reference, the chosen site for a camp under canvas. And it is now early December. I go to this place, find it pitted with shellholes and waterlogged, and point out there must have been some mistake, a wrong map reference.

Round two: Army informs me in writing that no mistake has been made, that I have had my orders and any further delay will not be tolerated. Counter-punching, I reply in writing that the chosen site is utterly unsuitable even for seven hundred and fifty fit men, that many of our men, British and Germans, are not fit and that I have on my hands a number of sick prisoners, some of them running temperatures.

Round three: a carload of red tabs and brass hats arrives, important chaps with staring eyes and those voices that are the equivalent in sound of hard stares, and ask what the devil I think I am doing, who the devil I think I am, and that they are giving me one last chance before I find myself facing a court-martial. Covering up and hanging on, in boxing terms, I mutter that the place they have chosen, which I cannot believe they can have seen for themselves, is impossible, that I cannot accept the responsibility of moving these men there, that my war is over and if the Fifth Army wants to court-martial me, let them get on with it. They stare at me again, climb haughtily into the car and drive off.

Fourth and last round: I lead with some smart left jabs, for now I have found, not too far from the site they chose, the widespread ruin of a German hut encampment, and promise that if the Army will leave us alone, then, without incurring any expense or demanding any help from the Engineers, out of this wreck my Germans will build their own camp. To my surprise, I am given a grudging consent, along with a few more warnings. Subaltern wins on points.

Not trusting my halting German on this occasion, I addressed the warrant officers and senior noncoms through the chief interpreter, a red-haired schoolmaster from Bavaria, and explained that their men had a chance to build a decent snug camp for themselves, to house them through the winter, if they worked hard and at full speed. Now among these hundreds of prisoners we had scores of skilled men, and, whatever faults the average German may have, he cannot be accused of a lack of application and diligence; and as I bustled around, entirely out of character for once, I saw with delight a new camp, solid and weatherproof rise almost magically out of those ruins I had discovered.

From the morning I planned the move from Calais until the day this camp was finished, I had lived, most happily too, the sort of life known to men very different in temperament and outlook from me. I had unexpectedly enjoyed glimpses of roads I had never even thought of taking. I had let loose a part of myself I did not even know was there; for a few astonishing and rewarding days I played the man of action not long before settling down, from that time to this, to live by putting words together and passing round the hat.

During the first three months of 1919 I was still with this P.O.W. company, no longer shouldering any real responsibility, glowering at the major, who now kept popping into Lille to visit a 'pretty little French gal', drinking a bit too much out of boredom, and now feeling more like a trapped civilian than any kind of soldier. We officers round there were now sharply divided into those, like me, who ached to leave the Army and get on with their real lives, and senior men, like the major, who knew when they were on to a good thing and dreaded the bowler hat. (There was a rumour, before I left, that it was taking three full colonels to run a laundry in Lille). As he regarded me as a nuisance, the major was glad to forward various applications I made for demobilisation. Finally, I was told I could go home, not because I was already enquiring about an educational grant, but because I had been a casualty three times and came into some category that had a slight priority of release.

The day arrived. Our own noncoms, with whom I had worked during that move and camp-building afterwards, seemed genuinely sorry to see me go. 'The only bloody officer we ever had who was any good: I overheard one of the men say, 'an' now of course he's off.' The Germans, through the red-haired interpreter, made me a solemn speech of thanks and farewell, and presented me with two group photographs, which I still have. No regrets from the Fifth Army or, for that matter, from the major, who now had two subalterns, almost half-witted, prepared to listen to his Eastern 'yarns' and 'pretty little gal' reminiscences ('It's all the etceteras I like best on these occasions, my boy'), until their eyes glazed over with whisky and sleep.

There had been trouble on the special night-trains running from Lille to Boulogne, crammed with men from all manner of units on their way to be demobilised. It was said there had been mutinous outbreaks, riot and damage. A lot of these men had had as much of the British Army, with its insistence, often at the wrong time, upon 'keeping the men up to the mark', as they could take.

When I reported to the R.T.O. at the station, with the train there already packed and uproarious, I was astonished and shaken to learn from him that not only was no senior officer travelling that night – whether by accident or design I never knew – but that I was in fact the only officer going on that train. I was to be responsible for all the men on it, hundreds and hundreds of them, embittered and sober, roaring and drunk, and responsible too for their seemly arrival at the Boulogne rest camp next morning. It was like suddenly being put in charge of eight circuses, short of pay, food and water. As time passed and we did not pull out, for all these worn-out trains hated to make a move, the atmosphere became curiously sinister. Discipline, always harder to maintain when men were away from their units and came from every branch of the service, had worn so thin you could hear it cracking. It was almost like an army disintegrating in a revolution. I spoke to a few N.C.O.s who seemed steady types, and put it to them that I did not expect anything fancy but that the less trouble we had the sooner we might go home.

Somehow we got by, the train rumbling through the night, in my imagination, like a volcano that might blow up. About the middle of the morning, wonderfully bright and fresh after that train, my mob came tumbling out at Boulogne, breakfastless and bleary-eyed and not standing any more bloody nonsense from anybody. They had to be marched to that camp on the hill. There was not a hope of getting them into two dressed lines, smartly forming fours (as we did then), and moving off like a well-drilled infantry column. I gave it out that the shortest cut home was by way of that camp, that if they formed themselves into some sort of column of march, followed me and kept together, no time and temper would be wasted.

So off we went, at an easy pace, for some of the men were weighed down with kit and in no shape to march properly, and finally arrived, moving together, at the entrance to the camp. A little fusspot of an adjutant came charging out, gave me a glare in passing, and, his voice rising almost to a scream, began shouting 'Left, right! Left, right!' The men stopped, looked him over, then either hooted with laughter or told him what he could do with his Left, right. Having created a situation he did not know how to control, he hurriedly retired somewhere, not the place where I reported the arrival of self and party. Had he met the train in this badly-timed regimental mood, either he or about half the men would not have seen the camp that day.

This anecdote, a trickle of small beer, is not related here to suggest that in me a man of action was lost to our time. I was a bewildered and secretly terrified subaltern of twenty-four, probably rather naive even for his years and status, who was handed a packet one of his seniors should have had, and just got by after using a little common sense, behaving more like a civilian than a British officer and temporary gentleman. No, the spotlight here is on that little adjutant who did not understand what was happening, barked at the wrong time and fled from his humiliation. He is the last military figure we shall meet, and he has remained in my mind a symbolic figure. He will do as well as another to represent what seemed to me to be wrong from first to last in the British Army of the First War.

The development of the familiar 'lions led by donkeys' theme can be left to those indignant younger men now appearing as military historians. But as one who served in that Army, not brilliantly and with a lot of luck but bearing some share of the jeopardy and misery, I should like to add a few observations to the record. So far as that war was won at all – and a negotiated peace in 1916 might have saved our world from one catastrophe after another – I believe that in the end it was chiefly won on the ground by a huge crowd of young Britons who never wanted to be soldiers, hooted at all traditions of military glory, but went on and on, when American forces were still not fully deployed and the French were fading out, with courage and endurance and tenacity we should remember with pride. And nobody, nothing, will shift me from the belief, which I shall take to the grave, that the generation to which I belonged, destroyed between 1914 and 1918, was a great generation, marvellous in its promise. This is not self praise, because those of us who are left know that we are the runts.

The British Army never saw itself as a citizens' army. It behaved as if a small gentlemanly officer class still had to make soldiers out of under-gardeners' runaway sons and slum lads known to the police. These fellows had to be kept up to scratch. Let 'em get slack, they'd soon be a rabble again. So where the Germans and French would hold a bad front line with the minimum of men, allowing the majority to get some rest, the British command would pack men into rotten trenches, start something to keep up their morale, pile up casualties and drive the survivors to despair. This was done not to win a battle, not even to gain a few yards of ground, but simply because it was supposed to be the thing to do.

All the armies in that idiot war shovelled divisions into attacks, often as boneheaded as ours were, just as if healthy young men had begun to seem hateful in the sight of Europe, but the British command specialised in throwing men away for nothing. The tradition of an officer class, defying both imagination and common sense, killed most of my friends as surely as if those cavalry generals had come out of the chateaux with polo mallets and beaten their brains out. Call this class prejudice if you like, so long as you remember... that I went into that war without any such prejudice, free of any class feeling. No doubt I came out of it with a chip on my shoulder; a big, heavy chip, probably some friend's thighbone.

Compelled throughout all my early twenties to live close to all kinds of men, as few of us have to do in civilian life, I came to some rough and ready conclusions that have stayed with me ever since. Out of any ten men chosen at random for you to live with, I decided that, unless the luck was running hard against you, one of them would be your sort, according to your type and temperament, a man you could call a friend, often, sometimes surprisingly, pure gold. The next eight would be average decent fellows, conventional, timid and a bit shuffling perhaps, but capable of responding to a reasonable appeal. The tenth would be no good, except to a saint or a teacher-leader of genius; he would be twisted somewhere inside, malevolent, life-denying, incapable of innocent happiness and so always anxious to smear it, blacken it, destroy it.

In an army, and no doubt in many large-scale organisations, this type wants some kind of authority, power over other men, so badly that all too often he gets it, not on any grand scale but sufficient for unwearying malignancy, becoming The Enemy. In an army, or any other service that offers him the cover and opportunity of discipline, he cannot be mistaken. But he exists outside, where names are not taken so quickly and punishment does not follow so fast. He is still around, still busy. But if democracy is not done for, the other eight are still with us...

One morning in the early spring of 1919 in some town, strangely chosen, in the Midlands – and I have forgotten both the date and the place – I came blinking out at last into civilian daylight. I made no great resolutions; I was wondering if I could go on a walking tour in the Dales and sell some pieces about it to the Yorkshire Observer; I was also deciding to buy a gramophone and some recordings of string quartets. No awards for gallantry had come – or were to come – my way; but I was entitled to certain medals and ribbons. I never applied for them; I was never sent them; I have never had them. Feeling that the giant locusts that had eaten my four-and-a-half years could have them, glad to remember that never again would anybody tell me to carry on, I shrugged the shoulders of a civvy coat that was a bad fit, and carried on.[122]

## PART II

# The Inter-War Years

# Chapter 4
# A wilderness of smoke and fury

From early September 1914 until the middle of March 1919, I was in the Army... When I look back on my life, seeing it as a road I have travelled, these four-and-a-half years shrink at once; they seem nothing more than a queer bend in the road full of dust and confusion. But when memory really goes to work and I re-enter those years... they suddenly turn into a whole epoch, almost another life in another world.

I can well believe that younger men and women feel much the same about the Second War. But I think the First War cut deeper and played more tricks with time because it was first, because it was bloodier, because it came out of a blue that nobody saw after 1914. The map that came to pieces in 1939 was never the apparently solid arrangement that blew up in 1914. Any intelligent European born, let us say, after 1904, reached the teens in what he or she knew to be a dangerous and cruel world. But if you were born in 1894, as I was, you suddenly saw a great jagged crack in the looking-glass. After that your mind could not escape from the idea of a world that ended in 1914 and another one that began about 1919, with a wilderness of smoke and fury, outside sensible time, lying between them.[123]

*Priestley had written little during the war. The only pieces that have survived from that period – a collection of poems,* A Chapman of Rhymes *– are far from typical of his later work and Priestley later tried to suppress them. He undoubtedly shared the 'survivors' guilt' of those who had lived through the war when so many did not, and, whatever its literary merits, his poem,* To Dead Comrades, *is a valediction to those many friends who died.*

I

Tonight bring neither lights nor wine
But close the door and turn the key;
This coming hour shall prove divine,
For dead men bear me company.

Their voices tremble in the air,
They leave their far-off dim abodes,
And seem to crowd about my chair,
These comrades of the long, grey roads.

In days of feast, when men drink wine
And raise each brimming glass on high,
One toast alone is always mine:
"The men who taught us how to die!"

Oh! Comrades! are you wrapt in sleep,
Unmindful of each passing day?
Or do your deathless spirits keep
Their sentry o'er some starry way?

II

For you, God work'd His will in dreadful hours,
Hammered in Hell and fraught with all its pow'rs;
And young and laughing-eyed, you passed away,
While we were mazed and wondered why you lay
So quiet and still among the trodden flow'rs.

You passed in flame like gods, but we shall weep
At half-remembered things, and, mumbling, creep
Into the chimney corners, there to die
The common easy death, while years go by
Like shadows in a dreamer's troubled sleep.

Now Death's grey tattered banners are unfurled
Above the depths where once our hearts were hurled,
So you must cherish things we erstwhile spurned;
Within a little hour you have unlearned
The old and bitter wisdom of the world.

You knew a way that youth could never mar,
A light that ever beckoned from afar;
Your souls are fluttering toward that light,
To you, a dawn already breaks the night
With dreams you lost upon another star.[124]

*The war was over but for Priestley, like his character Gregory in the novel* Bright Day, *'something of him will be caught, fastened, left behind while he goes on.'* [125] *He never returned to live in Bradford; that era was over – lost and gone like most of his friends – and like many veterans, he neither wrote about, nor talked about the war for many years. Much later, with the wisdom of hindsight, Priestley sought to explain his failure to address the war years more in his writing.*

I came out of the Army a divided young man, one half of him too bookish, the other half, across a gap not properly bridged for years, outside any tradition, committed to nothing except fairly sharp and often comic observation, reading only in that book of men. I came out of the war divided too in another way, not having one attitude towards it, as many men who wrote about it had, but two opposing attitudes I did not know how to reconcile during the years when I too ought to have been writing about it. Now I believe I can explain what puzzled some people, who began to imagine there was something mysterious, even sinister, about the way in which I, a fertile and energetic writer at least, and one who had soldiered as long as most of my fellow writers, shrugged away the war as a grand theme.

I could muster some not unreasonable excuses. During my first few years out of the Army, I wanted to get on with my life, to look forward and not back. And I was then giving my bookish half a freer run. Then came, during the next few years, a barrage of war reminiscences and novels – the best of them, by Graves, Sassoon, Blunden, Williamson, Aldington, to name no more, truly and powerfully written by my contemporaries – and I could claim that now I felt I had waited too long. But the real explanation, I believe, is concerned with that other division I have mentioned, those opposed attitudes that I, now merely attempting fiction and no great master of it, did not know how to reconcile.

Unlike most of my contemporaries who wrote so well about the war, I was deeply divided between the tragedy and comedy of it. I was as much aware as they were, and as other people born later can never be, of its tragic aspect. I felt, as indeed I still feel today and must go on feeling until I die, the open wound, never to be healed, of my generation's fate, the best sorted out and then slaughtered, not by hard necessity but mainly by huge murderous public folly. On the other hand, military life itself, the whole Army 'carry-on', as we used to say, observed closely, seemed to me to be essentially comic, the most expensive farce ever contrived. To a man of my temperament it was almost slapstick, so much gigantically solemn, dressed-up, bemedalled custard-pie work but with tragedy, death, the deep unhealing wound, there in the middle of it...

I agree that if I had ignored this division and hurled myself not at but into the job – trusting some creative reconciling function of the unconscious, where burning boats perhaps smell sweetly, I might, I just might, have pulled it off. But on my terms, making full allowance for the comic as well as the tragic aspects, nobody else did, and the closest anybody came was not in books written in English or concerned with the British Army. And now it is altogether too late, that is of course for me; any one of our novelists who is fascinated by the First War, believes he has the weight and staying power to tackle it, and is still only in his middle thirties (a good age for such work), can remind himself that he is as well placed as Tolstoy was when he began War and Peace, and indeed has far more material at his disposal. As for me, I let this chance go by, and now I think I was wrong.[126]

*Priestley used a modest ex-officer's grant to fund a degree in Modern History and Political Science at Trinity, Cambridge, and in 1921, while still a student, he married Pat Tempest, a Bradford librarian and neighbour of the Priestleys in Bradford, who had written to him and visited him in hospital during the war.*

*Priestley turned down the chance of an academic appointment in Cambridge and made the bold decision to move to London in search of freelance work as a journalist, where he began to build his literary career. He and Pat had two daughters, Barbara and Sylvia, born in 1923 and 1924, but during the Caesarean section to deliver Sylvia, doctors discovered that Pat was suffering from an untreatable cancer. She died on 15 November 1925, eighteen months after Priestley's father, Jonathan, had also succumbed to the disease. Priestley was left as a twenty-nine year old widower with two small children.*

*Perhaps hardened to adversity by the war years, it is a tribute to his resolve that he was able to maintain sufficient output of essays and articles to pay the bills, while working on the novels,* Adam in Moonshine, Benighted *and then* The Good Companions, *that made his name and fortune. Nor was he alone for long. Even while Pat was still alive, Priestley had embarked on an affair – the first of a procession of extramarital affairs – with Jane Wyndham-Lewis, who was in the process of divorcing her first husband. Priestley married her in September 1926, less than a year after Pat's death. They had three children, daughters Rachel and Mary, and a son Tom.*

*The humour, the optimism, the rapport with and championing of all the people, the instinctive dislike of humbug, cant and political '-isms' of any sort, already evident in Priestley's wartime letters, marked his work throughout his career. Yet he continued to avoid writing about the war and his experiences, and when he did do so, his first approaches to the subject were tentative, expressed in reviews of other's work, like 'At the Verdun Film'.*

It was very kind of the Gaumont Company to invite me to the Marble Arch Pavilion to see the great film Verdun. I don't know why they did it. Most of the other guests seemed to be political or military men (and the number of military bigwigs who look like first cousins of Alice's White Knight is surprising.) There were hardly any literary gents there, though I did catch sight of one famous novelist. I will not tell you his name; I will only say that I kept wondering what he thought about this tragic shadow show, whether it was inducing in him first-class sensations or merely second-class sensations, and how his human machine was running that night. I also caught a glimpse of the pale and handsome face of Sir Philip Gibbs [a famous war correspondent of The Times], and thought it was very clever of the management to have him here, for where there is a war – and there is a war in Verdun – there must be Sir Philip Gibbs...

When we had nodded and smiled and settled in our seats, the lights went out and we found ourselves back again in the War, the War with the capital letter, the real one. Verdun is a masterpiece. It is the work of a man and an artist. It does not show you the military and amorous antics of a crowd of actors, actresses and dressed-up supers, assisted by a few men from the local firework factory; it shows you the War. It has been conceived in no narrow and catchpenny spirit of nationalism – the Germans are as sympathetically treated as the French and English – and it has been carried out with real imagination and amazing skill. The difference between Verdun and the average American war film, such as The Big Parade, is the difference between the Eroica and 'Over There' or 'Keep the Home Fires Burning.' The success enjoyed by The Big Parade was a disgrace to the English public, who ought to have more sense. That film may have dealt with a war, but if it did it was some war between film studios. It was a war of actors. You saw actors marching, actors resting in billets and indulging in comic relief, actors making love to a pretty film star, actors being rushed to the front in theatrical lorries, actors being killed by property shell-fire. It was obviously an army rationed with hair-oil, sticks of greasepaint, and press-cuttings.

There are no actors in Verdun, at least you never think of its personages as actors. The soldiers and peasants look and act like soldier and peasants. The shell-fire and machine-gunning are the real thing. If you are curious about such matters you can read an account of the immense pains taken by the producer, but it is not necessary you should, for the film itself is there. The one objection I have to the film – apart from a few lapses into sentimentality of the French kind, which is even more bludgeoning than ours – is that, being a genuine work of art, it has a dangerous tragic beauty.

I thought at first that here was a film that would knock the belligerent nonsense out of people. It would be a good idea, I told myself, to show this film to the mouthing dictators, the drifting politicians, the youngsters who sigh in secret for a new and exciting life, the old men who at heart are ready for a sensation even at the expense of millions of lives. When they all begin to talk about the stout-hearted legions of patriots, the honour of the nation, the necessity for expansion, and the rest of it, let them be shown this film at once, I thought, and told it is this they are wanting all over again. (Though if the worst and loudest of them were at once hustled into a shallow trench and then shelled and bombed by a battery and squadron appointed by the League of Nations, it might be more effective.) Then I saw that this film would not serve such a purpose, or at least would not serve it as well as it might be served. No film, no matter how realistic in its conception and execution, can suggest the muddle and monotony, the waste without end, the long obscenities of war. Verdun, after all, is art, and it is too cleanly tragic. It has beauty, a dangerous beauty.

It is film full of great things, but perhaps the greatest is the Fort Vaux episode. The ceaseless bombardment, the had-to-hand fighting, the gas attacks, all were superbly pictured, and it was impossible to believe that these men of the beleaguered garrison, which still held out when the Germans were actually holding the top of the fort, were merely playing parts. We sat there, choky and hot-eyed, watching them trying to signal, rationing out the last drops of water, and then saw, at last, the final surrender, when the French commandant surrendered his sword through the window and the Germans presented arms as the survivors of the heroic garrison reeled past. It was horrible, horrible; that fort was a hell; and yet I for one found in it all a queer fascination, like that of the ground that has been shelled over and over again, until it was as remote from humanity as the face of the moon, horrible, hellish, but with a terrible austere beauty of its own. It holds my imagination yet, thunders there like the last scene of Hamlet. The men who made this film were soldiers, and there runs through it that grave pride of soldiers.

Verdun was one of those places – the very emperor of them – that made all its visitors Freemen; when you had been there you knew you had got down to bedrock and that after that you could shrug your shoulders at the worst hell the theologians ever invented; you had 'been through it'. Every man who did any real soldiering knows what I mean; he remembers that strange ecstasy. He also knows, as I know, that it will not do. That is why Verdun will not do simply as a piece of anti-war propaganda; it is too high and clean and tragic for that. But what a film! When I caught sight of M. Leon Poirier, its creator, afterwards, I had quite a shock. It was as if one had just run up against Prospero, a Prospero who had exchanged the enchanted island for a blasted heath.

*When Priestley did begin to draw on his wartime experiences, it was in novels and drama not non-fiction, though the views expressed by some of his fictional characters were unmistakably his own.*

I'm not going to talk about the War. You know all about that. It killed my father, who died from overwork. It killed my elder brother, Jim, who was blown to pieces up at Passchendaele. He was the best fellow in the world, and I idolised him. It was always fellows like him, the salt of the earth, who got done in, whether they were British or French or German or American.

People wonder what's the matter with the world these days. They forget that all the best fellows, the men who'd have been in their prime now, who'd have been giving us a lead in everything, are dead. If you could bring 'em all back, fellows like Jim, hundreds and hundreds of thousands of 'em, you'd soon see the difference they'd make in the place. But they're dead, and a lot of other people, very different sort of people, are alive and kicking...[127]

How queer it was that there was something inside you that could relish, grinning with irony, the most damnable situation you found yourself in, pointing out how damnable it was! He'd discovered that in France, when, as now, something in him was afraid and something else wasn't, something shook and something grinned. Some of the old faces came popping up, smiled, and were gone; fellows he thought he'd forgotten; a spectral parade; and he wanted to keep one steadily before him so that he could cry 'It's a good war', and once again hear it call back to him, just one of the daft old slogans: 'Jam for the troops, mate.' He would feel better after that.[128]

*There was an obvious reason behind Priestley's reluctance to address the Great War more directly, and one that he shared with many survivors of the conflict: the experiences that they had undergone were so scarring, so horrific, so traumatic, that many never wished to put themselves back into those dark places again, even in their imaginations. Priestley's sleep was troubled throughout his life and in one piece,* The Dark Hours, *published in 1928, he offered glimpses of the reason, and even briefly addressed his war service.*

This last week I have had a succession of bad nights. It is not merely that I cannot easily find sleep. This I never could do, except during those times when I have spent the whole day in the open. Who, having enjoyed them, does not remember those hours of sleep, a divine unconsciousness, that fell on him, came down like a vast benevolent sandbag on the top of his head, at the Front? Sleep then was not simply a dark little anteroom through which one passed in order to arrive at the next morning's breakfast table, but a sojourn in the Blessed Isles.

I remember – it must be twelve years ago – the best sleep I ever had. We had been three weeks or so in the trenches, the clayey kind, full of water and with hardly a dug-out; and though there had been no real fighting, there had been any number of those daft alarms and excursions that hearty generals, talking over the wine and cigars in some distant chateau, praised to one another, in the belief that Englishmen always preferred magnificence to war. We had been so long without adequate sleep that our eyes were for ever hot and staring under leaden lids.

Well, one dark night we were relieved at last, and went swaying down miles of cobbled road. Some of the fellows dropped out, others slept as they staggered on, and finally a remnant of us arrived at some place that was nothing to us but a dark assemblage of barns and windowless houses, familiar enough yet as unreal as a place on the moon. A gulp or two of hot sweet tea, a moment's glow of rum, then down we fell, so mud-caked that we were as stiff as mummies on the hard floors, and down too came the lovely velvet curtain, blotting out the whole lunatic show of babbling statesmen and lads with glazing eyes. I slept for eighteen hours.

In the ordinary way, however, I have to woo my sleep, and that is one reason why I have read so many books, chasing Morpheus down innumerable labyrinths of eighteenth-century moralising or twentieth-century introspection. Those no-sooner-have-I-touched-the-pillow people are past my comprehension. There is something suspiciously bovine about them. When they begin to yawn about half-past ten, as they always do when I am with them (and I make you a present of the inevitable comment), I feel that they forfeit all right to be considered as fellow-creatures, spirits here for a season that they may exchange confidences at the hour when all the beasts that perish are fast asleep. I do not complain about having to approach sleep so stealthily, tiptoeing through a chapter or so. After all, this is only to prolong the day, and I cannot help thinking that such a reluctance to part for ever from the day, though it be only an unconscious reluctance, is proof of an affectionate nature, unwilling to dismiss a servant, however poor a thing.

Nor do I complain – though I like it less – about waking too early, beginning the day before it is fairly ready for me, nothing but a grey little monster with the chill on it and still opposed to all our nobler activities. I have been told that as the years wither me away, I shall have more and more of these early wakings, and I cannot say that the prospect pleases me. But for the moment I will submit to it without complaint, for there are worse things, and all this last week I have been suffering from them. I have been finding myself awake, not at the end of one day nor at the beginning of another, but sometime between them, in the mysterious dark hours.

Now this I do most bitterly resent. I have accustomed myself to prolonging the day, and I will try hard to resign myself to beginning it before it is worth beginning, but this other thing, this awful interloping piece of time, neither honest today nor splendid tomorrow, is a horror. You suddenly wake up, open your eyes, expecting welcome daylight and the morning's post and the savour of breakfast, only to discover that it is still dark, that nothing is happening. You roll over, turn back, then over again, curl your legs up, stretch them out, push your hands under the pillow, then take them out, all to no purpose: sleep will not come. You have been thrust, a dreadfully alert consciousness, into some black No Man's Land of time...

The dark hour, belonging to no day, swoops down and claims you as its own. No longer do you float easily on the kindly tide of ordinary human affairs. There is nothing tangible that you are afraid of, and, indeed, a burglar or a little outbreak of fire would seem a blessing. Nor are you, in melodramatic fashion, the prey now of your conscience. But you are alone, completely alone, really; feeling for once that you are imprisoned in your consciousness. At ordinary times we seem able to reach out of ourselves, sometimes entirely forgetting ourselves; and that way lies happiness. In these dark hours there is no escape, not even by any dizzy ladder of thought, and your mind goes round and round, drearily pacing its cage.

Life is nothing but a pulse beating in the darkness, or, if not that, then only the remembrance of a vague happy dream, bright faces fading and suddenly dwindling laughter, surrounded and conquered by terrible night. But this is only life, as it were, outside yourself. Inside you, there is life too, something alive, sensitive, shuddering, a bird beating its wings against the bars.

This self-consciousness of the dark hours, unable to fasten on anything outside itself, for ever denied communication, its thoughts wearily jangling round the old circus ring of the mind, is a glimpse of Hell. These are the terrors with which the preachers should threaten us.

The old-fashioned place, we know, would soon become companionable. I have no doubt that it would not take us long to develop a taste for molten metal and brimstone, and that the fiends themselves would soon prove to be most entertaining companions. But these dark hours of the night and the spinning mind, if prolonged, would only gain in terror and despair. They are the true nightmare.

The very thought that even now they are probably lying in wait for me is infinitely depressing. And, for the time being, I am avoiding a certain kind of fiction, if only because it has a curious suggestion of this torment. The kind I mean consists of quite clever stuff by youngish contemporary novelists, who work entirely and very elaborately through the mind of one central figure, whose self-consciousness, inability to escape from self, are so extreme that he or she is really a solipsist. Never once do these unhappy creatures forget themselves. They are for ever watching themselves, and relating everybody and everything to that image. And always they are depressed and depressing. In theory these novels would seem to grapple very closely with life, but somehow in practice, as actual representations, they fail badly, as everybody who still clings to the unfashionable practice of comparing literature and life must recognise. I realise now, however, that they do represent something with tolerable accuracy, and that is the night's vengeance on the unsleeping consciousness, the dark hours.[129]

*Only with the publication of* English Journey *in 1934, did Priestley reveal the extent of his disgust at the betrayal of the hopes and dreams of those who had fought in the Great War and his belief that a fairer society must emerge. Those feelings were triggered by his attendance at the first reunion dinner of his old 'Kitchener's Army' Battalion, men who he had not seen in seventeen years.*

The reunion battalion dinner, which had brought me here when I ought to have been continuing my journey elsewhere, was held at a tavern on Saturday night. The battalion was the 10th Duke of Wellington's, of the 23rd Division, which did good work in France and then in the later stage of the war did equally good work on the Italian Front. It was not specifically a Bradford battalion. Most of the fellows I had known as a boy had not belonged to it, but had joined a Bradford 'Pals' battalion that had been formed rather later. There were a number of these 'Pals' battalions, and as a rule the young men in them were well above the average in intelligence, physique and enthusiasm. They were all sent to the attack on the Somme on July 1st, 1916, when they were butchered with remarkable efficiency.

I spent my boyhood in a rapidly growing suburb of Bradford, and there was a gang of us there, lads who played football together, went 'chumping' (i.e. collecting – frequently stealing – wood for the bonfires) just before the Fifth of November, played 'tin-can squat' and 'tally-ho' round the half-built houses, climbed and larked about on the builders' timber stacks, exchanged penny dreadfuls, and sometimes made plans for an adventurous future. If those plans had been more sensible, they would still have been futile; for out of this group there are, I think, only two of us left alive. There are great gaps in my acquaintance now; and I find it difficult to swop reminiscences of boyhood.

'The men who were boys when I was a boy,' the poet chants; but the men who were boys when I was a boy are dead. Indeed, they never even grew to be men. They were slaughtered in youth; and the parents of them have gone lonely, the girls they would have married have grown grey in spinsterhood, and the work they would have done has remained undone. It is an old worn topic: the choicer spirits begin to yawn at the sight of it; those of us who are left of that generation are, it seems, rapidly becoming mumbling old bores. It is, however, a subject that has strange ramifications; probably I should not be writing this book now if thousands of better men had not been killed; and if they had been alive still, it is certain that I should have been writing, if at all, about another and better England.

I have had playmates, I have had companions, but all, all are gone; and they were killed by greed and muddle and monstrous cross-purposes, by old men gobbling and roaring in clubs, by diplomats working underground like monocled moles, by journalists wanting a good story, by hysterical women waving flags, by grumbling debenture-holders, by strong silent beribboned asses, by fear or apathy or downright lack of imagination. I saw a certain War Memorial not long ago; and it was a fine obelisk, carefully floodlit after dark. On one side it said Their Name Liveth For Evermore; and on the other side it said Lest We Forget. The same old muddle, you see: reaching down to the very grave, the mouldering bones.

I was with this battalion when it was first formed, when I was a private just turned twenty; but I left it, as a casualty, in the summer of 1916 and never saw it again, being afterwards transferred to another regiment. The very secretary who wrote asking me to attend this dinner was unknown to me, having joined the battalion after I had left it. So I did not expect to see many there who had belonged to the old original lot, because I knew only too well that a large number of them, some of them my friends, had been killed. But the thought of meeting again the few I would remember, the men who had shared with me those training camps in 1914 and the first half of 1915 and those trenches in the autumn and winter of 1915 and the spring of 1916, was very exciting.

There were bound to be a few there from my old platoon, Number Eight. It was a platoon with a character of its own. Though there were some of us in it young and tender enough, the majority of the Number Eighters were rather older and grimmer than the run of men in the battalion; tough factory hands, some of them of Irish descent, not without previous military service, generally in the old militia. When the battalion was swaggering along, you could not get Eight Platoon to sing; it marched in grim, disapproving silence. But there came a famous occasion when the rest of the battalion, exhausted and blindly limping along, had not a note left in it; gone now were the boasts about returning to Tipperary, the loud enquiries about the Lady Friend; the battalion was whacked and dumb. It was then that a strange sound was heard from the stumbling ranks of B Company, a sound never caught before; not very melodious perhaps nor light-hearted, but miraculous: Number Eight Platoon was singing.

Well, that was my old platoon, and I was eagerly looking forward to seeing a few old remaining members of it. But I knew that I should not see the very ones who had been closest to me in friendship, for they had been killed; though there was a moment, I think, when I told myself simply that I was going to see the old platoon, and, forgetting the cruelty of life, innocently hoped they would all be there, the dead as well as the living. After all, there was every excuse that I should dream so wildly for a moment, because all these fellows had vanished from my sight for years and years and in memory I had seen the dead more often than the living. And I think that if, when I climbed the stairs of the tavern, I had seen my friends Irving Ellis and Herbert Waddington and Charlie Burns waiting at the top, grinning at me over their glasses of ale, I would not have been shocked nor even surprised, would not have remembered that they had returned from distant graves. Sometimes I feel like a very old man and find it hard to remember who still walk the earth and who have left it: I have many vivid dreams, and the dead move casually through them: they pass and smile, the children of the sword.

Never have I seen a tavern stairs or a tavern upstairs so crowded, so tremendously alive with roaring masculinity, as I did that night. Most of the faces were strange to me, but here and there, miraculously, was a face that was not only instantly familiar but that at once succeeded in recalling a whole vanished epoch, as if I had spent long years with its owner in some earlier incarnation. We sat down, jammed together, in a dining-room that can never have held more people in all its existence. It was not full, it was bursting. We could hardly lift the roast beef and apple tart to our mouths. Under the coloured-paper decorations, we sweated like bulls. The ale went down sizzling. But we were happy, no doubt about that. We roared at one another across the narrow tables. The waiters, squeezing past these lines of feasting warriors, looked terrified and about half life-size. The very bunting steamed.

I was between two majors, one of whom was the chairman and (no cool man at any time, except no doubt at a crisis in the front line) now quite red-hot. With him, I exchanged reminiscences that seemed almost antediluvian, so far away were those training camps and the figures that roared commands in them. The other Major, unlike most of us there, was not a West Riding man at all, but a South Country schoolmaster, known to all his men as 'Daddy', and whose character and reputation were such that through him the whole affected tittering South Country was forgiven everything, In short, he was amazingly and deservedly popular. Rarely have I observed such waves of affectionate esteem rolling towards a man as I did that night. Those rough chaps, brought up in an altogether alien tradition, adored him; and his heart went out to them. I caught a glimpse then – and I am not likely to forget it – of what leadership can mean in men's lives.

I had seen it, of course, in the war itself; but long years of a snarling peace, in which everybody tended to suspect everybody else, had made me almost forget its very existence. And I do not suppose that in all the years that had passed since the war, any of those men had found themselves moved by the emotion that compelled them that night to rush forward, at the earliest opportunity; and bring themselves to the notice of 'good old Daddy'. In other words, they had known this endearing quality of affectionate comradeship in war but not in peace.

It is more than sentimentality that asks, urgently and bewilderedly, if they could not have been given an outlet for this deep feeling just as easily in a united effort to help England as in a similar effort to frustrate Germany. Are such emotions impossible except when we are slaughtering one another? It is the men – and good men too – who answer Yes to this who grow sentimental about war. They do not seem to see that it is not war that is right, for it is impossible to defend such stupid long-range butchery, but that it is peace that is wrong, the civilian life to which they returned, a condition of things in which they found their manhood stunted, their generous impulses baffled, their double instinct for leadership and loyalty completely checked. Men are much better than their ordinary life allows them to be.

The toast in memory of the dead, which we drank at the end of the dinner, would have been very moving, only unfortunately when we were all standing up, raising our glasses and silent, there came from a very tinny piano in the far corner of the room what sounded to me like a polka very badly played. I tried to think, solemnly, tenderly, about my dead comrades, but this atrocious polka was terribly in the way. I sat down, bewildered. 'Damn fool played it all wrong,' growled the major, our chairman, in my ear. 'Should have been much slower. Regimental march, y'know.'

That little episode was just like life; and I suppose that is why I am at heart a comic writer. You stand up to toast your dead comrades; the moment is solemn and grand; and then the pianist must turn the regimental march into something idiotically frivolous, and ruin the occasion. I am certain that if my friends ever want to drink to my memory, something equally daft will happen; and I shall murmur 'What did I tell you?' from the great darkness.

Now more men came in; the temperature rose another fifteen degrees; the waiters shrank another six inches; and there were songs and speeches. The chairman made a good speech, and in the course of it told the lads that the last battle in which the battalion had been engaged, on the Italian Front, was the greatest pitched battle in the whole history of the world. As he talked about this battle and its momentous consequences, I stared at the rows of flushed faces in front of me, and thought how queer it was that these chaps from Bradford and Halifax and Keighley, woolcombers' and dyers' labourers, warehousemen and woolsorters, clerks and tram conductors, should have gone out and helped to destroy for ever the power of the Hapsburgs, closing a gigantic chapter of European history. What were the wildest prophecies of old Mother Shipton compared with this!

I had arranged to meet, in a little anteroom, the survivors of my original platoon, and as soon as I decently could, I escaped from the press of warriors in the big room, to revisit my own past. There were about eight of us present, and we ordered in some drinks and settled down to remember aloud. I had not seen any of these fellows for seventeen years. I knew them all; of course, and they seemed little older. The difference was that before they had all been soldiers, whereas now their respective status in civilian life set its mark upon them, and now one was a clerk, another a tram-conductor, another a mill-hand, and so forth.

Nearly of all them remembered more than I did, although I have an exceptionally good memory. Details that had vanished for ever from my mind were easily present to theirs. Why? Was it because a defensive mechanism in my mind had obliterated as much as it could from my memory; or was it because much more had happened to me since the war than had happened to them and, unlike them, I had not gone back over and over again to those war years? (A third explanation, of course, is that, living in the same-district and often running across one another, they had talked over those years far more than I had.).

As figure after figure, comic and tragic, came looming up through the fog of years, as place after place we had been in caught the light again, our talk became more and more eager and louder, until we shouted and laughed in triumph, as one always does when Time seems to be suffering a temporary defeat. Frensham, Aldershot, Folkestone, Maidstone, Bully Grenay, Neuve Chapelle, Souchez, how they returned to us! Once again the water was rising round our gum boots. We remembered the fantastic places: that trench which ran in front of a graveyard, where the machine-gun bullets used to ricochet off the tombstones; that first sight of Vimy Ridge in the snow, like a mountain of despair.

We recalled to one another the strange coincidences and dark premonitions: poor melancholy B. who muttered, 'I'll be lying out there tonight,' and was, a dead man that very night; grim Sergeant W. who said to the draft, 'This is where you can expect to have your head blown off,' and had his own head shattered by a rifle-grenade within three hours. And little Paddy O, who had always seemed such a wisp of a chap, with everything about him drooping, who looked the same as ever, ready to drop at any moment, though he never had dropped and the Central Powers must have spent hundreds of thousands of marks trying to kill him, little Paddy, I say, came close to me, finished his beer, and asked me, stammeringly as ever, if I remembered sending him from the front line for some water for the platoon, on a summer morning in 1916.

'Nay,' he stammered, 'I wasn't gone more than t-ten minutes, and when I c-come back, where you'd been, Jack lad, there was n-nobbut a bloody big hole and I n-never set eyes on you again till tonight.' And it was true. I had sent him away on a ten minutes' errand; immediately afterwards a giant trench mortar had exploded in the very entrance to the little dug-out where I was dividing up the platoon rations; I had been rushed away, and was gone before he returned; and it had taken us more than seventeen years to find one another again.

Several of us had arranged with the secretary to see that original members of the battalion to whom the price of the dinner was prohibitive were provided with free tickets. But this, he told me, had not worked very well; and my old platoon comrades confirmed this, too, when I asked about one or two men. They were so poor, these fellows, that they said they could not attend the dinner even if provided with free tickets because they felt that their clothes were not good enough. They ought to have known that they would have been welcome in the sorriest rags; but their pride would not allow them to come. (It was not a question of evening clothes; this dinner was largely for ordinary working men.)

I did not like to think then how bad their clothes, their whole circumstances, were; it is not, indeed, a pleasant subject. They were with us, swinging along while the women and old men cheered, in that early battalion of Kitchener's New Army, were with us when kings, statesmen, general officers, all reviewed us, when the crowds threw flowers, blessed us, cried over us; and then they stood in the mud and water, scrambled through the broken strands of barbed wire, saw the sky darken and the earth open with red-hot steel, and came back as official heroes and also as young-old workmen wanting to pick up their jobs and their ordinary life again; and now, in 1933, they could not even join us in a tavern because they had not decent coats to their backs. We could drink to the tragedy of the dead; but we could only stare at one another, in pitiful embarrassment, over this tragicomedy of the living, who had fought for a world that did not want them, who had come back to exchange their uniforms for rags. And who shall restore to them the years that the locust hath eaten?[130]

*Priestley's mourning for the 'lost generation' killed in the Great War was compounded by his anger at the poverty and humiliation of so many of those who had fought and survived, fuelling his conviction that never again should there be a betrayal of the promise of 'homes fit for heroes' for Britons going to war. He developed his theme in a series of newspaper and magazine articles that displayed both his humour and his gift for expressing complex ideas in simple, everyday, but memorable terms.*

Supposing your wireless set suddenly, stopped working properly. Well, perhaps you understand wireless sets. If so, you would set about mending it yourself, and if you have a glimmer of sense you would obviously go to work fairly slowly, methodically, patiently. If you don't understand wireless sets, you would call in somebody who does. But I don't imagine you would call in a large angry man with an axe who would give one yell and then reduce the set to broken glass and firewood. He might be a fine strong brave fellow – you might take a pride in the set of his shoulders and the thrust of his chin – but obviously if he was simply going to be angry and use his axe, he would not mend your wireless set.

A much smaller, milder man - perhaps a nice boy of twelve, who wouldn't look anything like so imposing and wouldn't be such an exciting person to have about the place - might be far more useful at mending the set. A little knowledge, a little patience, a little quiet skill, and the trick's done; the set's working and all's well.

Right. Now the political, economic and social systems of this world are far more complicated than any wireless set. And they are not working properly – we are all agreed about, that. What are we going to do about it then? Well, I suggest we don't want any strong men with axes. They are not going to mend complicated world systems. They are very imposing and exciting, they make us want to clap and cheer, but they are not going to be able to do the job. Like the broken set, the broken systems are going to need knowledge and skill and patience to put them together again.

Heroes of the good old-fashioned kind are useless. Nobody admires them more than I do – partly because I'm not at all like one – but in the present situation I'm afraid they are useless. In fact, some of them are just a nuisance; they are in the way. With the world as it is, we are not in need of fine brave eager fellows who are ready to die for something or other, their country, their flag, their leader. What we are in need of is people with knowledge, sense, good humour, and patience, who are willing to live and work for humanity. At the moment, one wise teacher is worth fifty dashing cavalry generals. The set's broken down and it's got to be put together again. Let's keep that in mind.

Our need is desperate. But a lot of things simply won't do any good at all, any more than the angry man with the axe. Among these things, in my opinion, are uniforms, flag-waving, processions, fiery speeches, patriotic songs, or revolutionary hymns accompanied by the organ, secret police, murder, chasing your opponents down side streets and clubbing them, saluting, supermen who think about Napoleon, sentries and passwords, bombs; mass meetings, censorships, lies for propaganda's sake, looting, storming of Bastilles, tearing rich men to pieces, hitting poor men with truncheons, and shouting at the top of your voice.

It's a pity that some of these things won't do any good, because they are amusing and would brighten one's life, probably. But they are about as useful in settling the world's problems as standing on your head in Piccadilly Circus. They belong to a world of violence, and, no doubt when you are as exasperated and nervous as most of us are these days, it is a relief to plunge into that world of violence, but it is quite hopeless, except as a means of suicide. It was the world of violence that brought us to the mess we are in, and if we're going to get out of this mess, then it's no good appealing to the world of violence. You hear impatient people roaring about Action, Action. But what's the use of making violent moves when you don't really know what you ought to do? You might just as well send Carnera [Primo Carnera, a huge heavyweight boxer] with a hammer into a watchmaker's.

All over the world there are millions of decent men and women who now find themselves without any security, without any hope, nearly starving in a world that is bursting with food and goods of every kind. It's probably the most maddening situation that the human race has ever found itself in, but simply being maddened and behaving like madmen won't get us out of the situation.

I have been talking so far to people – mostly younger people – who feel it is time something was done and want to do something. I have not been talking to those people – and there are still plenty of them in this country – who don't want to do anything, who believe the world will right itself for you if you only sit about and wait long enough. I don't propose to talk to those people. I don't think anybody ought to talk to them. It's obviously a waste of time. Give them a little light music, before the end comes - that's all you can do. The rest of us, who are worried, must consider what this bewildered world of ours stands most in need of.

I have already told you at some length what, in my opinion, it doesn't need. I have suggested, too, what seem to me the necessary qualities – knowledge, skill, patience, good humour. Above all we need some constructive thinkers and behind them a public that will free itself from prejudices. Just consider how few new ideas you ever find in the political-economic world. The other week I read a collection of' short things in prose and verse by some young men who announced themselves, rather self-consciously, as the latest arrivals. They pointed out that they were the real post-War generation and a new sort of people altogether and that the rest of us were already mere relics of the past – quaint survivals.

The human race, I gathered; was beginning all over again. That didn't worry me much. If the world could really settle its affairs happily, I for one would be content to survive in it as a dim comic figure from the past, perhaps as a sort of droll museum piece. But what I did expect, after this fanfare, was that these young men would have something really new to say to me, that I would meet ideas of startling novelty. But all they offered me were the usual remarks about the Capitalist system breaking down and a little mild Communism. I was dreadfully disappointed. Why, a comparatively elderly man like H. G. Wells is more up to date in his thinking than the whole crowd of them. Post-War indeed! Their Communism was nineteenth-century.

I have stopped regarding this chatter about the class war as thinking; it's all parrot stuff, and out of date too. I'm not a political-economic thinker, and don't pretend to be. I'm a literary man who takes the interest in these problems that every educated man ought to to do. But I'm not going to hesitate to say this, that it's time we did some thinking along really new lines in this field. I don't like the chaotic capitalistic system. Nobody with any sense does. It's like living in a place crowded with brigands and racketeers. I believe, too, that it's all breaking down. But I can't see why the only alternative should be Communism, which seems to, me terribly faulty, inflexible, old-fashioned. I feel sometimes that we are simply being bullied into imagining that there aren't any other alternatives. There must be. And this is where our constructive thinker sets to work. And he has got to work because he has a passion for the good life, because he is haunted by a vision of men leading full and happy lives.

Too many of our present political activities have their mainsprings in bitterness and hate. The Haves hitting out in fear of the Have-nots; the Have-nots hating the Haves. All this breeds anger and violence, and – I repeat once more – our complicated problems will not be solved by anger and violence any more than your wireless set can be mended with an axe.

That does not mean, as some people seem to think it does, that every problem will instantly be solved if we are all suddenly converted. Even if we were all saints, we should still have to find out the best way of ensuring that colliers in South Wales, salmon canners in British Columbia, coffee growers in Brazil and dairymen in Denmark, all exchanged their products to their mutual advantage. It is not simply goodwill that is going to do the trick. It is a combination of goodwill and brains. That is precisely what the world needs now.

I heard once of a family of children who used to say: 'Would you rather be good like mother or clever like father?' Well, what we want now are some people who are as good as mother and as clever as father, and – this is important – when we have found them, we have got to back them up. Tolerance and good humour come in, too. This statement will make a lot of people I know very angry. They believe that tolerance and good humour are characteristic English vices, and that we shall never get anything done until we have got rid of them.

This seems to me to spring from a confusion of thought, from supposing that tolerance and good humour, on the one side, and sheer sluggish indifference, on the other, are the same thing. They aren't. As I said before, I am not talking now to the merely apathetic, to giant sloths, to human puddings. I am talking to people like myself, who are worried, anxious, nervous, all strung up about it all. And once you are like that, the line of least resistance is that of some wild extreme, with anger and violence thrown in. The hardest thing is to keep your, temper and to set to work patiently.

We don't want any martyrs and heroes. We want some constructive thinkers who will have the ear and attention of a sensible, good-humoured public that won't sway in the breeze of every passing prejudice, like a monstrous captive balloon. And here's a tip. Welcome every appeal that is made to you as a rational individual. Suspect every appeal to herd instinct, no matter what side makes it. We have all gone roaring and trampling in herds too long, destroying in one silly mad rush what it may have taken years and years of patient work to construct.[131]

# Chapter 5
# And the men who were boys

*Throughout the 1930s, Priestley exchanged letters with his close friend Edward 'Teddy' Davison, who was living in the USA, and he often wrote with a frankness that was not always possible in his published work. In a letter written in June 1932, Priestley even expressed satisfaction with the Great Depression, a sentiment that, if publicly stated, would have caused serious damage to his reputation in the US.*

The collapse of America is a good thing for humanity, because it has completely broken the legend of American success and the spell of a mechanical material hog-philosophy. I was reading last night a new book by an intelligent German, who was emphatic on the point that Europe has to save itself by becoming more European, that Russia and America (which have different theories but the same intolerant material practice) have to be avoided like the devil, and that a satisfactory solution is more likely to come from England than from anywhere else. I hope this is true. Let us all come out strong on the side of the humanities, for quality against quantity, man against machines, poetry and fun against dreary materialism.[132]

*As war clouds began to gather over Europe once more, the warmongers' self-fulfilling prophecy of preparedness for the next conflict at first provoked fury in Priestley. His views expressed in 'The Lost Generation', written for a Quaker publication, and 'You and Me and War', for a popular daily newspaper, were diametrically opposed to those of the most prominent of those Siren voices, Winston Churchill, 'a voice in the wilderness' throughout the 1930s calling for Britain to rearm.*

'And the men who were boys when I was a boy will sit and drink with me.' Thus the poet. I hope he was luckier than I am. I belong to the wrong generation. Most of the men who were boys when I was a boy can not sit and drink with me. Loos and Gallipoli and the Somme did for them. They went and saved something and never came back. What it was they saved I cannot exactly tell, but I do know that I have never seen anything since 1918 that was worth their sacrifice.

When people wonder what has been wrong with England these last twelve years, it seems to me they forget the war. It is all very simple. The men who would be assuming leadership now, in politics, the professions, the arts, business, if there had been no war, are dead.

Who can tell what genius was poured down that vast drain? We can only guess, but those of us who remember those ardent and generous spirits, nearly always the first to go, can make tragically shrewd guess. We flung away brilliant young manhood as if it were so much dirt, and now we are paying the price for it. There is still a flourishing, pre-war generation, and there is, of course, a flourishing, if not markedly vital, post-war generation. But in between there was a generation that belonged to the war itself, that grew to manhood in the trenches, and now it is a remnant.

This is the generation to which I belong, for I celebrated my 21st birthday in 1915 in the front line. I have a few good friends and a great many acquaintances; but sometimes I feel like an old man, for I seem to know intimately more dead men than living ones. To think about an old playing field is to see a crowd of ghosts. I know very well that a man may have been killed in battle and yet have been a poor creature.

Yet it is not sentimentalism that makes me declare emphatically that the most eager, promising and finest members of my generation were lost to us through the war. I know it for a fact. I knew them, was with them. We who are left – the lucky ones – are a miserable remnant; and sometimes I wonder if any of us are quite sane, even though we may never have appeared in a police court and pleaded our war service.

I doubt you can grow to manhood under such circumstances – you can spend the most impressionable years of your life among shells and bloodstained barbed wire, and be quite normal. There are wounds of the soul as well as wounds of the body. In the life of a young man there is a period – let us say between the ages of nineteen and twenty-three – when, though he may be working hard at a university or learning a business, he can lead what is on the whole a carefree, cheerfully

Army memorabilia. Clockwise from bottom left: JB Priestley's Regimental shoulder tab; officer's commission (Second Lieutenant, Land Forces, Temporary); red wallet; Field Message Book; Field Service Pocket Book; army issue red wallet for documents; military medal miniatures.

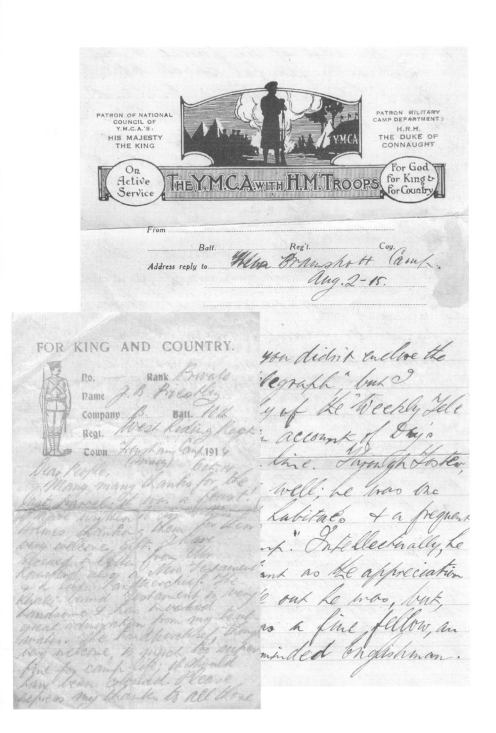

Priestley's army letters, often written on paper from the YMCA, almost always began 'Dear People', embracing his father, stepmother, sister, aunts, uncles and grandparents.

Priestley's 'innocent pudding face' – a photograph in lance-corporal's uniform taken just before he embarked for the Western Front.

Lord Kitchener, who became Secretary of State for War on 5 August 1914. Two days later he appealed for the first hundred thousand men. Priestley at once decided to answer Kitchener's call and volunteer, even though he had written an anti-war article only twelve months previously.

The famous 'eight horses or forty men' trucks in which Priestley and so many other British soldiers were transported to the Western Front.

British horse-drawn artillery on the Western Front. Priestley later stated that 'humping along cobbled roads, choked by the dust of military transport, was murderous'.

Signallers at work in Sausage Valley before the Somme offensive. Priestley wrote about 'old trenches that had simply been wired off, and when we explored them we found them filled with bloodstained clothing, abandoned equipment, heads, legs and arms'.

The grim devastation of trench warfare, epitomised by German troops in action near Arras.

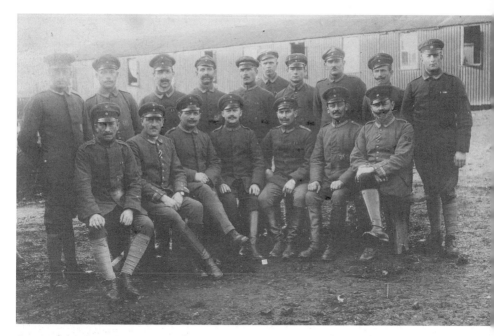

Some of the German prisoners of war under Priestley's supervision.

Under the supervision of a British officer, German prisoners of war mend roads in Northern France. Priestley was put in unwilling charge of a contingent of PoWs and, overseeing the construction of a new camp 'let loose a part of myself I did not even know was there; for a few astonishing and rewarding days I played the man of action not long before settling down, from that time to this, to live by putting words together and passing round the hat.'

The football team formed from the prisoners of war under Priestley's charge. He is sitting to the left of the Major.

Convalescents' fancy dress concert party at Hambleton Hall, Rutland, in 1916. Priestley is second from the left holding a toy dog.

Army Form B. 2079.

**WARNING.**—*If you lose this Certificate a duplicate cannot be issued.*

Certificate of discharge of No. *12398* (Rank) *A/Cpl.*

(Name) *John Boynton Priestley.*

(Regiment) *West Riding Regt*

who was enlisted at *Bradford.*

on the *7 - 9 -* 19*14* .

He is discharged in consequence of *his being promoted to commissioned Rank. Authy. W.O.
Letter no. 43/40/1516. (M.S.) P. 3) dy - 18-2-18.*

after serving *three* years *145* days with the Colours, and

*—* years *—* days in the Army Reserve.

(Place) *York.*

Signature of
~~Commanding~~
Officer *ho 2 Infantry Record York.*

*I Walker
Capt. for Col.
or Col. York.*

(Date) *29 - 1 - 1918.*

*Description of the above-named man on *29 - 1 - 1918.*
when he left the Colours.

| | Marks or Scars, whether on face or other parts of body. |
|---|---|
| Age *23 yrs - 139 days.* | |
| Height | |
| Complexion *Fresh.* | |
| Eyes *Blue.* | |
| Hair *Dk. Brown.* | |

*Should agree with the description on Character Certificate, Army Form B. 2067*

(A8856) Wt.W9155/M2138. 200,000. 9/17. D. D. & L. Sch.44. Forms/B2079/22.

Priestley's certificate of discharge from the ranks.

Members of the Officer Cadet Battalion to which Priestley was posted in 1917. He is standing in the middle of the second row.

Priestley, still in uniform, as an undergraduate at Cambridge.

Priestley in his study at Well Walk, Hampstead, probably late 1920s.

Hitler, photographed soon after the end of World War I. Priestley averred that his rise to power was due to 'some deep-seated weakness in the German character, addressing himself always to the dark face of his people'.

Hitler on steps of Vienna Town Hall, April 1938, receiving messages of allegiance from all thirty-one German provinces. Dr Goebels is behind him. Throughout 1938, Priestley's letters became ever more dark in mood.

Neville Chamberlain returning from his 1938 Munich visit, with the historic 'piece of paper' – 'Peace in Our Time'. Chamberlain's government embodied everything that Priestley disliked about the state of Britain in the 1930s.

Priestley and his second wife, Jane, outside Broxwood Court, Herefordshire, during World War 2. The building acted as a hostel, which Jane ran for mothers with small children evacuated from the bombed cities.

In the study at Broxwood Court, with the inevitable pipe.

Priestley and Jane at the head of the garden steps at Broxwood Court.

121. **Price, George Ward,** 17.2.86 Sonderkorresp. vom „Daily Mail",
London, RSHA IV B 4.
122. **Price, Morgan, Philips,** 1885, Politiker, RSHA VI G 1.
123. **Pries, Viktor,** 21.8.03 Hamburg, Schlosser (Am-Apparat), RSHA
IV A 2.
124. **Priestley, John Boynton,** geb. 1894, Schriftsteller, RSHA VI G 1.
125. **Prince, Edmund Matthew,** 21.9.96 London, Geschäftsführer, vermutl.
England, RSHA IV E 4, Stapo Wesermünde.
126. **Pringsheim, Ludwig,** 4.3.16 Halle/Saale, Wehrpflichtiger, London,
RSHA V — D 2 f, Ger. d. Kommand. Berlin.
127. **Prins,** zuletzt: Den Haag, jetzt: vermutl. England, RSHA IV E 4.
128. **Pritt, Denis Nowell,** geb. 1887, London, L. C. 4, 3 Pump Court,
RSHA VI G.1.
129. **Prochazka, Karl,** 25.4.05 Brünn, ehem. tschech. ND.-Offiz., vermutl.
England, RSHA IV E 4, Stapoleit Prag.
130. **Prochownick, Vilma, Dr.,** 1904, ledig, Ass., Cambridge (Univers.),
Emigrant, RSHA III A 1.

Priestley's name was included in a Nazi death-list of people to be eliminated immediately after an invasion of Britain.

Hitler and Benito Mussolini. It was Priestley's contempt for them that earned him a place on the Nazi death-list. He referred to the fascist tyrants as 'characters in ... an evil fairy-tale, turning all Central Europe into a haunted, bloodstained forest'.

irresponsible existence.

It is the age at which young men sit up very late at night, smoking brand new pipes, drinking beer and gigantically settling the affairs of the universe. It is also the age at which, very idealistically, they first fall in love, and take to writing sonnets, after illuminating experiences at college dances.

My generation missed all that. It spent that period watching its dearest friends be killed. And when, after the war, it came back, blinking, bewildered, it had to grab a livelihood, and do it when everybody seemed to be greedy and grabbing. Can you wonder then that we seem at times a trifle hysterical, rather bitter? Perhaps we don't; perhaps we seem jolly, healthy-minded fellows, but then you are not there when two or three of us are gathered together.

Writing then, as one of this remnant, possibly half-witted, I will confess that I do not understand this world at all. I do not understand people's sense of values. I cannot gather exactly what it is they want to get out of life. Take this war business as an example. Learned and industrious men, after burrowing away among documents for years, give us long books on the causes of the Great War, and you pay your money and you take your choice.

But the real cause of the war could be set down on a postcard. It was the inevitable result of people standing about, their fingers on triggers, expecting a war. Everybody who was in the trenches will remember how, one night when all was quiet, some young ass of a sentry would fire a few quick rounds at nothing, just to warm his hands. So a German sentry would loose off a few rounds. Then more English, more Germans. The machine-guns would join in. Then the light artillery and the trench mortars on both sides. Then the heavy artillery would be called in and finally the night would be a daft inferno. That is war. And that is how the war started.

The most dangerous lunatics we have had to do with this century have been the 'Be Prepared' agitators. To be prepared, you have to amass big guns and little guns and heaps of explosive. Once you have done that, the rest flows. Some fool gets a fright and pulls a trigger – and then you are off. You can't have dangerous weapons without wanting, at some time, to use them. We are not in the habit of killing each other where I live, being nice, peaceable ratepayers; but suppose we were told that murder was inevitable and all began to go about armed to the teeth, what do you think would happen? Why, very soon the place would be littered with corpses. All those people who go about saying that war is inevitable and giving interviews on the next war are either dangerous lunatics or criminals. They ought to be locked up and fed on bread and water.

I hardly ever go to a cinema without wondering if there is a glimmer of sense in this world, for at the cinema, in the news reels, they are fond of showing you the latest developments in the techniques of mass murder, the airplanes that will drop unheard of bombs, the tanks that can cross rivers, and so forth.

And these people sit, placidly looking on, eating chocolates and holding hands. Nobody says 'Wait a minute! What are these things for? When that airplane buries or suffocates the population of half a city, when those tanks shatter men's spines or drive men's bodies deep into the mud, what is to be the new excuse?'

In other cinemas, in other countries, they are proudly exhibiting pictures of their own new bombing planes or tanks, and everybody there is placidly looking on too. And nobody says 'Why? Why? Why?'

But one dangerous fool, whose finger has been itching at the trigger too long, will fire a shot. And next time, there won't be any learned or industrious men writing any books on the causes of it all. There won't be any learned or industrious men and there won't be any books.

There will only be a few idiots gibbering among the ruins. And sometimes, even now, I feel like one of them.[133]

It is no use. I had hoped to be able to keep off this subject, but events have been too much for me.

Let me admit at once that I am no expert. I am an ignorant layman. Moreover, I am apparently a sentimentalist. I am, it seems, incapable of reasoning clearly. I am, you see, one of those people who believe that the very worst way to preserve peace is to prepare for war. Incapable as I am of reasoning clearly, blinded as I am (unlike our clear-sighted statesmen) by the mists of sentimentality, I propose to try and reason a little on this subject of peace and war, armament and disarmament. There is still time before the first shot is fired, if we make a quick dive for the essentials of the problem.

It is obvious that there are two schools of thought, and that the fundamental conflict is between them. There are those like myself who believe that if you prepare for war, you get war. Then there are those like our ministers, who believe that you can only be peaceful by being warlike. This is called the clear-sighted, rational, realistic view.

Let us see just how clear-sighted, rational and realistic it is. We British, it says, are a pacific race, unlike the sinister foreigners. If we arm ourselves, we do it for the good of the world. Our battleships, bombing planes, tanks, are quite different from the nasty battleships, bombing planes, tanks of the foreigners, although we are ready to supply them with these articles at a fair profit. But our bombs and shells, unlike theirs, will only explode in a Good Cause, for Freedom and Justice and things like that.

Now just because we are Better than other nations, so we ought to be Stronger, so that if they do not understand the moral force of our arguments (and they are often very stupid), they will have to appreciate the physical force of them. And as they will be terrified of our physical force (one of us being equal to ten of them), they will not dare to oppose us, and we shall all enjoy the blessings of peace. This is the clear-sighted, rational, realistic view, that of stout men of the world, who call a spade a spade and won't have any of your darned nonsense. None of your literary man's highfalutin' about it. Just plain common sense.

The fact is of course, that this argument is so silly and sentimental that compared with it a Christmas card reads like a laboratory report on a blood test. It is so silly and sentimental that foreigners laugh or grow indignant and talk about 'English hypocrisy.' They cannot believe that men who talk in this idiotic strain can be sincere. To them it sounds like smooth villainy. But it is not. It is often sincere and always silly and sentimental.

It is we, who are called the sentimentalists, who are realistic in this matter. To begin with, we realise that our armaments look to foreigners exactly as theirs do to us namely, like sinister, menacing preparations on the part of a mistrustful, unfriendly power. They do not understand that our battleships are nice good battleships. Why should they? Battleships are battleships, and are not there for fun. Therefore, the foreigner declares that he must defend himself – and Freedom and Justice and the other things – against this menace. He must have more of whatever arms he fancies, not because he likes such things, not even because his cousin has shares in the firm that makes them, but because the Fatherland, the Motherland, the Home of Truth, Beauty and Goodness, must at all costs be defended. So he immediately increases his army, navy, air force. And so do his neighbours.

Bewildered, rather hurt, feeling misunderstood, Britain once more finds herself comparatively unprotected. These nasty foreigners are apparently armed to the teeth. We have a moral obligation, because we are Better than they are, to be Stronger, for the good of the world. We are not belligerent. All we want is peace. So in the name of peace, we must build still more battleships and bombing planes.

Once again the wretched foreigners do not understand. They imagine we are threatening them more ferociously than ever. Every nerve must be strained to reply to this new challenge. They cannot afford to fall out of the dreadful race. On they go again.

By this time, a good many important things have happened. To begin with, an atmosphere of intense fear and suspicion has been created everywhere. It is rather like the atmosphere of the saloons in the old mining camps, where every man carried and used a gun, where a fellow had but to make an accidental movement towards his hip for a fusillade of shots to ring out. Every nation is bristling with arms, and standing on the alert.

Moreover, once a country's armaments are big enough, the professional fighting men become very important members of its councils. Thus, pre-war Germany was practically an armed camp, with the inevitable result that the General Staff of the Army bossed the country. Unfortunately, professional fighting men have a bias, and rarely think on broad, statesmanlike lines. If peace is what you are after, they are not good men to have about. Their natural element is a state of war. They are only playing at soldiers during peacetime. They would like to get on with their job. When they feel that they are controlling a superb fighting machine, which at a touch will devour the opposing forces, they itch to set the lovely thing in motion. They are like a young man who has been given a new racing car.

So that, what with a general atmosphere of fear and suspicion, fighting men itching to be at it, fingers trebling on triggers, war is inevitable. You have all prepared for it. To prepare for something is to set Time bringing it towards you. The war that we expect will surely arrive. It needs only the most trivial excuse.

We have just reached the end of a 15-year period when there were international quarrels sufficient to start fifty wars, but there was no war. There was no war because the preparations were inadequate. The greater powers were not ready for war. If everybody is thoroughly unprepared, there never will be a war. Let every power be convinced that its own army, navy and air force are all in a shocking condition and vastly inferior to its neighbour's, and nobody will want to fight. Though international affairs are one long squabble, still nobody will want to fight.

It seems that now we have reached the end of that period. In the name of Peace, the nations are beginning to prepare for War again. The old race has begun. It has only one goal – War. And there is only one way to stop his lunacy, and that is for the people, who have no fundamental quarrel with the folk of other nations, to stop it themselves.[134]

*The pessimism of such articles was far from typical of Priestley, whose belief in the innate qualities and decency of ordinary Britons was unwavering throughout his life; 'I did not discover the proletariat at Oxford or Cambridge, for the West Riding [of Yorkshire] working class was in my blood and bones'.[135] He was a lifelong socialist, but a moderate one – 'I am a pink,' he once declared, 'and a pleasant, healthy colour it is too'[136] – and years later, writing in his autobiography,* Margin Released, *he outlined his political creed and its roots in his upbringing.*

Bradford, the birthplace of the Independent Labour Party, was one of the earliest socialist strongholds. My father and many, though not all, of his friends were socialists. They were not Marxists – and I doubt if there was a student of economics among them – but were all in the looser and warmer English tradition of socialism. This was largely unplanned, too vague, too hopeful, but it was able, as some intellectual improvements upon it have not been able, to generate enthusiasm. It could create an atmosphere in which immediate and fairly radical reforms seemed possible. It may have moved towards an impossible goal, but on the way it could do more good than harm. In this respect it was unlike those movements that produce and are ultimately led by dedicated revolutionaries, men of steel, who soon begin to hate everybody, even the very people they are trying to rescue from poverty and despair.

I grew up in this English socialist tradition, and at heart I still believe in it. Liberalism is modem man's nearest approach to real civilisation; as soon as most of it was sneered away, the power men took over, the secret police arrived, torture came back. This old-fashioned English Left was liberalism with the starch out of it, the fire lit, the company it could assemble more varied, easier and warmer-hearted, not incapable of a song and a chorus. It was life-seeking, life-enhancing, a protest, perhaps too late, on behalf of the feminine principle.

I grew up listening to political argument – some children enjoy adult talk, and I was one of them – and later I joined in, for though I have never been a compulsive talker, I cannot keep silent long. But during these later teens I found myself in a position where I have remained more or less ever since.[137]

*Priestley's liberal-socialist views put him at odds with the British Establishment, many of whose members were tacit and sometimes overt admirers of the fascist regimes of Italy, Germany and Francoist Spain, seeing them as bulwarks against the tide of 'creeping Bolshevism' that threatened their wealth and privilege. Priestley had no time for any accommodation with extremists of the Right or the Left and was horrified by the excesses of Hitler, Mussolini and Stalin, but he was emphatic that extremist creeds in Britain should be countered by debate and force of argument, not state repression.*

It is because I do not like Fascism that I urge that it should be left alone in this country, allowed to march and speak when and where it likes. I dislike Fascism because it gives itself military airs, is politically retrogressive, settles no important problems; and when successful has always shown itself to be the enemy of political and intellectual liberty.

Even in the country of its birth, Italy, for which it may be peculiarly suited. I doubt it has done more good than harm. Tourists are loud in praise of Italian Fascism because it has given them a punctual train service, new roads and great public works to admire. They do not hear any grumbling from the Italians themselves because a great many of the most forceful grumblers have been removed and the others are frightened of opening their mouths.

We do not know what Fascism will do to Germany, but so far it has succeeded in alienating that country from the rest of the world. Both these two countries, Italy and Germany, are centuries behind this one in political experience. It is not true, as some people are always telling us, that the Italians and Germans have advanced beyond democracy. The truth is that they have not arrived at it yet.

It is pitiful to see young Britishers so slavishly imitating the political tactics of Italians and Germans. It is enough to make our grandfathers turn in their graves. No doubt the Italians and Germans can teach us a great deal, but not about politics. There is not a fundamental problem, economic or social, that Fascism really attempts to solve. And where it is successful it destroys that liberty of thought and speech which is not only a solid good in itself but without which no fundamental problem can be solved....

It is Communism that has produced Fascism and without one we should never have had the other. This is a fact some people might remember. A good many acquaintances of mine have been loud in their condemnation of the Nazi Revolution this year because the Nazis behaved with such brutality towards their political opponents and showed themselves to be so ferociously intolerant. But some of these same people have long been quite sentimental about the Bolsheviks who employed precisely the same tactics and whose proscriptions and executions were on a much larger scale.

There is, as Mr. H.G. Wells has said, a book-burning Nazi 'oaf.' But there has also long been a book-burning Bolshevik 'oaf.' The fact is, of course, that all these brutally intolerant folk are oafs, whether they are wearing red, black or brown shirts. Now we are not going to turn this country, which still has some professions to civilisation, into a battleground between snarling Communists and roaring Fascists. We do not want the War of the Shirts here. Britain will not be saved by either gang. Neither has anything of real value to say to us.[138]

*Through his Bradford roots and his European travels before the Great War, Priestley had been steeped in German culture, literature and music, and he mourned its perversion and near-extinction under the Nazis.*

There was a time when our histories were too contemptuous of economic motives. That was corrected, and indeed during these last twenty years I think it has been over-corrected. Human beings are something more than economic limits. We need now a little psychology in our history.

Thus I do not believe that the rise of Hitler can be explained by economic motives alone. He also appealed to and gained his power through some deep-seated weakness in the German character, addressing himself always to the dark face of his people.

It simply will not do to see Hitler and his friends, and all the saluting and screaming youths who obey them, as ordinary men with a few grievances who want to see their country as one of a settled, prosperous order of nations in a peaceful world. They are dragon-slayers with magic swords. They are characters in a fairy-tale, but now it is an evil fairy-tale, turning all Central Europe into a haunted, bloodstained forest.[139]

Artists and scientists and scholars need secure conditions and a wealthy community. They cannot work properly if the secret police are pestering them and their families all the time. The concentration camp is a poor environment for culture. Great works of art will not be conceived and executed under skies dark and noisy with bombing squadrons.

The cultural history of the totalitarian states is almost a complete blank. Mussolini brags about his bayonets, not about his philosophers. A screaming Goebbels cannot accomplish what a serene Goethe could do. No matter how powerful and efficient your dictatorship is, how supreme your Will, you cannot command into existence the finer things of the human spirit. The mind will not blossom to order. A cultural desert is the price you pay for all those big heavy boots marching and counter-marching.[140]

For many of us the emergence of Hitler's Germany has been a double tragedy, for just as we detest this new Germany, so we loved the old Germany that we have lost. Here is something that the Nazi propagandists have been careful never to mention. The people who out of their love for the old Germany, protested the most against the treatment of the post-war German Republic, who were the most sympathetic during those 'seven long years' that Hitler for ever refers to, were the very people over whom the Nazis have always poured their bile and hate - Socialists, Radicals, Liberals, Bolshevised folk, Jew-ridden theorists. These - and these alone - were the friends of that stricken Germany. And they are the people today who most deeply regret the disappearance from their lives of the Old Germany.

Every nation has two faces – one charming, the other detestable. Now, the two German faces are in very sharp contrast. The dark face is heavily brutal, touched with sadism, humourless, clever but completely unwise, whining in defeat and insufferable in victory, the face of a neurotic sergeant-major. The other face, at once so affectionate and contemplative, is the face behind the earnest metaphysics and the lovely string quartets that you used to see in the innumerable happy and devoted families that made Germany one of the kingdoms of the spirit.

And the tragedy – not only for Germans but for all of us – is that dark face has eclipsed the bright face. Never before in history can a great people have been so completely dominated by their own evil genius as the Germans have been these last five years. Nearly everything that has made Germany shine in the minds and memories of men has been destroyed. It had a great culture and it is rapidly being obliterated. It had a charming and deeply affectionate family life which is being poisoned. It had for imaginative people everywhere a fairy-tale quality, but now the enchanted pages are wet with blood and tears.

The Jews, with their strong humorous sanity, were a very valuable leaven in German public and cultural life. Perhaps no people really needed the Jews more than the Germans did, and it is a fact beyond dispute – outside the reaches of the Gestapo – that the German Jews were not only patriotic citizens, but that their roots went deep into German life, deeper, I suspect, than the roots of Jews settled elsewhere went into the lives of their respective countries. It was characteristic of the evil genius that has been at work that the Jews should be the chief victims of oppression.[141]

*Priestley's work was also banned by the Nazis, joining a long list of other authors of left wing views or Jewish origins.*

What a world! I have lately received news that my last novel, 'They Walk in the City,' cannot be brought out in a German translation by my publishers in Berlin. An evening paper, the other night, said that the Nazis must have banned my book because I am a Socialist, and the President of the International P.E.N. Club. It is true, I have long been a Socialist of sorts. But I am not the President of the P.E.N.; but only the President of the London Centre of that club. The International President is a French writer, Jules Romains.

Well, here I am, banned from Germany because I am a Red. I have never had any of my books published in Russia, presumably because I am not Red enough. And, unless we are careful, it looks as if, very soon, anybody who tries honestly to tell the truth as he sees it will be published nowhere, banned as a dangerous fellow throughout the whole crazy world."[142]

*Priestley's opinions, expressed in scores of articles and broadcasts as well as the novels and plays that had made him famous, also earned him a more sinister approbation from Hitler's regime: his name was added to a Nazi death-list of those to be executed in the wake of an invasion of Britain. But his hatred of Fascism and Nazism did not make him a Marxist sympathiser or fellow-traveller; indeed he argued that Communism had actually created the necessary conditions for the rise of Fascism.*

I dislike Marxism, believing it to be based on a false materialism. Its economics do not frighten me, but I dislike it as a substitute for a general philosophy. And its effect on the mind of its converts is not reassuring. (Marxist criticism of literature and art for example, is the most dreadful bosh.) I do not believe in its dialectical process. Even if this were true, it would be necessary now to admit that the process has continued past the point at which Marx said it would stop, for militant Communism called Fascism into existence, and now Fascism must be producing something that has no name yet.

In spite of the conversion of many young intellectuals, I doubt if Marxism will go very far here. It does not suit our book. Its nonsense is not our nonsense. And I have noticed among many extreme left-wingers a Central European rather than an English air and atmosphere. They do not seem at home on this soil. You know at once they would rather be playing chess in a cafe than darts in a pub. I do not see their kind ever leading the English people.

The earlier English Socialism, from Owen to Morris, was the product of middle-class compassion and idealism rather than of proletarian resentment. The men and women who demanded this social revolution did not do so because they were trying to compensate themselves for some deep-seated feeling of inferiority. They were not moved by vindictiveness disguised as the reforming and crusading spirit. There is much to be said in favour of this earlier Socialism.

One school of left wing thought takes the view that the privileged classes cannot be gradually ousted out of power and that they will fight desperately, shedding much blood, before they will climb down from their seats. This view, which frequently finds its way into print, seems to me by no means true and certainly dangerous.

No matter what end it has in view, violent revolution seems to me both horrible and futile. It has been compared to a surgical operation. Let there be a period of fear, pain, bloodshed, so that the social body may be preserved. This is, I think, a mistaken notion, a false analogy. We know now how horrible a violent revolution can be.

To explain exactly why I hold it to be equally futile, always bringing about results quite different from those first imagined, would take us too far from our present subject; but briefly, roughly, let me say that I believe that the terror and hate brought into play by such revolutions prevent the imagined end from being achieved. Instead of moving up a spiral, you merely swing a pendulum. You cannot create good by adding to the world's evil.[143]

*Priestley's constant expression of traditional Liberal-Socialist ideals and values, and his urging of the need for individual freedoms to be preserved and enhanced, gave the lie to right wing mutterings that he was a 'Red'. As the threat of war loomed, he acknowledged that some of our cherished freedoms might have to be temporarily curtailed, but warned of the danger of imposing state controls on too many areas of British life.*

I remember an article in the Left Book Club News that attempted to prove that there was more freedom in Russia than in England. What the writer really meant was that the worker's life in general seemed to him better in Russia than in England. But to lump all that together and call it 'freedom' is absurd. Surely it would be at once more accurate and sensible to say that though the Soviet Republic offered its workers better prospects and in some respects much happier conditions at present there was not more than less freedom than in England. For example, you cannot go there and start a Right Book Club and prove in its Monthly News that everything is much better in England.

The value you give to freedom depends upon your temperament. I place a high value on it myself because by temperament, though not by conviction, I am strongly individualist, independent, perhaps a trifle wayward. In practice, though not in theory, I hate the herd instinct. I dislike processions, mass-meetings and the military way of life. I don't want a Leader myself and don't want to be anybody else's. I sympathise with people who won't fit into a pattern. I would rather do without motor-cars than work myself in a mass production factory - I am depressed and not exhilarated by the spectacle of five thousand persons drilling together.

This is, I think, a very English temperament, though I suspect it is not as marked as it was a generation or two ago. We like freedom more than most nations, but not as much as we used to do. The reason why the English set great store by freedom is that their instinctive way of life demands it.

'What governs the Englishman,' said Santayana in his fine essay on us 'is his inner atmosphere; the weather in his soul...' And later: 'It is a mass of dumb instincts and allegiances, the love of a certain quality of life to be maintained manfully.'

If you are to grow like a tree and not be set up like a telegraph pole you need space. This space is what we really mean by freedom. At the moment it looks as if to protect our right to grow like trees we shall have to be set up like telegraph poles; or to be plain, we are being asked to give up more and more of our freedom in order to preserve our freedom. A compromise is possible and we seem to be making it. But I suggest that if freedom must be curtailed in this direction, then it should be enlarged in that; in short that a wise government, if it has to tighten one rein, will let some others go slack. We all need room to put out a new branch or two 'where the birds might nest and sing.'[144]

*Priestley spent the winters of 1936-37 and 1937-38 in the USA, wintering in Arizona for the sake of Jane's health. While there he continued a series of letters to Teddy Davison, charting the progress towards war.*

17 March 1936

We sail a fortnight this Saturday, April 4th, and I must say I am longing to be off now, not because I am tired of America but simply because I long to be home again. The situation over there is not pleasant but I do not think there will be war yet, though obviously it looks as if it were on the way The only good thing is that people now are so war conscious – as they were not in 1914 – that it is possible that it will threaten for long time and yet be avoided. But the whole continent wears a horrible look.[145]

31 December 1936

... I've talked to people back from the Spanish Front, and they tell me that the Russian Planes chased the German ones out of the sky. This must be making Hitler think a bit. I'm all for telling him 'where he gets off.' There must be a bust-up of some kind soon.[146]

1 February 1937

... I believe Germany must either fight or collapse, and if Hitler sees everything sliding, he may gamble on war, just as Ludendorf gambled on one big push in 1918. I fancy our own government is playing for time, partly to rearm, and partly because Germany is getting worse. Spain was a Nazi-Fascist job, of course. The only thing is an Anglo-French-Russian alliance. But these fantastic trials don't make me feel easy about Russia, and I don't move a step nearer to communism. With all our nonsense, we've got something precious in England – a non-hating, decent spirit – and we must preserve that. I shall be interested to see what Roosevelt makes out of his second term.[147]

3 November 1937

The news of the world is bad, but I doubt if it is as bad as the Press makes it out to be. I have noticed before that as soon as one gets over here, things in Europe seem on the verge of war. It doesn't seem as bad actually in Europe. The predatory powers have got themselves definitely in line, and are out to bluff as hard as they can go. The real danger is that their internal situation (for Germany, Italy and Japan are in a bad economic position) may get so bad that they will risk a war.[148]

10 February 1938

The state of the world makes any big attempt in fiction almost impossible. 1 am toying with the idea of writing a longish novel out of our own time, not a historical novel, but making the time and place rather undefined – say, somewhere in Central Europe about the beginning of the 19th Century – in order to concentrate on things that, with a modem setting, instantly become journalistic and controversial. It isn't so much a matter of escape, as of getting away, for once, from the newspaper front page. Nobody can say I haven't attempted to have a look at our own age.

To my mind, the news gets steadily worse. I have just been reading a book, published by Harpers, called The House That Hitler Built, written by an Austrian professor, and it's terrifying, and as it happens the most recent news from Germany makes it more terrifying still. The Germans of 1914 were quiet, sane, reasonable people compared with this lot. These people must make war; they cannot organise for permanent peace, only for approaching war, therefore it is inevitable that they will make war, and that pretty soon.[149]

17 March 1938

I agree with you about the Chamberlain business. (As I write he looks like falling). Nobody wants war, but I feel the only thing is to put on a bold front with these madmen (who in my opinion are really not to be reasoned with, are lost in some vast Teutonic Siegfried dream of victory and conquest – read 'The House That Hitler Built' as a damned good exposition of all that) and to tell them definitely to toe certain lines. On the other hand, I am weary of the endless sneers in the American Press, which jeers at us because we arm and look like being embroiled in war, and yet jeer again because we won't fight at the drop of a hat. When all's said and done, if these very people hadn't ratted on Wilson when he went to Versailles, none of this need have happened, and the League could have been a reality with America in it. I still blame this country more than any other for this tragic state of things, though now I think it might as well stay out of the dogfight.[150]

*Back in England, Priestley continued to write to Davison, his letters growing ever more dark in mood.*

4 December 1938

The political situation keeps us in a nightmare here, not so much of fear, as of despairing effort. Will I keep the families of several Catalan authors? Will I rescue an Austrian dramatist, now in Prague, from the Germans, who will beat him up? Will I write an introduction to a pamphlet on the refugee problem? Will I give something towards another Spanish food ship? Will I subscribe something for Czech authors? And so on and so on Meanwhile though I detest our present government and mean to help fight them (by speaking etc.) during the next election, I am rather impatient with American criticism Indeed, if Chamberlain felt – and it is a big IF – that Hitler meant to fight, then he did right to give in, because in a week Czecho-Slovakia would have been overpowered and London, totally unprepared, would have been a shambles.

The only people who could have possibly saved Czecho-Slovakia were the Russians, and they showed not the least desire to do so. Why? Nobody has ever told me yet. The Russians claim to have the largest army and air fleet in Europe. Why weren't they willing to use it? I don't take the view that Chamberlain is a Machiavellian pro-Fascist He is, I think, a rather stupid, quite honest, Birmingham business man, who does not really understand what Nazism is about, and of course is terrified by the famous Red menace Whether he is foolish to believe in 'promises' made by Hitler and Musso, 1 don't know. He is probably playing for time there, and hoping for an internal crack-up in both countries. (Conditions are worse, I believe, than is generally imagined.) The trouble is, that if a war comes, it will be an immediate stalemate on land, and develop into a senseless aerial affair.[151]

3 July 1939

It is, as you can imagine, terribly difficult to make any plans here because of the constant threat of war and we are all living in a kind of hand-to-mouth fashion which is extremely unsatisfactory. Incidentally, if you have not read it, get hold of Drucker's 'End of Economic Man', which I think is the best book I have read so far on the significance of Nazism...

I am not very grand myself. The doctor says I am suffering a little from nervous exhaustion, probably due to years of overwork and worry, with the result that I tire very easily and find that it requires twice the usual effort to get any work done. I wish I were coming out to your conference in Colerado, but that is quite impossible not only as I have so much to do here but also because we simply dare not go far from home now and until things are cleared up - and how they will be cleared up I can't imagine – we shall simply have to stay on this side of the water.[152]

*While he was as clear-eyed about the evils of Stalinist Russia as of Nazi Germany, Priestley saw the Soviet regime as an essential ally in any conflict with Nazi Germany and was horrified at the way the 'anti-Red' bias of much of Britain's political and military leadership had isolated the Soviet Union.*

*The Conservative government of Neville Chamberlain embodied everything that Priestley disliked about the state of Britain in the 1930s, not least the lack of genuine democracy in what he saw as government by cabal, dominated by landed and corporate interests. At times, even Priestley's perennial optimism gave way to despair about the state of his country and, as Britain sleepwalked towards war, he wrote a series of articles for the* News Chronicle *under the general heading 'Britain, Wake Up!' that 'brought me floods of letters and the offer of about twenty constituencies as Independent Progressive Candidate.'* [153]

What is wrong with us the British? As I see it, the rot set in when the post-war period ended in nothing, or, if you like, in making-do and muddling as a substitute for creation. A tradition, based chiefly on a profound feeling of security, perished in the summer of 1914. For the next five years it was a matter of struggle and endurance.

Then came the post-war period, when weary returned soldiers

hoped something would happen, but had to start their own lives over again, and the youngsters were all cynical and disillusioned, the Arlen-and-Coward era, and the elderly men, some of whom are still with us, thought they could put the date back to early 1914.

Out of this post-war period of chaos should have sprung a New Britain, no doubt with much of its old leisurely charm gone for ever, but alert, purposeful, courageous and richly creative, both politically and culturally. And it didn't...

Our ruling and official classes never at any time had much respect for any form of culture, but recently they have had less. Every triviality of mind is encouraged, and anything likely to make men think and feel deeply is discouraged. We still go on telling ourselves that the most wonderful thing that can happen to an Englishman is to own the horse that wins the Derby. And we no longer even play our games very well. All we do is to chatter, chatter, chatter about them.[154]

During the last few years our national life has been riddled with complacency, snobbery, hypocrisy, stupidity. Never before have we made such a fuss about trivialities. Never have we congratulated ourselves so often about nothing. If we all awoke one morning to find ourselves paralysed, some of our newspapers would congratulate us: 'Let foreigners go moving about,' they would say, smugly, 'but the ordinary decent British citizen has wisely decided to stay in bed.'

Every possible triviality of mind has been encouraged, and anything likely to make us think and feel deeply has been discouraged. And this is not Hitler's and Mussolini's doing. It is our own. And as I see it, the rot set in when the post-war period ended in nothing, in making-do and muddling and cynical pottering as a substitute for creation. A tradition, based chiefly on a profound feeling of security but containing within itself certain valuable seeds of growth, perished in the summer of 1914.

I am not myself conservative-minded and have no respect for the past, yet I do not hesitate to declare that the England of 1914 was superior, in every important department of national life, to the England of today. But it had to go. For the next five years it was a matter of struggle and endurance, during which our loss of first-rate manhood was comparatively high and terribly damaging. But something much better, one felt, would emerge from all this.

Our social system had had a good shake-up. The old snobberies were leaving us. Between them the young men who had fought and the young women who had worked would achieve something. They didn't, but there seemed to be plenty of time. After all, the weary men who came back had to start their lives all over again, as I know only too well, having been one of them; and the young women were anxious to be nice settled wives and mothers. The still younger people were immensely cynical and disillusioned. We achieved the post-war period, the Arlen-and-Coward-and-night-club era.

Throughout this period the elderly men of the ruling classes were quietly working out the very difficult problem of putting the date back to early 1914. They did not really notice anything happening in the world after the Russian Revolution of 1917. Significantly, this was the last event that meant anything to them. Just before the gates of their minds closed to all new and profound impressions, in slipped a terrible figure, dripping with blood-the menacing Red.

This then was the post-war chaos, which lasted about ten years. At the end of those ten years or so there should have emerged a new Britain, with much of its old leisurely charm gone for ever, robbed of many an antique grace, but alert, purposeful, courageous and richly creative both politically and culturally. And it didn't. Instead of going forward, the country halted, hesitated, wobbled, then tried to move backwards. What should have been an advance turned into a retreat.

English political life, which had not been improved by the Khaki Election of 1918, slipped down to a new low level in 1931, the year of the faked financial crisis, of the Labour Prime Minister who turned Tory overnight, of the bogus National Government, of an election swung by the nastiest lie yet, the one about the Post Office Savings raid [the right wing press had claimed that if Labour won the 1931 Election, they would raid people's Post Office savings accounts for money to deal with the financial crisis facing the country]. My own feeling is that English life, political, social, cultural, took a turn for the worse about then and has shown little improvement since. It was now we began to see ourselves wearing that gross, vacant face of the tired rich old man. And brightness fell from the air.

Our commonest error of speech is our description of this country as a democracy. It is not a democracy and never has been; though it is worth observing that it is farther away from true democracy than it was twenty years ago. Indeed, I think we were nearer to being a democracy back in 1912. Just after the War, it did look as if we were about to say good-bye to feudal Britain for ever, but very soon the ranks of privileged persons closed up and common people had to keep their distance. Neither politically nor socially is this country a democracy. Hardly anybody here thinks or feels like a democrat. if you begin to talk like one in public, there is a rumpus...

We are not a democracy, but a plutocracy roughly disguised as an aristocracy. All our real government is done by the Right People... You can see the private income outlook at work. It does not by any means necessarily coincide with the best interests of the country. There is a natural tendency to suppose that whatever protects the drawer of dividends is sensible and wise. These men are probably quite unlike the heavy villains of capitalism who figure in the Left Wing prints. But they cannot help seeing things from their own narrow angle.

Moreover, being men of financial substance, perhaps born to it, they are apt to live in a style that cuts them off from the mass of the people and probably brings them into contact with a small, wealthy and privileged class. What is worrying some agreeable fellows at the club, some nice chaps from the City, will soon begin to seem much more important than whatever happens to be worrying a hundred thousand poor devils somewhere in the industrial regions. And as four newspapers out of five are owned and directed by the same sort of people, it follows that the weaknesses of such political gentlemen will not be mentioned and corrected by most of the Press. All this explains in part why quite nice but rather stupid fellow-countrymen of ours can behave in a fashion that makes the simpletons of the extreme Left see them as deeply scheming villains, planning to dragoon and starve the people.

Unless we are fortunate, then, we are not really free to express ourselves politically even at elections, and there are not many elections and between them we have only the ghost or political power. That we were once a little more of a democracy is shown by the fact that there still lingers some faint trace of Government sensitiveness to public opinion, but anybody who cares to examine in detail Baldwin's handling of the electorate in 1935 will see that genuine representation of that opinion has become a mockery. And now, in the new style of doing things it is not even Parliament, not even the Cabinet, but the Prime Minister and two or three or his chosen senior Ministers, who make all the decisions for us. We do not know until long afterwards what those decisions are.

We may not be compelled to make a fancy salute every time Chamberlain passes us, and the secret police do not come round to see that we are carefully listening to him on the wireless – and if that means democracy, then we have one – but the fact remains that we ordinary English citizens have known no more about what Chamberlain has been doing than the Germans and Italians know about Hitler and Mussolini...

The tradition of a feudal aristocracy and landed gentry hangs over our life like the pall of smoke over London... The country house routine, with its solemn arrangements for slaughtering creatures at stated seasons, is regarded as one of the great goals, life at its fullest. Our more energetic, acquisitive, cunning citizens will scheme and toil half their lives in order that at last they may change their names and lead this fancy-dress existence. Their children have hardly heard of the dark towns from which the money came. And the towns themselves, where the muck remains, reap no harvest, not even of dead pheasants.[155]

*Priestley also gave vent to his anger and frustration that, while even his moderate Liberal-Socialist views were routinely described as 'Left Wing propaganda', the 'smooth and constant kind of Right Wing propaganda' passed without comment or criticism.*

We are always reading remarks of this kind: '...... stated that some of their authorities were concerned about the subversive propaganda being spread through the primary schools and the teachers of primary schools. The Teachers' Federation in Australia was said to have been captured by the Communist wing of the Trades Hall, and the subversive propaganda was spreading right through the educational system .....'

At a first glance it looks all right. 'Subversive propaganda'! We can't have that. Nobody wants subversive propaganda in schools or anywhere else. What should they be given in schools then? Oh – the facts, the plain truth. But where is this plain truth to be found? What you might call the facts, I might call propaganda.

When a communist begins talking to you about the class war, he is quite certain that at last you are being given the truth about our history. He is taking you, he feels, away from the dope of capitalist propaganda, and giving you the bare facts. But all the anti-communists cry, 'Now, now! Stop that subversive propaganda!'

Each party compares its own simple truth with the elaborate lying propaganda of the other side. So much is evident. But there is one difference, in the capitalist democracies, between the Left and the Right Wings, and that is that while Left Wing propaganda is always being recognised and denounced as such, what is equally propaganda from the Right Wing is taken for granted. A finger is pointed at the teacher with the red tie, but the teacher with the old school colours passes unnoticed.

I remember that about three years ago the Film Censor warned the film trade against 'introducing politics' into the cinema. I wrote an article about it at the time. I have no doubt that the Film Censor, whoever he was, felt that he was only doing his duty by uttering this warning, and he did not realise that when he said 'politics' he meant Left Wing opinions, and that a great many of the non-political films that he approved of were themselves a kind of propaganda. In short, like nearly everybody else, he took a certain smooth and constant kind of Right Wing propaganda for granted.

The Press, books of every kind, films, lectures, plays, are pouring out an enormous stream of Right Wing propaganda day and night. They are telling you directly or indirectly that a society in which the acquisitive instinct is the most highly prized and rewarded is a fine civilised society. They ask you to take their word for it, that business is sacred, and that patriotism means a bit of drilling and flag waving, and does not mean that you should stop selling raw material for munitions to potential enemies.

We are governed by an oligarchy. We are no nearer to being a true democracy than we were thirty years ago; indeed, we are further away. Our present government... is government by the rich and privileged. It is about as much like a true national government as Mr. Chamberlain is like the Birmingham Symphony Orchestra. It is not even government by a party but by a clique within a party, and one condition of remaining a member of the clique is that you do not show any signs of having strong and independent views.

And if any schoolmaster, having to talk to the boys on 'How we are governed', put his textbook on one side and told a few of these home truths, he would be denounced by somebody or other as a Red propagandist. Yet the schoolbook itself, covering the facts with a lot of fine talk about our democracy, would never be described as propaganda. To show what propaganda can do when nobody calls it propaganda, I offer you the following instance.

Millions of decent folk here sincerely believe that the reason why we are now in such a pickle is that we could not stand up to the dictators earlier because we were not strong enough. And we were not strong enough because a lot of muddle-headed Liberals, Radicals, Socialists ('fellows like you, Priestley') would not allow Britain to rearm. This is swallowed hook, line and sinker, without any mention of propaganda.

But the real reason why we did not stand up to the dictators long before we were in this pickle is that the Tory Right Wing, which dictated our foreign policy, did not want us to stand up. All our present strategic weaknesses are the result of their bad policy. We were in the fantastic situation of seeing a dominant group here making friends all the time with the very enemies of our Empire; Manchukuo, China, Abyssinia, Spain, Austria, Czecho-Slovakia, these are the milestones along that rotten road.

This is the truth. It is also, of course, Left Wing propaganda, and probably subversive. About this time of year, a few dozen ex-Service bigwigs present school prizes and at the same time hand out great slabs of Right Wing propaganda. Subversive too. If we are not careful, it may prove to be subversive of European civilisation. But I never hear any complaints that the minds of the young are being polluted. Yet let some elementary schoolteacher be caught speaking his mind for ten minutes, and the word goes round that the very playgrounds have been painted red.

The other day I read a letter from a noble lord, given great prominence in an important daily, protesting against the Nazi Spy film now showing at Warners Theatre. Although it is founded on fact, it is, of course, propaganda. But what about the other films that are in effect propaganda for a narrow and militant imperialism, for things as they are, for silliness and greed and callousness?

Let it be made plain that as men are today, living in highly organised communities, there can be no natural order of things, some arrangement settled for us by our guardian angels. People who protest against the present organisation of our society are not wilfully setting their faces against some God-given division of wealth, privilege and power. They are not simply trying to inject too much red into an exquisite harmony of shades. What they are saying is: 'Try a little red in place of all this blue, into which everything has been dipped.'

All this is not as fanciful as it may first appear. It is a very clever trick – and you can see it working everywhere – to pretend that the man who wants to improve on one man-made system, which is not functioning properly, by substituting another, is really a mere mischief-maker, an agitator, a born rebel, a dangerous propagandist.

This artful assumption makes the whole vast stream of counter-propaganda, the blues against the red, seem the natural tide of affairs. It is the big brother of the other old Tory trick of claiming the national flag as the emblem of your party, although that same party may have been busy bringing dishonour to the flag.

But sometimes the propaganda appears in the wrong place. The other week I read something like this in a morning paper: 'Yesterday of course there was a very slender House of Commons because of the Eton-Harrow match.' Now I call that Left Wing propaganda, and it could easily be subversive too. Only it appeared, in all innocence, in a Tory paper.[156]

# Chapter 6
# A terrible awakening

*Priestley's novels, plays and screenwriting had made him a popular and influential figure in the United States, and, as Europe slid towards war and American isolationism reasserted itself, his articles and radio broadcasts were instrumental in correcting American misconceptions about British attitudes, and in influencing public opinion about potential US involvement in the coming war.*

*On 2 February 1939 he wrote to his friend Teddy Davison: 'I've just agreed to write a long article for* Harpers Magazine *explaining the progressive attitude in England, and it should clear up some prevalent misconceptions in America. Please be assured of this: the English people are strongly antifascist now, and are not – as some American journalists (who get their ideas from Mayfair) suggest – hysterically afraid.*[157]

*In his long examination of 'Where England Stands', Priestley showed his customary humour, insight and acute analysis, but the article also took a prescient view of problems that would come to dominate the post-war agenda, including the vexed question of Britain's place in Europe. Chamberlain's government was lambasted but Priestley reserved his strongest ire for the isolationism of 'Little Englanders' led by Lord Beaverbrook, and the knee-jerk anti-Communism that had prevented any serious diplomatic overtures being made to the Soviet Union, a potential ally against Hitler, but being driven into his arms by the hostility of the West.*

Ever since last September a great deal of what I have read about England in American periodicals has left me feeling annoyed. The writers were not deliberately misrepresenting the facts. They were not misinformed. (Though here and now I will admit that I think there is a strong tendency among American journalists to exaggerate both the power of the Reich and our fear of it.) But they were annoying because they were telling their American readers about an England that does not exist. They did not, in fact, mean England itself. They were not writing about the English people. They were writing about Neville Chamberlain and his friends.

Chamberlain and his party, which is still supposed to be a coalition, officially a National Government, but which is really Tory, have a large majority in the House of Commons. But this does not mean that the country itself is solidly Tory in sympathy. The fact is that our electoral system, hopelessly out of date, prevents any genuine representation of the people. Indeed, one of the first things a progressive government must do in Britain is to reorganise the whole system of Parliamentary elections. We have no proportional representation or even the alternative vote. What happens over and over again in many constituencies is that the progressive vote is split between a Liberal and a Labour candidate, while the Tory grabs the seat. Thus it is possible for more people to vote against Chamberlain and his policy than vote for him, and yet Chamberlain's man may win the seat.

At one recent general election it was calculated that in a certain section of the country the Tories polled roughly a million and a half votes and the various Progressives about a million. But that same section of the country was represented by no less than eighty-four Tory members to one solitary Progressive. Anybody who did not understand our electoral conditions would assume, quite wrongly, that all these people were overwhelmingly Tory in sympathy. Moreover, even within our present system there is a distinct need of reform, for the seats are by no means equally divided among voters. A vote in Cheltenham, for example, is really worth four votes in some big industrial boroughs, and it is significant that this bad inequality nearly always works to the advantage of the Tories.

Unless these electoral anomalies are kept steadily in mind it is very easy completely to misunderstand English politics. Thus there is only a tiny group of Liberal members in the House of Commons, and you might suppose from this that the great Liberal Party, which had been long in power at the outbreak of war in 1914, has now withered away. This would be quite untrue. The Liberal Party is very much alive, and I am not sure that at the moment of writing it could not perhaps command more talent, not narrowly political but in general ability, than any other party. The liveliest newspaper in England, from a political point of view, is the News-Chronicle (once the Daily News and first edited by Dickens), and this is a Liberal paper. What might be called Liberal opinion, to which we shall return later, is found everywhere, frequently and loudly expressed. Yet a survey of the House of Commons would suggest that Liberalism was almost dead.

Moreover, not only does the House of Commons fail to represent public opinion, but now the Government itself does not really represent the House of Commons. We are no longer even governed by a Cabinet. We are governed by an Inner Cabinet. Our policy is being decided, not by public opinion, not by the House, not even by the whole Cabinet, but by Chamberlain, Simon, Hoare, and Lord Halifax. We voters can make our opinion felt, within the limits of a very bad system, at the next General Election; but until that time comes we have about as much say as to what Britain will do as one of Hitler's Germans has as to what the Reich will do. The ordinary German or Italian citizen has no idea what Hitler or Mussolini will spring upon him next, but then neither have I, who am supposed to be a member of a democracy, the least idea what Chamberlain and his friends are going to do next. (And some of these friends, who go about with mysterious authority, men like Montagu Norman and Sir Horace Wilson, are not even elected persons.) Thus when Chamberlain went to visit Mussolini in January he was not delegated to go by the British people, who did not understand at all why he went. Indeed, I am certain that if there had been a referendum on the question of that visit there would have been a decided majority against it...

It would not be true to say that the English people as a whole are now anxious to reverse Chamberlain's policy, simply because the English people as a whole do not think about policies. They are not, in fact, many of them, politically-minded at all, which is one reason why they make such poor democrats. Even to this day, with gas masks hanging in the kitchen, they are less interested in foreign affairs than they are in football pools, cricket matches, dog racing, and the local cinema and dance hall. And the trouble is, as we have seen over and over again, that this thoughtless mob can be stampeded into voting for the Tory interest at a General Election simply by some last minute catchpenny cry. (Remember that the Tories control about four-fifths of the Press.)

But when we come to that cross-section of the English people that is politically conscious, the people who give at least part of their mind to national and international affairs, then I do not hesitate to declare that the majority of them condemn the part Britain has played during these past few years. They were for the League of Nations and bitterly resented Mussolini's invasion of Abyssinia. They were for a bold stand, together with France and Russia, against Hitler. They were against the Anglo-Italian pact. They were decidedly anti-Franco. They were appalled by the Munich Agreement. They do not believe in Chamberlain's 'appeasement'.

In home politics these people may be Liberal, Labour, Socialist. (Our Communist Party is so small that it may be ignored.) But they take the same point of view of our foreign affairs. And it must be remembered that it is very easy for the most experienced and conscientious London correspondent of an American newspaper to underestimate both the numbers and the depth of feeling of these people; for the journalist, busy gathering news and views in Westminster, the City, and the West End of London, is not coming into contact with them, but cannot help seeing much more of the comparatively small group that has been pursuing a policy condemned in hundreds of thousands of homes all over the country.

The foreign correspondent has another weakness, against which his readers should be warned. He has to be readable, lively, dramatic, and have something of the triumphantly penetrating style of a detective in the last chapter, when all the suspects have been gathered together in the library. Now it is difficult to be all this and yet write truthfully about what is a vast muddle. The result is that many of these specialists in foreign affairs pretend there is no muddle and put in its place an elaborate pattern of deep-laid plots and far-reaching policies. Bewildered and not very bright statesmen, who are actually wondering what on earth to do next, are turned into tremendous machiavellian figures. This is particularly so with the chief muddlers, the English.

Thus we read that the real explanation of the antics of Chamberlain and his friends is that they are plotting to achieve Fascism in Britain. I do not believe this for a moment. There is of course a small group, very small though not without influence, that would like to see some form of Fascism established in this island. It is indeed difficult for the thoroughgoing Tory mind not to have some tenderness for such an authoritarian and intolerant form of government. But I am convinced that Chamberlain, Simon, Hoare, and Halifax are not plotting to introduce Fascism and that indeed they have no great liking for it. But why then do they behave so curiously?

The answer – and very disappointing it is too – is muddle. They are all in a dreadful muddle. There are various good reasons for this, and the first is that they are suffering from a very bad time-lag. When Chamberlain talks about 'appeasement', he is referring to a Germany and an Italy that do not exist. He is solemnly trying to settle the world of 1909, not 1939. The result is that he is always two or three moves behind in the game. Thus he imagines that there must be either peace or war, just as his father, Joe Chamberlain, would have thought. He still does not realise that the Fascist trick is continually to create a state of affairs that is neither peace nor war but something uneasy and unpleasant in between, a state of demands and loud threats and mobilisation and bad nerves all round. It was by similar devices that the dictators came to achieve power and they use the same technic to enlarge that power.

The very last thing they want is a settled Europe, in which each country attends to its own affairs, because they do not know how to attend to their own affairs but only how to acquire more power. Nearly all their familiar grievances are really excuses. Thus we are told that Germany has no raw materials because Britain and France have such large colonial possessions. Meanwhile this same poverty-stricken Germany, instead of buying raw materials in the open market, contrives to pile up armaments on a scale beyond anything the world has hitherto known. It is a country at war that must have immediate access to raw materials, and by their emphasis upon their lack of these materials the Nazis reveal what is at the back of their minds.

Hitler was helped to power by the feeling among the Germans that they had not had a square deal. (But please notice that the very Tory apologists for Hitler, who now point out the German grievances, were the very people who were most obdurate in refusing to relieve the pressure upon Germany before Hitler's accession. They will listen to Hitler but they closed their ears to Stresemann.) But it is a mistake to suppose that the Nazi leaders would be satisfied now with a square deal. Their aim is world domination.

There has just come into my hands, as I write this, a summary of the main ideas in Dr. Rauschning's Die Revolution des Nihilismus. The author has been for years a member of the Nazi Party and was President of the Senate in Danzig. The ideas he puts forward are those that are held by or are influencing the Party leaders, who have now moved a long way from Mein Kampf, which was, after all, an early work and intended for popular consumption. According to Rauschning, National Socialism is a dynamic, revolutionary movement, not merely aiming at the redressing of obvious wrongs, but with aspirations that cannot be satisfied with anything short of world domination. It is prepared to ally itself with other 'dynamic powers', but even then only temporarily; for even when there has been a considerable redistribution of territory and power, the revolutionary and dynamic character of the movement will lead to further expansion, until at last, Germany is master of the globe. Already one of the S.A. songs ends with the line: 'Today Germany is ours, tomorrow the whole world.'

To these theorists of the geopolitical school, Britain's Empire is as good as lost already: we are the Venice of the Twentieth Century. France, they hold, is now a dying nation, and it may not be necessary even to fight her; she can be bled to extinction. The smaller European states are incapable of real independence, and can easily be mopped up. Once Germany controls all central and north-western Europe, with Italy controlling the whole Mediterranean, the next move will be toward world domination. Meanwhile there is no settled policy (even an alliance with the Soviet Union is possible), except that the great military machine must be kept whirring menacingly, the world's nerves must be continually jangled, and the old game of unscrupulous opportunism, disorder, and bullying, at which these men are masters, must be played for all it is worth. And let us remember that so far it has been played successfully.

If there is any truth in all this, as we think there is, then obviously it is folly to deal with Nazi Germany as if it were merely a country that had at last found a form of government that suited it and was anxious to redress a few wrongs before settling down comfortably with its neighbours. You might as well regard an Al Capone as a wine merchant who happened to have been a little rattled by some of his competitors...

I am not in Mr. Chamberlain's confidence – we members of the British electorate have not that honour – but as he has sources of information at least as good as, if not better than, most of us have, we may assume, as we are compelled to do at times if only out of sheer fatigued bewilderment, that he is not foolish all the time and may occasionally be playing a game of his own. First, he may be stalling, desperately gaining time; for the machinery of rearmament has been working very slowly here, for various reasons, among them the downright inefficiency of the Chamberlain Government officials. But now the graph of production is rising steeply, and before the end of this year the Nazi theorists who are banking on our military decadence may have a terrible awakening. (And it must be remembered there is such a thing as quality as well as quantity in airplane manufacture.) Second, Chamberlain may well be influenced by a feeling that these vast dreams of imperial power in which the dictators are losing themselves may not necessarily be shared by the mass of their people, who are already paying a very stiff price for these heady talks over the atlas. This is the only reasonable explanation of his fondness for making personal visits to the dictator countries; to show himself, the pacific elderly gentleman with the umbrella. You can fake or censor the news; you can shout down the broadcasts from over the frontier; but you cannot hide from your people the gigantic fact that the British Prime Minister has arrived in person to try to patch things up for his people and yours.

There are signs that this trick has not been without success. But there seems to me, who am no military expert, one strong objection to this policy of trying to detach their people from the dictators. It is the existence – the ace of trumps in the dictators' hands – of the bombing plane. If there were no such thing as aerial warfare (which may well prove to be the curse of our age), both Hitler and Mussolini might find it difficult and dangerous to arm all their people and set them going in wearisome campaigns beyond the frontiers; but the air forces, where the young hot-heads are, can be depended upon to strike at the first word of command; and as soon as there are retaliations for their bombing, the angry people are united at once and will believe anything they are told. While the very threat of aerial warfare, as the dictators know only too well, makes war more terrible than ever to contemplate in anticipation, once it actually begins, I believe the very cruelty and horror of it will breed such fierce resentment and hate that wars, instead of being shortened, will be lengthened, fought between fairly equal combatants to a bestial finish, with nothing to show in the end but universal ruin. Thus I never see an airplane now without feeling that humanity, which might by reason of its scientific and mechanical achievements be thought to be approaching a real and enduring civilisation, has also reached an "all-time high" in idiocy.

But if, as we believe, the Nazis and Fascists are inspired by this evil philosophy of dynamic revolution, there are other foolish attitudes toward it besides that of the advocates of 'appeasement,' There is, for example, the policy of isolation that is forever being presented to us by some sections of our press, notably that controlled by Lord Beaverbrook. These isolationists tell us that Britain is not a European power, that we have no concern with the old French-German quarrel or with the fate of all these Central European powers, that we should turn our backs on them and can concentrate upon our Empire, merely taking care to defend ourselves and our dominions and colonial possessions. And it is typical of the muddled minds of these people that when the League of Nations was trying to function as a first attempt at some form of collective security they never lost an opportunity of sneering at it and attacking it, without asking themselves whether, if collective security failed and the world became a dogfight again, we could defend this enormous scattered Empire of ours with its long and dangerous lines of communication.

And the same muddlers of course opposed any understanding with that other immense empire, which, unlike Germany and Italy and Japan, had shown no signs of envy of our possessions – I mean of course the Soviet Union. Again, they smiled upon Mussolini's Ethiopian adventure and were horrified at the suggestion that we should dose the Suez Canal and call his bluff. Again, they were enthusiastic supporters of a policy that enabled Germany and Italy, under cover of aiding Franco, to make at least a show of controlling the whole western end of the Mediterranean and to threaten to cut one of the lifelines of this precious Empire of theirs. And lastly, they talk as if Britain itself, the whole island, could be towed into the middle of the Atlantic, completely ignoring the unpleasant fact that for quick bombing purposes Britain is in Europe. So much for isolation, a donkey's creed.

But this does not mean that all this can be regarded as a purely European affair. This is a mistake still made by some sections of the American public, who persist in referring to these recurring crises in much the same tone that we English used to employ when we talked about 'those perpetual squabbles in the Balkans.' These Europeans, it is suggested, are queer, quarrelsome, murderous folk.

They – or is it we? – may be, but that is not the point. The dictators, with their ally, Japan, are thinking in terms of world domination. And they are not people who will wield power tactfully, graciously. This is especially true of the Nazis. America, I imagine, is beginning to find them almost unendurable now. Let them have more power still, and every continent will shrink from the sound of their iron-heeled boots. During the past twenty years the globe seems to have dwindled, chiefly because of its new lightning communications. It may be a long time before the United States could be in any serious danger from a Nazi Empire, even if there is to be a Nazi Empire; but on the other hand, the United States will find itself on the same dwindling globe as this insolent and unscrupulous power, and probably with the other end of the Axis now moving farther and farther down the Pacific.

The fact is that nobody can afford to be indifferent to the movements of the dictators. The very Eskimos and South Sea Islanders may yet have their lives changed because of some move planned in Berlin or Rome. Nor do I believe that America can afford to be indifferent to the fate of the British Empire, for as things are, if that Empire were smashed, the world would soon look a very different and more hostile place. Not of course because the Empire could not be improved, but because while it exists, it means that thousands of miles are policed and kept tranquil by a power, Britain, with which America is not likely to have any real quarrel. Let those same spaces be suddenly inspired by that 'dynamic revolutionary movement,' and the United States, from New Orleans to Boston, San Diego to Seattle, will find itself facing a new and bristling world.

But we in the Liberal and Labour parties here are more concerned now about Britain itself than about the Empire. It is not only the foreign policy of our present Government that has been at fault. There has been a dreadful inertia, a complete absence of any inspiring creative idea, at home. There is about this Government, as there must be about any Tory Government here, more than a suggestion of the mentality of a tired, rich old man. We see ourselves often in foreign eyes as a tired, rich old man, dozing over his money bags, but occasionally starting up in alarm. This is the England of a privileged governing class, the money lending England of the 'invisible exports', an uncreative and lethargic England. Among some of these people there may be a certain tenderness toward a Fascist order ('Look at the way that chap Mussolini has made the trains run on time – what!'), but what chiefly influences them – and you may see it at work in the Government policy these past few years – is a deep-seated fear of 'the Reds'.

It is as if the last great political event that made any real impression upon them was the Russian Revolution. Not much is said about this fear in public. But it explains many mysteries. Imperial Britain – and all these people are Imperialists – had everything to gain and nothing to lose if the Spanish Government were triumphant and Franco defeated. Nobody suggested that Russia would establish submarine bases and keep bombing squadrons along the Spanish and North African coasts. Moscow was not going to use Spain as a lever in a demand for more territory. Nevertheless, it was better that Franco should win. Why? Because of the terrible 'Reds'.

In the same muddled fashion, Russia as a possible ally was heavily snubbed and then ignored, though it was obvious that the immense Soviet forces, or the mere threat of them, would be of inestimable value. But it seems we would rather perish than accept the hand of the 'Reds', though, oddly enough, some of these very people are always pointing out, when Germany and Italy are mentioned, that it is none of our business how a foreign people should choose to be governed. And there can be no doubt – for I know it from first-hand experience – that many of our Tory strategists based everything on the hope that Hitler would move eastward, become embroiled with Russia, and then dog would eat dog. But we have heard less of this lately, when there have been many anxious glances at news items that suggested a possible German-Russian understanding. As they have been saying across political dinner-tables – 'We can pull through so long as Russia doesn't sign the anti-Comintern pact.'

At the time of writing – and I must emphasise this, because the situation changes so quickly – the position here is as follows: There is a very real and widespread dissatisfaction with the present Government, chiefly on the score of its foreign policy but also with its muddling and inertia at home. I know myself how great this is because not long ago, after writing a series of articles for the News Chronicle, I was snowed under with letters, nearly all in enthusiastic agreement, from every part of the country. We feel that the only chance of changing our government, because of the peculiar electoral conditions already referred to, is to form a Popular Front party, in order that Progressive candidates should not help to defeat one another. This party would range from Liberals to the extreme Left, not excluding the Communists.

The first task of such a party, if it achieved power, would be to try to form a determined democratic bloc, beginning with France and the Soviet Union, but bringing in as many states as possible, to oppose firmly any further threats by the Fascist powers. It is not a question of the Haves banding together to keep down the Have-nots. (As a matter of fact, this Have and Have-not account of the matter simply will not do, for it overlooks the dictators' insistent demand for a high birth-rate and also that 'dynamic, revolutionary movement' already mentioned.) We are ready to have all these questions of colonial possessions and raw materials thrashed out in a world conference.

This means, if it is not to be idle talk, some form of collective security. There will have to be some sovereignty representing civilised world opinion and interests to keep a merely predatory state in check. If civilisation is to endure, then 'dynamic, revolutionary movements', based in public on nonsensical theories of race and in private on mere ambitious brigandage, must be arrested. If this means living in an armed camp for a few years, with money urgently needed for social services being taken for airplanes and deep shelters, then we must put up with it. What cannot be endured any longer is this elaborately exploited, almost universal state of nerves and 'jitters', in which the dictators, who keep it in existence, bluff their way from one dingy triumph to another. Nor is it possible to endure much longer a world in which German and Italian and Japanese airmen swoop down and spray with lead thousands and thousands of women and children with whom they have no real quarrel.

This Popular Front party will have to agree about a home policy as well as a foreign one, and though naturally here there will be grave differences of opinion, there is widespread agreement that the democratic Britain to be defended must be worth defending and must be really democratic. The comfortable old privilege must go. Creative, working Britain must be given the preference over lethargic, dividend- or pension-drawing Britain. We must tackle, as this Government apparently cannot do, our huge unemployed problem, substituting national work (and there will be plenty to do) for the profitless and contemptible dole.

Here I should mention the people, who have been well represented in my correspondence lately, who would be with us in our reforms but not in our defence. I mean the out-and-out pacifists who believe – with Aldous Huxley – that war itself is the greatest of evils, and that even against the dictators in their most menacing moods the resistance should be only passive, in the manner of Gandhi and his followers.

These theorists, however, overlook the fact that the British in India, though neither conspicuously tolerant nor gentle, are but half-hearted conquistadors. The spectacle of moral idealism will not move these advocates of a dynamic, revolutionary technic, as we have already seen.

The British reluctance to re-arm, following a period of a definite reduction of arms, is accepted in Nazi and Fascist circles, as we know, merely as a sign of decadence. If we are all decadent, these black-shirted toughs will argue, then so much the worse for us. While the philosophy of the sword is still taught and learned, then it is still not time to throwaway your shield. When that philosophy is finally abandoned then we can all begin to live like sensible human beings. There were plenty of peace-loving, passive idealists in Germany, just as there are in England and America and elsewhere. But where are they now? Who hears their voices?

Even if all the Progressives were already united, the difficulties would be immense; but actually at present they are far from being united. The trouble is that the official Labour Party – usually called after its headquarters, Transport House – obstinately opposes any alliance with a Popular Front. The official Labour men say: 'We are the party at present in opposition. We have a fine organisation, and a definite program of our own. Anybody is at liberty to join us. But we don't propose to throw away years of hard work by becoming entangled now with Liberals on one side and Communists on the other.' With the result that, at the time of writing, Transport House is still refusing to withdraw its candidates from constituencies in which these candidates have no chance of success but where a United Progressive candidate might take the seat from the Tory. If this deadlock continues, the Tories – for the 'National Government' is a mere facade – will sweep the country again at the next General Election. There are many different objections to delivering the whole Progressive movement to Transport House. My own objection, shared by many, is a mistrust of Trades Unionism as the basis of a national party. There is nothing wrong with Trades Unionism in its own field of industrial relations. But the typical Trades Union mind is an uncreative mind, equally incapable of long views and bold planning. And now, if we are to save ourselves, we need courageous and creative intelligences.

We have a double task. We have not only to defend our democracy from outside aggression but also from internal collapse. For in one very important matter the dictators have an immense advantage over us. This new and horrible game is being played according to their rules, not ours. A condition of military preparedness, a country that is like an armed camp, a people permanently mobilised – all this suits dictatorship, which indeed cannot flourish in any other atmosphere. Not so democracy. It is terribly easy to lose your democracy by agreeing to defend it. In order to remain a free man, you find yourself submitting to conditions that finally take away your freedom. We can counteract this only by heightening the consciousness of democracy in the citizens we ask to defend it.

In short, the Britain we must defend will have to be more democratic, less tolerant of privilege, with a wider vision of its own destiny, than the Britain that has been muddling and messing about for the past few years. But let nobody, least of all any American, imagine that this second Britain, which has received so much attention in your Press, really represents the mass of decent citizens here; for they have as yet shown no signs of hysteria and panic, have not willingly let other democracies go to their doom, and, I believe, are ready now to make a firm stand against the dictators. For they know – as we all must know – that at the heart of the Nazi and Fascist movements there is an evil principle, something that will have to be destroyed before humanity can go forward again into the sunlight.[158]

*Although he had criticised the warmongers in the early 1930s, Priestley recognised the evil of fascism far earlier than most of his contemporaries, and saw that war against Hitler's Germany would be inevitable. By the summer of 1939, even the most die-hard appeasers were coming to share that realisation.*

*His political views were a long way from those of Winston Churchill, but Priestley saw that the qualities that might make Churchill a liability in peacetime, made him invaluable in war, and on 10 July 1939 he published an article, 'We Are Being Held To Ransom', urging Churchill's inclusion in the Cabinet.*

It is time we restated a few facts and had a good look at them. People wonder when war will break out. Strictly speaking, war started at least three years ago. It was started not by the people of Germany, Italy and Japan, but by the crazily ambitious and quite unscrupulous groups that controlled those people. The leaders of this war of Axis aggression are the Nazis.

If any readers are still in doubt as to the real aims of the Nazis, I advise them to examine two books, 'The War Against the West', by Aurel Kolnai, and the more recent 'Germany's Revolution of Destruction,' by Hermann Rauschning. In both these books, please note, the damning evidence has been entirely gathered from Nazi sources. The gang is allowed to condemn itself.

It is about as sensible and safe to imagine that the Nazi leaders are merely patriotic Germans dissatisfied with the Versailles Treaty as it would be to mistake a man-eating tiger for a rather large pussycat. These men, and their Axis allies, are engaged in a gigantic campaign of filibustering. Brigandage is now their national industry. It is useless asking them to settle down and become nice peaceful neighbours. They couldn't do even it if they wanted to. You might as well have asked Al Capone to have settled down as the proprietor of a soda-fountain. Nazi Germany must go on expanding, not because it needs lebensraum (that is just Goebbels' nonsense), but because it is now organised for conquest and absorption and for nothing else.

What do they want? The answer is: anything they can get. But reliable evidence (see the two works already mentioned) suggests that the Axis now sees as its finest and fattest ultimate prey the British Empire, which it believes must disintegrate very soon. Many of the moves in this undeclared war of the last three years have been directed against the British Empire. I do not think they would have succeeded if these Axis strategists had not had the assistance of our own Imperialists, who are anxious, for reasons best known to themselves, to commit suicide.

When Japan spread itself over the Far East, when Mussolini spread himself in Africa and the Eastern Mediterranean, when Hitler began swallowing Central Europe, when Hitler and Mussolini together turned Spain into an Axis base of future operations, there were cries of 'Bravo!' from the City, the Carlton Club and Mayfair. And if the Axis powers could have continued at the same rate of progress, within five years some of these same people would have been saying, 'I think your Gestapo are wonderful', and half the staff of this newspaper would have been on the run.

Since our end of the Munich appeasement policy was found to bear some likeness to the reception of a well-directed kick in the pants, our intensely patriotic National Government has decided to resist further aggression. But even now the strange suicidal impulse seems to be still there. The charming Von Ribbentrop still has his friendly correspondents in London, who tell him not to mind us. There are discreet little conferences in the City. And nearly every day in The Times there are persuasive letters, from good addresses, telling us it is all a slight misunderstanding and that if we knew the Gestapo better (as we may do soon) we should discover that they are fine, stout fellows.

We are, of course, spending fabulous sums on armaments. But your High Tory, with his big business connections, has always believed in doing this. After all, for every penny he pays out on arms he may possibly have sixpence returned. And to show there is no ill-feeling, we do not mind supplying Japan with the munitions of war, or even of doing a deal or two with the Germans in material that may easily be turned against us. There can, it seems, be no treason in big business. It is its own justification.

The Nazi method, imitated by its allies, is not to risk everything on a huge naked conflict, a war like the last, but to continue, with ever-increasing pressure, the present campaign. The trick is to keep the whole nation on almost a war basis, to run the propaganda machine for all it is worth, to promise anything to the idiots who will believe you, to create disorder in the countries to be attacked, to corrode and disintegrate, and then by a sudden move and the threat of overwhelming force to take what you want. We should all recognise the method by this time. It has nothing to do with the old-fashioned relations between States. It belongs to a different world, and in this world we are now living. Any member of any government who does not openly acknowledge these facts proclaims himself either a fool or a knave, a downright traitor to his country.

The only way to live like men is openly to acknowledge these facts and to behave accordingly. We must state quite clearly that we are ready to treat with the German people, to settle such real grievances as they may have, when they cease to be herded and marched by this gang of liars, cheats and bullies, and not before. We must treat with contempt the screaming propaganda machine. We must regard all men who do not publicly disown the Nazi Party as dangers to our commonwealth.

There are other and better tests of the sincerity of our Government's protestations than huge armaments, National Service, a form of conscription, for the Tories have always wanted these things. They are only too glad of an excuse to rush them through. But are they ready to set their boasted patriotism – to argue the matter on their own lines – above their party and personal prejudices? If they are, then why is the definite public demand for the inclusion of Mr. Winston Churchill in the Cabinet being so obstinately resisted?

There are three good reasons why he should be included. First, he is a man of outstanding ability and experience, and nobody except the leaders of our present Cabinet believe it to be rich in those qualities. Secondly, the people want him there. Thirdly, his presence will at least do something to show the world, which has no confidence whatever in our statesmen, that we are in earnest.

The same arguments, with a few differences, apply to the return to office of Mr. Eden. Bluntly stated, he was dropped simply to please Mussolini, as part of a miserable policy that made us the laughing-stock of the world. The policy failed, as it deserved to do, so now let us forget it. Let us have Mr. Eden back, and suggest, for a change, that Mussolini throws overboard his mischievous Ciano (who will undoubtedly ruin him) and Hitler his Ribbentrop.

Nobody can say whether there will be a real world war or not, because in these unhappy times our fate depends not on the judgement of respectable statesmen but on the whims and moods of megalomaniacs and hysterical gangsters. But what we can be certain of is that wobbling and double-faced antics, talking one way in public and another way in the City, the Carlton Club and big country houses, can bring nothing but disaster. It has lost us every move in the game so far, flung away strategical advantages, ruined our prestige, and we cannot afford now to drop another point. The score is advantage to server, and it is not we who are serving.[159]

*On the eve of the war Priestley had a dream, recorded in* Rain Upon Godshill, *which was perhaps, a premonition of the ruin and destruction that was about to be unleashed, but which ended on a note of great optimism.*

I dreamt I was standing at the top of a very high tower, alone, looking down upon myriads of birds all flying in one direction; every kind of bird was there, all the birds in the world. It was a noble sight, this vast aerial river of birds. But now in some mysterious fashion the gear was changed, and time speeded up, so that I saw generations of birds, watched them break their shells, flutter into life, mate, weaken, falter, and die. Wings grew only to crumble; bodies were sleek and then, in a flash, bled and shrivelled; and death struck everywhere at every second. What was the use of all this blind struggle towards life, this eager trying of wings, this hurried mating, this flight and surge, all this gigantic meaningless biological effort?

As I stared down, seeming to see every creature's ignoble little history almost at a glance, I felt sick at heart. It would be better if not one of them, if not one of us all, had been born, if the struggle ceased for ever. I stood on my tower, still alone, desperately unhappy. But now the gear was changed again, and time went faster still, and it was rushing by at such a rate, that the birds could not show any movement, but were like an enormous plain sown with feathers.

But along this plain, flickering through the bodies themselves, there now passed a sort of white flame, trembling, dancing, then hurrying on; and as soon as I saw it I knew that this white flame was life itself, the very quintessence of being; and then it came to me, in a rocket-burst of ecstasy, that nothing mattered, nothing could ever matter, because nothing else was real, but this quivering and hurrying lambency of being.

Birds, men or creatures not yet shaped and coloured, all were of no account except so far as this flame of life travelled through them. It left nothing to mourn over behind it; what I had thought was tragedy was mere emptiness or a shadow show; for now all real feeling was caught and purified and danced on ecstatically with the white flame of life. I had never before felt such deep happiness as I knew at the end of my dream of the tower and the birds, and if I have not kept that happiness with me, as an inner atmosphere and a sanctuary for the heart, that is it because I am a weak and foolish man who allows the mad world to come trampling in, destroying every green shoot of wisdom. Nevertheless, I have not been quite the same man since.[160]

# PART III
# The Second World War

# Chapter 7
# Let the people sing

*On the evening of the day that war was declared, 3 September 1939,*
*Priestley was due to broadcast the first episode of his novel,* Let the People
Sing, *written specially for the BBC. 'I groped my way to Broadcasting*
*House through an appalling blackness, my very first taste of it, and almost*
*felt I was back in the First War when in Broadcasting House, I found*
*myself among sandbags, bayonets, nurses in uniform.'* [161] Let the People
Sing *is an upbeat novel that avoids mention of the looming war, but it is*
*impossible to miss the martial echoes in some sections, and the hope for a*
*better world emerging from the conflict.*

And now they swung into it, and the tune came alive, and people of all
colours and customs seemed to come out of their dungeons and mud
huts and slums and ghettos and stifling workshops and dark factories
and wharfs and fields and mines, and they marched out of cities and
across deserts and mountains, singing in a triumph that was the only
real triumph the world had yet seen, for it was not the victory of some
cunning megalomaniac over tyrants less cunning, it did not celebrate
the ascendance of one state above its neighbours, but it was a triumph
of Man himself, who had found at last a way to live and now came into
his inheritance of the fruitful globe.

The little hall shook with soaring and thundering sound. Men left
the billiard tables and dartboards in the club next door, and came in to
listen and stare and finally to sing. In the mean street outside men and
women stopped to listen and to hum the tune while the children, like
tiny conquerors, strutted and swaggered up and down to its lilt. Here
at least something was happening in Dunbury. Perhaps a bit of
magic....

To be an artist is to be more alive than ordinary men but to feel
more incomplete than they do, so that the artist feels that he is
nothing, or worse than nothing, a kind of criminal, unless he is
practising – and successfully practising his particular art. It is a mistake

to suppose – as we Europeans so often do – that the English are rarely artists. The official tradition in England is hostile to art, and so I think is the social tradition based on the prejudices of a ruling landed class, the feudal England. But a great many of the English, because they are dominated by what lies in the unconscious, are genuine if only half-developed artists. In this they are the opposite of the French, who are controlled by their conscious minds, and appear to be more deeply artistic than they really are. If England were to be conquered, were suddenly to lose nearly all its wealth and power, I think the English would soon be famous throughout the world as a race of poets, painters and actors, and life on this strange misty island, which is essentially romantic in its atmosphere, would seem to the Americans, Russians, Chinese, who by that time would do the world's manufacturing, to be a fairy tale of art and dreams.

*In the following months, Priestley's letters to Teddy Davison set out to correct the misapprehensions that many Americans then had about the war and Britain's part in it.*

11 October 1939

Although I have little sympathy with the common American point of view that suggests this is all a sensational entertainment devised for the American public, I agree with you that we have handled our stuff very badly. Actually it has been even worse done at home. Two reasons for this: the Ministry of Information was extremely badly organised, and contained far too many civil servants and not enough journalists (there are no authors employed at the Ministry at all); secondly, it was not given the power to decide when the public should be given news, the older ministries still exercising their right of censorship. The truth is that the people in power have not yet fully understood that this war depends more on public opinion and morale than on anything else. Deep down they have the mandarin's contempt for the general public. Thus, in any other country but this, a man of my experience and knowledge* of the English public mind would at least have been consulted at some time or other, but neither I nor any other author has been asked for even the shortest report on the psychological aspect of things. They turn these matters over to lawyers, Treasury officials, and the like. (* this sounds pompous and conceited, but I don't mean it that way. Took myself as nearest example) ...

It is wrong to suppose, as some people do, that there is a kind of Munich flavour about our end of this war. You have probably heard this, so let me give you a fairly well informed opinion from the other angle. Poland collapsed for a variety of reasons – the obstinacy of her military people, who wouldn't be told anything; the flying start of the Germans (which enabled them to cripple the Polish Air Force); and, I understand, tremendous espionage inside Poland. Even if France had battered at the West at once, it would not have saved Poland.

Now for ourselves: the Navy had to combat the U boats, which were already lying in wait when war started, and this is being done very successfully, and the blockade is undoubtedly successful. The Army had to transport the most highly mechanised force in the world, for so we're supposed to be, across the Channel, a hell of a job, quite different from anything in the last war. The Air Force might have done much more, apart from the very valuable leaflet raids, but probably it would not have been possible to bomb the back areas of the Siegfried Line without killing civilians, and we did not wish to be the first to start that.

Moreover, time is on our side, for two reasons: first, of course, the blockade; secondly, Germany has already reached her maximum production whereas we, as I know from my own direct observation, are producing more and more every week. And all the military experts agree in believing that with equally well-armed forces, the advantage now is overwhelmingly with the defence. A huge frontal attack in the West would convert it into a gigantic slaughter-house.

This country entered the war more united than she had ever been in any major war for two centuries. There was not one political group of any importance that was against it. And people submitted very patiently to all the various tiresome restrictions. Since then, the Russian business has made a lot of extreme Left Wingers declare that they are now against the war, and to hear some of them talk, you would think Chamberlain and Daladier (no favourites of mine, as you know) were much more dangerous figures than Hitler. Again the German trick (very clever) of almost leaving us alone has made some idiots forget that these are the Hitler and Goering who were screaming threats at us when we showed no signs of fighting. (The great Nazi trick, so far successful, is 'not to play' with the rest of the world.)

When the democracies were obviously ready to sacrifice almost anything for peace, the Nazis pointed to their bombers and bayonets and shouted blue murder. Now our monkey's up, they ask why we want to plunge Europe into war, etc. If we demobilised, in six months they'd begin all over again.) But having been left alone, naturally the people here feel a bit let down with all these precautions about, and they begin to trot their grumbles about this, that and the other. Fifty bombs would clear all those grumbles away, but I doubt if Hitler is clever enough to realise that and to stay his hand.

As you will have gathered, the whole atmosphere is quite different from 1914 - no jingoism, no flag-waving, no bands, none of that hysterical Bank Holiday feeling, no romantic exaltation. This is a complete refutation of the charge that human nature doesn't change, for I never saw such a change. Apart from some young Nazis, if they haven't already learnt better, nobody even pretends to like war. It's just a damned nuisance, like having to tackle a huge raving drunk who threatens to set the house on fire. About as romantic as that. On the other hand, the few American papers I've seen – a copy of two of 'Life', for example – do tend to overemphasise the more hellish aspects. There's a sort of hysteria in much American journalism that tends to falsify the atmosphere of everything it deals with. I have always felt more worried about European affairs in America than I have here. So much of the normality is left out. Too many hellish high spots. Just as newsreels seem to exaggerate the noise of everything...

I can't give you news of friends because I hardly seem to see any. This war puts us all on desert islands, upon which, at six thirty, total darkness descends. But a bit of darkness won't do us any harm. Perhaps we can find ourselves in it.[162]

27 January 1940

I do hope you jump on the notion, very common in neutral countries, that the war is just another quarrel between Germany and the allied powers. Here, I can assure you, most people feel that it is a fight, possibly to the death, between two ways of living – one that has, with all its faults, some connection with Christian civilisation, and the other a hellish, soul-destroying tyranny. It simply isn't possible to live in the world with anything so horrible as Nazism. The people who advocate a patched up peace forget that life in that peace, with Hitler and Co ready to pounce at any moment, would not be worth living. Better to be fighting and to know where you are.

Many of us feel here that the testing time will come just after the war and it is for this reason that I am glad I am not in uniform again, for whatever small influence I have with people here is going to be badly needed then. I anticipate great social changes here, much greater than after the last war, owing to the long-continued and now murderously high taxation and the very real attempt to prevent big war profits. The professional and technical classes should have a great chance to assert themselves, and under modem conditions it is more and more they who run a highly organised country. I foresee an opportunity for a liberal socialism, of the type towards which the Scandinavian countries have been moving. It has a very different impulse behind it from that of communism. The chapter in Rain Upon Godshill on England will show you how my mind is working these years.

Although, as you know, I have a real affection for the American scene, I feel in myself no desire to join the émigrés of the last year who have given up Europe as a bad job. Europe is a bad job, yet I feel that if Western Europe could steer itself somehow out of this whirlpool it might rise to something not merely as good as but really better than America, and all the better perhaps for its terrible heartbreaks and awful disasters. I read more hysterical nonsense about air raids in 'Life' and 'Harpers' than I have read, heard or seen here for the last six months. And I still believe that the decency and steadiness of unintimidated citizens, which is what you get in Britain and France, can beat the Gestapo and the reign of terror. But if they can't, if the drilled robots and their secret police can beat the comparatively free citizens, then not only is Europe finished, but so is America, so is the world.[163]

*Priestley always berated the use of false propaganda on the domestic front, urging government to be more open and honest with the people, but he also warned of the dangers in allowing Nazi propaganda abroad to go unanswered. In the first weeks of the 'Phoney War' that followed the formal declaration of war with Germany, Priestley made a journey in which he discovered the views of ordinary people in different parts of the country. What he discovered caused him alarm, not only about the extent to which German propaganda had proved effective even in Britain, but also the failure of the British government to involve the people in what was already being termed 'a people's war'.*

I have just set out again after snatching two or three days at home, during which I had to grapple with the accumulated mail of the last three weeks. Many of the letters referred to these articles, and some of them abused me heartily. With one section I was unpopular merely because I put into print, as honestly as I could, what had been said to me about various topical problems. The rest grumbled about this and that.

Then, in addition, there were letters from friends overseas, who told me how things looked from their angle. Many of these letters – and especially those from friends outside this country – only confirmed certain suspicions that have been worrying me for the last two weeks. We have a magnificent case, but we are handling it very badly. Our presentation of it is – or has been so far – equally unfortunate at home and abroad.

But first, a word about Nazi propaganda. In my opinion its power is underestimated. Because it is so often widely untruthful, downright stupid, horribly overdone, we begin to have a contempt for the whole vast machine. This is a mistake. At least three persons out of four I have spoken to during these last few weeks have been influenced by Nazi propaganda. If this seems an extraordinary statement, please notice how many of your friends and neighbours agree, without any further thought, on the subject, that the Versailles treaty is the villain of the 1919-1939 piece, that the German Army in 1918 was finally let down by the civil population, that Hitler has done a great deal for the German people.

The general unqualified assent to these propositions is a tribute to the power of Nazi propaganda, which set out, several years ago, to make the world accept these dangerous half- and quarter-truths as whole truths. I say then that we are foolish to have a contempt for Nazi propaganda when we may observe some of its successful results all round us. It is, no doubt, a machine so enormous and clumsy that it often seems comic – a kind of Heath Robinson lie-scatterer. Nevertheless, it has been functioning day and night for years. And for one scrap of news, one photograph, that we have sent to any neutral country, the Nazis have sent hundreds. To imagine this does not matter is the height of stupidity.

Why has our own work in this field been so poor? To say that new and hitherto untried organisations have partly failed is not good enough. We must look further than that. It is my belief that the root reason is that our persons in authority may assent to the statement that this is a war in. which public morale is all important, may readily agree that our own people must be heartened and neutrals kept well-informed and friendly, but that in their heart of hearts they do not believe these things. They may think they care, but actually they do not care very much. Deep down they are wondering whether it is not all a lot of fuss about nothing. You cannot change the fundamental opinion of official persons overnight.

During this journey it has been necessary for me to make many applications to see and describe things not shown to the general public. I have no complaint to make. I have always been treated courteously and often with real friendliness. Some of the things I have wanted to describe have been denied me: not so much because there was any definite refusal but because I simply had not time to hang about until the bureaucratic machine delivered its permit. I have had less trouble on the whole than I anticipated.

Yet I have rarely escaped the feeling that my readers and I have been condescended to and humoured. What I was up to was not serious, just as books and plays are not serious. There are some men who always refer to women as 'the ladies' and imply that at the best they are only charming nitwits. Something of the same playful condescension has crept into the rather brief remarks addressed to me by officers of the higher ranks, senior civil servants, and the like.

Now this would not matter at all it it did not suggest that these important personages which decide our policy and are not given to welcoming outside assistance, only pay lip service to this new notion of a people's war and are not really converted to it. And this, more than the failure of new organisations, accounts for the over-stubborn censorships, the stiffness and creakiness of the machinery of information and propaganda, the half-heartedness of it all. The public cannot help feeling that the mandarins do not want to play.

Not that the Press has been perfect, although I think that as a whole it worked hard to counterbalance the official attitude during the first weeks. The greatest mistake of the Press so far has been its desperate and quite unnecessary attempt to humanise these first weeks of war by giving this war a false 1914 flavour. It might be called the Tipperary touch. And it is not wanted. It does not belong. It is 25 years out of date.

This war has its own atmosphere, and no matter how that atmosphere thickens and curdles, what it will never be is the hysterical Bank Holiday atmosphere of 1914. The whole set-up is different. Not only has the whole scene changed, but people themselves are different. They are far, far more serious now. I do not mean that they do not want a joke or a song, but I am certain that they want their own kind of joke and song. And what they want still more is to get on with the ghastly job, to stand their corner whatever that corner may be, but to do it in the hope of catching a glimpse of a saner and nobler world. And when people are in this mood, it is the terrible height of folly not to trust them. And if it came to a choice between giving the enemy a bit of information and keeping the whole public wondering and uneasy, for my part I would not hesitate long.

A final word about the Ministry of Information. It is not, as some people seem to imagine, staffed by authors. There is not a single author on its staff, I believe. (There are men who have written books, of course, but they are not authors first). Some of its appointments... seem to me quite good. There are other appointments that could only have been made because the officials concerned were on the public payroll and so work had to be found for them.

Its chief fault, I think, is that most of the people at the top are organisers, who know how to run a department but do not know much about the public mind, whereas the men in control ought to have been persons who understood what they were trying to serve. What is wanted in that Ministry is a little less Lincoln's Inn Fields and a bit more Gracie Fields.[164]

*Priestley had taken up arms to do his duty in the First World War; in the Second, he put the power of his mind – and his voice – at the service of the state, most notably in a series of broadcasts that boosted the morale of Britons but also advanced Priestley's own social agenda for the country.[165] He gave an early hint of this in a final letter to Teddy Davison, before the demands of wartime curtailed the correspondence.*

9 April 1940

One of the difficulties of the modern world is this: you cannot do anything now without a big rich organisation, but all the big rich organisations prefer to debase public taste instead of improving it. There's little doubt that the Beaverbrook-Rothermere press here, like your Hearst press, deliberately tries to keep its public half-witted and fixes their attention on rubbishy stuff – silly films, 'glamour girls' etc. I feel more and more that what is needed is a drive along all fronts together, not only political and economic but cultural. The general quality of life must be raised. It is, to my mind, one of the great weaknesses of our present Labour Party that it does not see this, has not kept before it a steady vision of a new urban civilisation. The Tories have their kind of life – with its country houses, etc., – but not the

Labour folk. I propose to write something about this soon. I think it's our particular job – I mean, yours and mine – to see that people don't become robots and spiritually dead, while our more methodical friends work out schemes of production and distribution of goods and services.[166]

*Priestley was already a famous and celebrated writer, but his 'Postscripts', broadcast on Sunday nights immediately after the nine o'clock news made him a household name throughout Britain. He also recorded a stream of other talks that were heard around the world.*

*Priestley was not the only 'Postscripter' – half a dozen other people broadcast in the same slot, but none had anywhere near the immediate nor the lasting impact. Although the BBC normally maintained a clear division between 'News' and 'Talks', the corporation took the unprecedented decision to schedule the Postscripts as part of the nine o'clock news, to ensure the largest possible audience. The broadcasts 'in which well-known speakers were to explain events in a reasonable way, admitting British shortcomings and avoiding "exaggerated propaganda",' [167] were nonetheless seen as having high propaganda value as a deliberate counter to the naturalised German William Joyce – 'Lord Haw-Haw' – who also broadcast on Sunday nights, and had secured a large British audience in the early stages of the war.* The Times *even published the wavelengths on which he could be heard, and when a BBC mandarin, Patrick Ryan, visited France in January 1940 he complained that 'Lord Haw-Haw is as popular with the British troops as with people at home.' [168]*

*The BBC had first tried scheduling its more popular light entertainment programmes against Lord Haw-Haw, but it was felt that something more was needed and Priestley 'one ordinary Englishman talking to other ordinary Englishmen' [169] was introduced in the belief that 'a contrast in voice, upbringing and outlook' to the normal BBC voices with their cut-glass 'Received Pronunciation', might ease worries about 'lower class morale' [170] – by implication the BBC clearly felt that the 'lower classes' would be the most susceptible to Haw-Haw's propaganda.*

*However, Priestley's first wartime broadcast was not a Sunday night Postscript but 'a kind of testing sample. I'd gone to the BBC and said I'd like to do some broadcasting, I'd often done broadcasting way back to Savoy Hill days... It was just after Dunkirk so I took the theme of Dunkirk and the idea of victory coming from defeat, which is a very English thing I think... and I always remember because one very prominent broadcaster, I met him in the corridor afterwards, and he was weeping.'* [171]

It was broadcast the day after Churchill's famous 'We shall fight on the beaches, we shall fight on the landing grounds, we shall fight in the fields and in the streets, we shall fight in the hills, we shall never surrender...' speech to Parliament, and though adopting a far more domestic and intimate tone than Churchill's oratory, it proved almost as effective in transforming public perceptions of Dunkirk from an unmitigated disaster to an epic, heroic turning-point.

Wednesday 5 June 1940

I wonder how many of you feel as I do about this great Battle and evacuation of Dunkirk. The news of it came as a series of surprises and shocks, followed by equally astonishing new waves of hope. It was all, from beginning to end, unexpected. And yet now that it's over, and we can look back on it, doesn't it seem to you to have an inevitable air about it – as if we had turned a page in the history of Britain and seen a chapter headed 'Dunkirk' – and perhaps seen too a picture of the troops on the beach waiting to embark?

And now that this whole action is completed, we notice that it has a definite shape, and a certain definite character. What strikes me about it is how typically English it is. Nothing, I feel, could be more English than this Battle of Dunkirk, both in its beginning and its end, its folly and its grandeur. It was very English in what was sadly wrong with it; this much has been freely admitted, and we are assured will be freely discussed when the proper moment arrives. We have gone sadly wrong like this before; and here and now we must resolve never, never to do it again. Another such blunder may not be forgiven us.

But having admitted this much, let's do ourselves the justice of admitting too that this Dunkirk affair was also very English (and when I say 'English' I really mean British) in the way in which, when apparently all was lost, so much was gloriously retrieved. Bright honour was almost 'plucked from the moon'. What began as a miserable blunder, a catalogue of misfortunes and miscalculations, ended as an epic of gallantry. We have a queer habit – and you can see it running through our history – of conjuring up such transformations. Out of a black gulf of humiliation and despair, rises a sun of blazing glory.

This is not the German way. They don't make such mistakes (a grim fact that we should bear in mind) but also they don't achieve such epics. There is never anything to inspire a man either in their victories or their defeats; boastful when they're winning, quick to whine when threatened with defeat – there is nothing about them that ever catches the world's imagination. That vast machine of theirs can't create a glimmer of that poetry of action which distinguishes war from mass murder. It's a machine – and therefore has no soul.

But here at Dunkirk is another English epic. And to my mind what was most characteristically English about it – so typical of us, so absurd and yet so grand and gallant that you hardly know whether to laugh or to cry when you read about them – was the part played in the difficult and dangerous embarkation – not by the warships, magnificent though they were-but by the little pleasure-steamers. We've known them and laughed at them, these fussy little steamers, all our lives. We have called them 'the shilling sicks.' We have watched them load and unload their crowds of holiday passengers – the gents full of high spirits and bottled beer, the ladies eating pork pies, the children sticky with peppermint rock.

Sometimes they only went as far as the next seaside resort. But the boldest of them might manage a Channel crossing, to let everybody have a glimpse of Boulogne. They were usually paddle steamers, making a great deal more fuss with all their churning than they made speed; and they weren't proud, for they let you see their works going round. They liked to call themselves 'Queens' and 'Belles'; and even if they were new, there was always something old-fashioned, a Dickens touch, a mid-Victorian air, about them. They seemed to belong to the same ridiculous holiday world as pierrots and piers, sand castles, ham-

and-egg teas; palmists, automatic machines, and crowded sweating promenades. But they were called out of that world – and, let it be noted – they were called out in good time and good order.

Yes, these 'Brighton Belles' and 'Brighton Queens' left that innocent foolish world of theirs – to sail into the inferno, to defy bombs, shells, magnetic mines, torpedoes, machine-gun fire – to rescue our soldiers. Some of them – alas – will never return. Among those paddle steamers that will never return was one that I knew well, (or it was the pride of our ferry service to the Isle of Wight - none other than the good ship 'Gracie Fields'. I tell you, we were proud of the 'Gracie Fields', for she was the glittering queen of our local line, and instead of taking an hour over her voyage, used to do it, churning like mad, in forty-five minutes. And now never again will we board her at Cowes and go down into her dining saloon for a fine breakfast of bacon and eggs. She has paddled and churned away – for ever. But now – look – this little steamer, like all her brave and battered sisters, is immortal. She'll go sailing down the years in the epic of Dunkirk. And our great grandchildren, when they learn how we began this War by snatching glory out of defeat, and then swept on to victory, may also learn how the little holiday steamers made an excursion to hell and came back glorious.[172]

*The broadcast was a tremendous success and the following Sunday, Priestley began a series of regular weekly talks after the news.*

Every Sunday found us heading for one of the small News Talk studios in a Broadcasting House that had changed incredibly from its pre-war charming foolishness of lush flower arrangements in the reception hall, a receptionist in a long evening dress and announcers in dinner jackets. Already the corridors were dim with too much use, the Concert Hall had been turned into a vast dormitory, and even many of the small studios had extra beds in them.[173]

A visitor to the BBC is apt to find himself edging his way into a wire cage past the bayonets of sentries. His pass is carefully inspected, steel doors are undone and he steps through a narrow aperture into the operational department of broadcasting. The general impression is of a mixture between a cinema studio and a bargain basement at sales time. Everyone is hurried, looking a little worried; doors open and shut as in a French farce; there is an ever-present aroma of fried fish and chips from the canteen which operates twenty-four hours a day. Beds and rolls of bedclothes, hair brushes and wooden crates litter the ship-like passages and the cell-like rooms; and the microphones look like nothing but microphones. Such is the background, unseen by the public, against which the Postscripts are delivered.'[174]

*While Churchill's broadcasts centred on great events on the world stage and the need for Britons to strain every sinew in the war effort, Priestley's talks focussed on simple, domestic themes – a celebration of Britishness and the British way of life, that was equally potent in reminding Britons why they were fighting and what they were fighting for.*

Radio became increasingly important. It was not simply that people turned to it for war news. Communications and travel became more difficult; newspapers were smaller and could not always be delivered; books soon ran out of print because of the paper shortage; and many people, after working long hours and then crawling home through the black-out, only wanted to stay in and switch on their loudspeakers. Radio at last had come into its own.[175]

*Priestley came from a middle-class background and was a Cambridge graduate, but he had never lost his Yorkshire accent and in an era of 'received pronunciation' and broadcasting of such formality that announcers wore dinner jackets, Priestley's unpretentious manner and warm North Country vowels were a breath of fresh air. His own military service in the Great War, his status as an 'outsider' – not one of the Establishment or a BBC apparatchik – his natural empathy with the concerns of ordinary Britons, male and female, and ability to give voice to them in vivid images and memorable prose, gave him an authority that few others could equal and he became a hugely popular broadcaster, a reassuring and familiar voice, and one of optimism, articulating the feelings of millions of Britons in dark and troubled times. 'By some law of survival, the voices are there, as the great fighting men are there, when the need is critical.'* [176]

Priestley's *blend of a feel for Britain's landscape and traditions, with an innate and optimistic belief in the basic goodness and decency of ordinary British people, and the destiny they shared, might have struck many as romantic, almost naive, but it resonated powerfully with his audience.*

Sunday 9 June 1940

I don't think there has ever been a lovelier English spring than this last one, now melting into full summer. Sometimes, in between listening to the latest news of battle and destruction, or trying to write about them myself, I've gone out and stared at the red japonica or the cherry and almond blossom, so clear and exquisite against the moss-stained old wall–and have hardly been able to believe my eyes; I've just gaped and gaped like a bumpkin at a fair through all these weeks of spring. Never have I seen (at least, not since I grew up) such a golden white of buttercups and daisies in the meadows. I'll swear the very birds have sung this year as they never did before. Just outside my study, there are a couple of blackbirds who think they're still in the Garden of Eden. There's almost a kind of mockery in their fluting.

I think most of us have often felt we simply couldn't believe our eyes and ears: either the War wasn't real, or this spring wasn't real. One of them must be a dream. I've looked out of my house in the country on these marvellous days of sun and blue air, and I could see the blaze and bloom of the Californian poppies and the roses in the garden; then the twinkling beaches and the stately nodding elms, and then, beyond, the lush fields and the round green hills dissolving into the hazy blue of the sky. And I've stared at all this – and I've remembered the terrible news of battle and destruction I'd just heard or read – and I've felt that one or the other couldn't be true.

Sometimes I've felt that I was really staring at a beautifully painted silk curtain; and that at any moment it might be torn apart – its flowers, trees and green hills vanishing like smoke, to reveal the old Flanders Front, trenches and bomb craters, ruined towns, a scarred countryside, a sky belching death, and the faces of murdered children. I had to remind myself that the peaceful and lovely scene before me was the real truth; that it was there long before the Germans went mad, and will be there when that madness is only remembered as an old nightmare.

Tennyson might have been prophesying this German madness in the spring when he wrote:

> The fields are fair beside them,
> The chestnut towers in his bloom;
> But they – they feel the desire of the deep
> Fallen, follow their doom.

But sometimes, too, I've felt that the unusual loveliness of our gardens and meadows and hills has come home to us because these things are, so to speak, staring at us – as you see so many women now staring at their soldier husbands, sweethearts, sons, just before the trains take them away. It's as if this English landscape said: 'Look at me, as I am now in my beauty and fullness of joy, and do not forget.' And when I feel this, I feel too a sudden and very sharp anger; for I remember then how this island is threatened and menaced; how perhaps at this very moment, thin-lipped and cold-eyed Nazi staff officers are planning, with that mixture of method and lunacy which is all their own, how to project on to this countryside of ours those half-doped crazy lads they call parachute troops.

This land that is ours, that appeals to us now in all its beauty, is at this moment only just outside the reach of these self-tormenting schemers and their millions who are used as if they were not human beings but automata, robots, mere 'things'. They drop them from planes as if they were merely bombs with arms and legs. They send them swarming forward in battle as if they were not fellow-men but death-dealing dolls, manufactured in Goering's factories...

The Nazis understand – and it is their great secret – all the contemptible qualities of men. They have a lightning eye for an opponent's weakness. But what they don't understand, because there's nothing in their nature or experience to tell them, is that men also have their hour of greatness, when weakness suddenly towers into strength; when ordinary easy-going tolerant men rise in their anger and strike down evil like the angels of the wrath of God.[177]

Sunday 16 June 1940

A night or two ago, I had my first spell with our Local Defence Volunteers or 'Parashots'. I'd been on the muster for the previous fortnight – but I'd been away, busy with other work, so I hadn't been able to see how our village was keeping watch and ward. Ours is a small and scattered village, but we'd had a fine response to the call for volunteers; practically every able-bodied man in the place takes his turn. The post is on top of a high down, with a fine view over a dozen wide parishes.

The men I met up there the other night represented a good cross-section of English rural life; we had a parson, a bailiff, a builder, farmers and farm labourers. Even the rarer and fast disappearing rural trades were represented – for we had a hurdle-maker there; and his presence, together with that of a woodman and a shepherd, made me feel sometimes that I'd wandered into one of those rich chapters of Thomas Hardy's fiction in which his rustics meet in the gathering darkness on some Wessex hillside. And indeed there was something in the preliminary talk, before the sentries were posted for the night, that gave this whole horrible business of air raids and threatened invasion a rustic, homely, almost comfortable atmosphere, and really made a man feel more cheerful about it...

The intellectual is apt to see these things as the lunatic end of everything, as part of a crazy Doomsday Eve, and so he goes about moaning, or runs away to America. But the simple and saner countryman sees this raiding and invading as the latest manifestation of that everlasting menace which he always has to fight: sudden blizzards at lambing time, or floods just before the harvest.

I think the countryman knows, without being told, that we hold our lives here, as we hold our farms, upon certain terms. One of those terms is that while wars still continue, while one nation is ready to hurl its armed men at another, you must if necessary stand up and fight for your own. And this decision comes from the natural piety of simple but sane men. Such men, you will notice, are happier now than the men who have lost that natural piety.

Well, as we talked on our post on the hilltop, we watched the dusk deepen in the valleys below, where our womenfolk listened to the news as they knitted by the hearth, and we remembered that these were our homes and that now at any time they might be blazing ruins, and that half-crazy German youths, in whose empty eyes the idea of honour and glory seems to include every form of beastliness, might soon be let loose down there. The sentries took their posts. There was a mist coming over the down. Nothing much happened for a time. A green light that seemed to defy all black-out regulations turned out to be merely an extra large and luminous glow-worm; the glow-worms, poor ignorant little creatures, don't know there's a war on and so continue lighting themselves up. A few searchlights went stabbing through the dusk and then faded. The mist thickened, and below in all the valleys, there wasn't the faintest glimmer of light. You heard the ceaseless high melancholy singing of the telegraph wires in the wind.

So we talked about what happened to us in the last war, and about the hay and the barley, about beef and milk and cheese and tobacco. Then a belt of fog over to the left became almost silvery, because somewhere along there all the searchlights were sweeping the sky. Then somewhere behind that vague silveriness, there was a sound as if gigantic doors were being slammed to. There was the rapid stabbing noise of anti-aircraft batteries, and far away some rapping of machine-guns. Then the sirens went, in our two nearest towns, as if all that part of the darkened countryside, like a vast trapped animal, were screaming at us.

But then the sounds of bombs and gunfire and planes all died away. The 'All Clear' went, and then there was nothing but the misty cool night, drowned in silence, and this handful of us on the hilltop. I remember wishing then that we could send all our children out of this island, every boy and girl of them across the sea to the wide

Dominions, and turn Britain into the greatest fortress the world has known; so that then, with an easy mind, we could fight and fight these Nazis until we broke their black hearts.

I felt too up there a powerful and rewarding sense of community; and with it too a feeling of deep continuity. There we were, ploughman and parson, shepherd and clerk, turning out at night, as our forefathers had often done before us, to keep watch and ward over the sleeping English hills and fields and homesteads. I've mentioned Thomas Hardy, whose centenary has just been celebrated. Don't you find in his tales and poems, often derived from the talk he listened to as a boy, a sense that Napoleon, with his threatened invasion by the Grand Army at Boulogne, was only just round the corner?

And I felt, out in the night on the hilltop, that the watch they kept then was only yesterday; that all this raiding and threat of invasion, though menacing and dangerous enough, was not some horror big enough to split the world – but merely our particular testing time; what we must face, as our forefathers faced such things, in order to enjoy our own again. It would come down upon us; it would be terrible; but it would pass. You remember Hardy's song: 'In Time of The Breaking of Nations':

> Only a man harrowing clods In a slow silent walk,
> With an old horse that stumbles and nods,
> Half asleep as they stalk;
>
> Only thin smoke without flame
> From the heaps of couch-grass:
> Yet this will go onward the same
> Though Dynasties pass.
>
> Yonder a maid and her wight
> Come whispering by;
> War's annals will fade into night
> Ere their story die.[178]

Sunday 23 June 1940

... Ever since the faked 'burning' of the Reichstag – ever since that 'weekend of the long knives,' when Hitler had so many of his associates murdered – I think I have known that in the end it must come to this: that there must come a night when I would find myself walking through a blacked-out London in an England that was being turned into a fortress.

I don't pretend to any notable consistency, but it's a fact – and cold print can prove it – that about Hitler and the Nazis I have always held the same opinion – the opinion that they were evil, and that the time must come when either we must destroy them or they would destroy us; they were no more to be compromised with than typhoid fever is to be compromised with. You might as well try to come to an amicable settlement with a pack of ravening wolves.

My feeling from the first, I think, had nothing to do with economics and politics, but was really moral – or, if you like, religious. Here, in these cruel figures who emerged from the underworld, who promptly destroyed the cultural life of their country, turned workers into serfs again, trained boys to be brutes, brushed away the last specks of honour, organised two vast new government departments – one for systematic lying, the other for equally systematic torture; and even perverted and poisoned the life of the family, so that school children became police spies at the very dinner table-here, I say, was something that cut deeper than the economic disagreements and political differences.

Here, I felt, was the growing corruption, the darkening despair of our modern world, shaping itself into one vast dark face – a German dark face, that would call to other dark faces elsewhere. Every nation has two faces – a bright face and a dark face. I had always been ready to love the bright face of Germany which speaks to us of beautiful music, profound philosophy, Gothic romance, young men and maidens wandering through the enchanted forests.

I had been to Germany before the last war, walking from one little inn to another in the Rhineland. After the war I went back, and wrote in praise of the noble Rhine, the wet lilac and the rust-coloured Castle of Heidelberg, the carpets of flowers and the ice-green torrents of the Bavarian Alps. But after the Nazis came, I went no more. The bright face had gone, and in its place was the vast dark face with its broken promises and endless deceit, its swaggering Storm Troopers and dreaded Gestapo, its bloodstained basements where youths were hardened by the torture of decent elderly folk – the terror and the shame, not just their shame, but our shame, the shame of the whole watching world, of the concentration camps...

And any country that allows itself to be dominated by the Nazis will not only have the German Gestapo crawling everywhere, but will also find itself in the power of all its own most unpleasant types – the very people who, for years, have been rotten with unsatisfied vanity, gnawing envy, and haunted by dreams of cruel power. Let the Nazis in, and you will find that the laziest loudmouth in the workshop has suddenly been given power to kick you up and down the street, and that if you try to make any appeal, you have to do it to the one man in the district whose every word and look you'd always distrusted.

And as I thought these things going home the other night, there came the recollection of a tiny paragraph I'd seen in the papers that morning. It said that a German woman — like so many thousands of others, the hopelessly mentally distressed victim of Nazi persecution – had been found drowned in the Thames and had left the following message: 'I have had much kindness in England, but I decided to leave this world. May England be victorious.' And I asked myself earnestly if really there was anything more to be said at this supreme hour than that.

If the kindness of England, of Britain, of the wide Empire forever reaching out towards new expressions of freedom, is overshadowed by that vast dark face, then we all might as well decide to leave this world, for it will not be a world worth living in. But, she cried, 'May England be victorious.' And we can only reply to that poor tormented spirit: 'England will be victorious.'[179]

*In his next broadcast Priestley took a sideswipe at officialdom, contrasting*

*the indomitable, defiant spirit of ordinary Britons with the pettifogging
rules, regulations and restrictions beloved of a certain kind of Whitehall
bureaucrat. It strengthened his populist credentials and generated an ever-
growing stream of appreciative letters to the press and the* Radio Times.

Sunday 30 June 1940

... On the second day of this war, I wrote an article called 'Two Ton
Annie.' I'd been watching some invalids from mainland hospitals being
evacuated to the Isle of Wight, and among these invalids was a very
large, elderly woman, who was sitting upright on her stretcher and
being carried by six staggering, sweating, grinning bearers, who called
her 'Two Ton Annie'.

She exchanged cheerful, insulting remarks with everybody. She was
a roaring and indomitable old lioness, and wherever she was carried
there was a cheerful tumult; and as she roared out repartee she saluted
the grinning crowd like a raffish old empress. Yes; she was old, fat,
helplessly lame and was being taken away from her familiar
surroundings, a sick woman, far from home. But she gave no sign of
any inward distress, but was her grand, uproarious self.

She did all our hearts good that day, and I said then that although
Britannia can put up a good fight, Two Ton Annie and all her kind can
put up a better one. I said that if it comes to a struggle between them
and worried, semi-neurotic, police-ridden populations for ever raising
their hands in solemnly idiotic salutes, standing to attention while the
radio screams blasphemous nonsense at them, these people will emerge
victorious because their sort of life breeds kindness, humour and
courage, and the other sort of life doesn't. Kindness, humour and
courage are mightily sustaining qualities. They prevent that breakdown
inside upon which our enemies with their screaming bogy-machines
always depend.

Well, that was Two Ton Annie, who gave me such a heartening
glimpse of our folk at the very beginning of the war. Since then, I'll
confess, I've had glimpses that were much less heartening-in fact were
even depressing.

For weeks, perhaps months, somehow Two Ton Annie and her uproarious stretcher-bearers and admirers disappeared, and instead I encountered another set of figures who might he described as Complacent Clarence, Hush-Hush Harold, and Dubious Departmental Desmond! These gentlemen have their places in our wartime scheme of things: this is not an attack upon them and their like; but often I couldn't help feeling, as a man who'd tried for years to understand our national character, that there was a real danger of these pundits and mandarins creating a rather thick, woolly, dreary atmosphere in which that national character of ours couldn't flourish and express itself properly.

The war, to which we have brought a unity of feeling never known before in our island history, was somehow not quite our war. Nobody told us right out to mind our own business, but often something of the sort was implied. There were too many snubs and cold-shoulders about. That was before the Blitzkrieg began. Since then, and especially since the danger crept nearer and the screaming threats grew louder and louder, I feel that that fog and its whispering figures have almost vanished, and that at any moment now I may encounter again my old friend Two Ton Annie.

Through the fading mists there emerge the simple, kindly, humorous brave faces of the ordinary British folk... on them, on us, on all of you listening to me now, there rests the responsibility of manning this last great defence of our liberal civilisation. Already the future historians are fastening their gaze upon us, seeing us all in that clear and searching light of the great moments of history. That light may discover innumerable past follies and weaknesses of policy and national endeavour, but here and now, as the spirit of the people rises to meet the challenge, I believe that it will find no flaw in the sense, courage and endurance of those people.[180]

*In a letter to friends, Priestley's wife Jane reflected on the popularity of the 'Postscripts' and the pride she took in his broadcasting work.*

Sunday 30 June 1940

Jack is doing simply magnificent work, broadcasting Sundays at 9.15 and any other evening he's asked to England and to the Dominions and USA on short wave Mon Wed Fri at 2a.m. London Summer Time. The English broadcasts are an abnormal success. They are a 'Good Companions' success. The Americans we don't know about. Does anyone listen to short wave?...

The comments one hears now are grand. 'Well we're in at the finals now and it will be on the home ground'. My very nervous little housemaid left us to work in an aeroplane factory and said 'Give in to the Germans? I'd rather die'. Our newsagent here: 'It's a comfort to know our chaps will be fighting here and not going off abroad'.

Jack is being simply magnificent. All he is doing – and he's at it 18 hrs a day – in articles, films (documentary films dealing with the war) broadcasts is inspired and if I'd never been proud of him before, I'd be most proud now...

We feel at any moment things will start here and so every hour of a day like this, every meeting with a friend is doubly precious. We pray and hope and are determined to sacrifice everything, if necessary rather than give in. It's not a bad moment to be alive in and I can't tell you how exalted and consecrated one feels England to be.[181]

*Priestley continued to find ways to use the minutiae of British life to inspire his audience; as he remarked himself, 'I think it's that tying up of the big war theme to the small, homely things that gave them their popularity.*[182]

Sunday 7 July 1940

I'll tell you the two most heartening and inspiring things I've seen this week. The first was a duck; and the second was a dig in the ribs!

Now, in order to appreciate the duck you have to have some idea of the whole setting of the scene. It was rather late the other night, and we were coming home to Highgate Village by way of High-street, Hampstead, and the Spaniards-road, which run, you might say, on the roof of London. We had to pass the Whitestone Pond.

Now I like the Whitestone Pond. On fine afternoons, boys sail their toy boats on it, and when there's a wind blowing across the Heath the toy boats have to battle with enormous waves – about three inches high. At night, this pond is like a little hand-mirror that the vast, sprawling, yawning London still holds negligently; and you see the stars glimmering in it.

Well, the other night was one of those mysterious nights we've had lately when there seems to be a pale light coming from nowhere, and the sky has a pure washed look. The dim lights of a few cars could be seen in the dusk round the pond, and some people, late as it was, were standing and staring. We stopped, and heard a solicitous quacking and a great deal of faint squeaking. Then we saw on the pond, like a tiny feathered flotilla, a duck accompanied by her minute ducklings, just squeaking specks of yellow fluff. We joined the fascinated spectators; we forgot the war, the imminence of invasion, the doubts about the French Fleet, the melancholy antics of the Bordeaux Government.

Our eyes, and ears, and our imagination were caught and held by those triumphant little parcels of life. This duck hadn't hatched her brood here; she'd hatched them in some hidden corner – nobody knows where – and had then conveyed them – and nobody knows how – to swim happily in the dusk on this summit of the city. She hadn't asked anybody's advice or permission; she hadn't told herself it was too late or too difficult; nobody had told her to 'Go to it' and that 'it all depended on her'. She had gone to it, a triumphant little servant of that life, mysterious, fruitful, beautiful, which expresses itself as a man writes a poem-now in vast galaxies of flaming suns, now in a tiny brood of ducklings squeaking in the dusk.

And if we forgot the war for a moment, afterwards we returned to think of it with a new courage, as if by that pond we'd been given a sign. For reduced to its very simplest but profoundest terms, this is a war between despair and hope; for Nazism is really the most violent expression of the despair of the modern world. It's the black abyss at the end of a wrong road. It's a negation of the good life. It is at heart death-worship. But there flows through all nature a tide of being, a creative energy that at every moment challenges and contradicts this death-worship of despairing, crazy men. Even the mallard duck, bringing from nowhere its happy little cargo of life, salutes us in the growing darkness and tell us to stand up and fight and be of good courage.

The second of these two most heartening and inspiring things of the week was, as I said, a dig in the ribs! It wasn't a dig in my ribs; and then again, it wasn't so much the dig as the grin that went with it. But I'd better explain. It happened on Thursday afternoon. I went to the House of Commons to hear the Prime Minister make his statement on the French Fleet. It was, as you all know by this time, a most exciting and heartening afternoon. The deepening undercurrent of excitement during the question time that preceded the statement, the rapidly-filling benches and galleries of the House, the sombre opening and triumphant conclusion of the Premier's speech, the tumultuous reception of it by the whole standing, cheering House. But all this you have heard already.

What specially heartened and inspired me was a tiny thing that happened long before these fireworks were exploded. Mr. Churchill entered the House, not to make his statement but to answer one or two questions. He was greeted, as well he might be, with that peculiar 'hear-hearing' that is described by parliamentary reporters as 'cheers'. His head was sunk into his broad shoulders, giving him that characteristic bulldog look. His face was set, unsmiling, grave. He looked indeed what we knew him to be – a man called upon to take terrible decisions, to remove the sword from the hand of a friend who is beginning to forget the solemn oaths with which that sword had been unsheathed.

Now, next to the place on the Front Bench towards which Mr. Churchill was now slowly making his way was Mr. Ernest Bevin, who had been answering questions on the paper – and answering them with promptness and vigour – a powerful, thick-set, determined figure of a man, a fine lump of that England which we all love; one of those men who stand up among the cowardices and treacheries and corruption of this recent world like an oak tree in a swamp. So Mr. Churchill, representing you might say the other half of the English people and English history, moved slowly to his place next to the massive, yeoman figure of Mr. Bevin; and for a second or so, still meditating deeply on what he had to say, he kept the withdrawn, unsmiling look with which he had entered.

But then, coming out of his reverie and recognising who was beside him, Mr. Churchill gave his colleague a sharp little punch of greeting – a little dig in the ribs; and as he did this there flashed across his face a sudden boyish, mischievous, devil-may-care grin. And I said to myself 'these are the men for me'. I said to myself as if I'd suddenly turned back twenty-five years and was a corporal of infantry again: 'That's the stuff to give 'em!'

You know, I'm always being asked by somebody or other to talk to you about these slogans that are produced by experts, but somehow I never quite take to them; but if they were anything like as good as 'That's the stuff to give 'em!' I'd talk about them until the microphone began to steam. And now after years I found myself crying exultantly again: 'That's the stuff to give 'em!'" because Mr. Churchill, a man in his sixties who has driven himself as hard as he could go ever since Omdurman, who has held high office for more than thirty years, and upon whose shoulders now rests perhaps the fate of Europe for centuries, could in this grave hour to which he had done full justice both in his private decision and his public utterances, let slip that wonderful, lightning grin which was like a miraculous glimpse of the inner man who, like so many formidable men, is still a boy at heart, still full of devilment. And I said to myself that this is the kind of man the English, and the Scots, and the Welsh, and for that matter the Irish, want at this challenging hour, and no weary gentlemanly muddling and mumbling of platitudes.

When I saw that grin and that dig in the ribs, I said: 'These are the men for us, but let them make haste, raise their voices and command the expectant people, who can, out of their kindness, humour and courage, yet defeat these cunning, ruthless but crack-brained and small-hearted Nazis.

Let them cry at once, with Shakespeare, to the waiting people:
"For there is none of you so mean and base
That hath not noble lustre in your eyes.

I see you stand like greyhounds in the slips,
Straining upon the start. The game's afoot:
Follow your spirit; and, upon this charge
Cry: "God for Harry, England and Saint George".'[183]

## Chapter 8
# A better England in a nobler world

*Priestley's early 'Postscripts' had been almost universally popular and were 'rapidly gaining the status of a British institution'.*[184] *Newspapers often printed extracts the next morning and even the right wing* Daily Mail *commented that 'as the hours grow darker, he grows brighter'.*[185] *However in his next broadcast, Priestley began to explore a theme to which he would repeatedly return, setting the scene for a battle between those who shared his vision and those who either viewed it as socialist propaganda, or deplored any distractions from a single-minded pursuit of victory in the war. Priestley later made a succinct statement of the core beliefs that informed this and every subsequent Postscript.*

I believed we had to fight that war, cost what it might. I also believed – though this brought me some powerful enemies – that we could not fight it simply to restore the same rotten world that had nourished Hitler and the Nazis. On those beliefs I took my stand whenever I faced the microphone.[186]

Sunday 14 July 1940

The other day I made the strangest journey I ever remember making in this country: I went to Margate. But of course it wasn't like any possible kind of visit to Margate that we could have imagined before this war; it was like some fantastic dream of a day trip to Margate. A dozen times during the day I told myself that in a minute I'd wake up from all this, and find myself back in the comfortable routine of a year ago. I didn't pinch myself – I believe people only do that in rather carelessly written novels – but I think several times I sort of mentally pinched myself, to discover if I were awake.

The start wasn't unusual except that we all had a lot of passes and permits, and we took tin hats along with us too; so that if a lot of stuff came down we'd have our portable little air-raid shelters. Some people despise tin hats – but not me. I remember them first arriving in the trenches – and very glad we were to see them, too.

Well, we set off for Margate – and for some time it was all quite ordinary, but after that it soon began to seem rather peculiar. Along the road there were things that weren't quite what they first appeared to be – if you see what I mean; the Bren guns seemed to be getting mixed up with the agricultural life of north Kent. The most flourishing crop seemed to be barbed wire. Soldiers would pop up from nowhere and then vanish again unless they wanted to see our permits. Some extra large greenish cattle, quietly pasturing underneath the elm, might possibly have been tanks. It was a rum sort of farming round there! And then as we came nearer the East Coast, the place seemed emptier and emptier. There were signs and portents. A field would have a hole in it, made at the expense of considerable time, trouble, and outlay of capital, by the German Air Force. An empty bungalow, minus its front door and dining-room, stared at us in mute reproach. An R.A.F. lorry went past, taking with it the remains of a Heinkel bomber.

We were almost on the front at Margate before I'd realised that we were anywhere near the town – although I was holding the map! I must say that if any invaders are going anywhere in particular, and not just wandering about, they're in for a very puzzling time; and I can't help feeling that while they're trying to make out where they are, whole packets of trouble will come their way.

But there we were at last – on the front at Margate. The sun, with a fine irony, came bounding out. The sea, which has its own sense of humour, winked and sparkled at us. We began to walk along the front. Everything was there: bathing pools, bandstands, gardens blazing with flowers, lido, theatres, and the like; and miles of firm golden sands all spread out beneath the July sun. But no people! – not a soul.

Of all those hundreds of thousands of holidaymakers, of entertainers and hawkers and boatmen – not one. And no sound-not the very ghost of an echo of all that cheerful hullabaloo - children shouting and laughing, bands playing, concert parties singing, men selling ice-cream, whelks and peppermint rock, which I'd remembered hearing along this shore. No, not even an echo. Silence. It was as if an evil magician had whisked everybody away.

There were the rows and rows of boarding-houses, the 'Sea Views' and 'Bryn Mawrs' and 'Craig-y-dons' and 'Sans Soucis' and the rest, which ought to have been bursting with life, with red faces, piano and gramophone music, and the smell of roast beef and Yorkshire pudding, but all empty, shuttered, forlorn. A most melancholy boarding-house at the end of a row caught my eye-and that one was called 'Kismet'. Kismet, indeed!

In search of a drink and a sandwich, we wandered round. and sometimes through, large empty hotels. The few signs of life only made the whole place seem more unreal and spectral. Once an ancient taxi came gliding along the promenade, and we agreed that if we'd hailed it, making a shout in that silence, it would have dissolved at once into thin air. An elderly postman on a bicycle may have been real or yet another apparition.

At last we found a cafe open, somewhere at the back of the town, and had no sooner had our roast mutton and green peas set in front of us, than the sirens began screaming. But after all this strange ghostliness, an air-raid warning didn't seem to matter much; and we finished our mutton and had some pancakes. The 'All Clear' found us in a small bar about two miles away, where one of the patrons – a fat man in his shirt-sleeves observed placidly: 'Well, I fancy there ought to be another one just about six.' After noting this evidence of the 'terrible panic' among the remaining inhabitants of the south-east coast of Britain, we returned to contemplate, still under its strange spell, this bright ghost of a Margate.

I remembered so vividly a day I'd spent here ten years ago, when the whole coast was crammed and noisy with folk and it was all a jolly, sweaty pandemonium. Had that been a dream? – or was this strange silent afternoon a dream? It seemed impossible that they should both be real. Yet here we were, alone, hearing our own footfalls on the lifeless promenade. The evil magician had muttered the enchanted phrase-and a wind had come from Hell and blown away all the trippers and paddlers and pierrots and hawkers – all that perspiring, bustling, rowdy, riotous holiday-making.

And as I stood there, half bemused in the blazing ironic sunshine, I asked myself what I would do if another and better magician should arrive and tell me that he had only to wave his wand to send time hurtling back, so that once again these sands would be thick with honest folk, the boarding-houses bursting again with buckets and spades and the smell of cabbage; the bandstands and stages as lively as ever. Would I agree? Would I say: 'Yes, let time go back. Let this melancholy silent afternoon be only a dream of an impossible Margate. Say the word, and let Margate-and Westgate, and Herne Bay and Broadstairs and Ramsgate and a hundred other resorts-be as they were a year ago.'

And I said 'No, I want no such miracle. Let this be real, so far as all this muddled groping of ours with the deep purposes of life can be considered real-and let time tick on. But if you would help us, then, if you are a great and wise magician, move our minds and hearts towards steadfast courage and faith and hope, because we're ready to accept all this: the silent town that once was gay; vanished crowds now toiling far from these vacant sands; this hour of trial and testing – if we know that we can march forward – not merely to recover what has been lost, but to something better than we've ever known before.'

That's what I would have said to that magician. And now I say to all of you who are listening, for in your common will there is an even mightier magician: This Margate I saw was saddening and hateful; but its new silence and desolation should be thought of as a bridge leading us to a better Margate in a better England, in a nobler world. We're not fighting to restore the past; it was the past that brought us to this heavy hour; but we are fighting to rid ourselves and the world of the evil encumbrance of these Nazis so that we can plan and create a noble future for all our species.

I think that in the coming time the hearts and hopes of men
The mountain tops of life shall climb, the gods return again.

I strive to blow the magic horn; it feebly murmureth,
Arise on some enchanted morn, fight with God's own breath,
And sound the horn I cannot blow, and by the secret name
Each exile of the heart will know, kindle the magic flame.[187]

*One of Priestley's biographers described him as 'haunted by a world. It is not a lost world, of the kind which keeps many writers trapped in visions of the past, since it never really existed. It is more a kind of ideal: a longing for the way things could be.'[188] His early 'Postscripts' had been largely uncontentious but he now began to articulate a vision of the war not merely as the means to defeat fascism, but also the opportunity radically to transform British society and bring that ideal a step closer.*

Priestley's matchless ability to make something special out of vernacular language, coupled with his roots in provincial radicalism, enabled him to produce a discourse in which the people and nation were one... Although he did not coin the phrase (and no one seems to know who did), Priestley more than anyone became associated with the notion of the 'People's War': that this was a war in which the active participation and commitment of ordinary people was paramount, and that this had implications for what war meant, for the way it was run, and for what would happen after it was over. Because of these sacrifices, and the betrayals and disappointments of the interwar years, the idea of the 'People's War' carried with it a strong hint of better things to come. But to be part of 'the people' as Priestley saw them, meant actively seeking that better life: actively participating in the war effort and in the shaping of the postwar world. This combination of rights and obligations, actively pursued, we might call "citizenship." For Priestley, citizenship had been at a low ebb in the Britain of the 1920s and 1930s, but in the summer of 1940 he thought he saw its rebirth...

The hope of radical postwar reconstruction grew out of despair at the condition of the nation in the 1930s... his social and political critique had gathered strength through the decade... and extended beyond the familiar Wigan Pier territory of unemployment and social conditions in the depressed areas, to bring in issues of democracy, culture, national identity and the distribution of power and status in British society... there was more to his wartime agitation than a shopping-list of legislation, and in any case he had always been sceptical of Five Year Plans, bureaucracies and social reconstruction from above. He was a visionary as much as a social reformer, and his vision was of a nation renewed below, 'bombed and burned into democracy'... offering a new, almost spiritual vision of a nation at last worthy of itself.[189]

*Priestley's views put him on a collision course with the Tory right wing and with Winston Churchill, already hostile to Priestley's critiques of pre-war Conservative policies, and implacably hostile to any debate about 'Peace Aims' before the 'War Aims' – total victory – had been achieved. Priestley felt that the two were not incompatible and, indeed, that a commitment to a transformed post-war British society would be a potent boost to wartime morale, and in a succession of 'Postscripts' he outlined and developed his theme of 'a better England in a nobler world'.*

Sunday 21 July 1940

I hadn't been in his room more than two minutes when this official and I were looking at each other as a cat looks at a dog. We just weren't getting on at all. I ought to have known we wouldn't get on. And we hadn't been together five minutes, this official and I, before I knew that he knew what I thought about him, and he knew that I knew what he was thinking about me. He saw me as an impatient, slapdash, dangerous sort of fellow, wanting everything done all at once, bringing out all manner of half-digested notions and bragging, swaggering, insufferably pleased with myself, rather a bounder and an outsider, really. And I saw him as a coldly conceited, ungenerous, sterile kind of chap, never throwing himself wholeheartedly into anything, always wondering how he was going to come out of it, and just as he'd call me a bounder I'd call him 'a stuffed shirt'.

Well, there we were, not getting on at all and taking a greater and greater dislike to each other. But his manners, being better trained than mine, hadn't worn quite so thin. He made those little movements that politely suggest to a caller that it's time to go. He said: 'We might be able to form a small sub-committee; then, perhaps you'd like to send in some kind of report, just a short memo, embodying...' And I said: 'No, I don't think so. Good morning,' and went. And he said to himself: 'Well, thank goodness I've got rid of that fellow, barging in here as if he owned the place. He can't begin to understand our difficulties, relations with the Treasury and so on'; and I said to myself: 'Stuffed shirts and Mandarins, oh dear, oh dear, oh dear, oh dear, oh dear.'

Two entirely different and opposed types of mind and temperament, you see, the warmly imaginative against the coldly rational, the slapdash against the punctilious, the impatient against the cautious, the creative against the administrative. Clearly we must have both types of mind working now at full pressure and it's absolutely essential that each should have its own sphere of activity. It's in the relation of eager, imaginative, creative minds and cool, punctilious, administrative minds that we've tended to go wrong. That abortive interview I've just described is probably typical of what happens.

Now, there are two ways of looking at this war. The first way, which, on the whole, we are officially encouraged to adopt, is to see this war as a terrible interruption. As soon as we can decently do it, we must return to what is called peace, so let's make all the munitions we can, and be ready to do some hard fighting, and then we can have done with Hitler and his Nazis and go back to where we started from, the day before war was declared. Now this, to my mind, is all wrong. It's wrong because it simply isn't true.

A year ago, though we hadn't actually declared war, there wasn't real peace, or the year before, or the year before that. If you go back to the sort of world that produces Hitlers and Mussolinis, then no sooner have you got rid of one lot of Hitlers and Mussolinis than another lot will pop up somewhere, and there'll be more wars.

This brings us to the second, and more truthful, way of looking at this war. That is, to regard this war as one chapter in a tremendous history, the history of a changing world, the breakdown of one vast system and the building up of another and better one. In this view of things Hitler and Mussolini have been thrown up by this breakdown of a world system. It's as if an earthquake cracked the walls and floors of a house and strange nuisances of things, Nazists and Fascists, came running out of the woodwork.

We have to get rid of these intolerable nuisances but not so that we can go back to anything. There's nothing that really worked that we can go back to. But so that we can go forward, without all the shouting and stamping and bullying and murder, and really plan and build up a nobler world in which ordinary, decent folk can not only find justice and security but also beauty and' delight. And this isn't a 'pipe dream', because many of our difficulties have arrived not because man's capacity is feebler than it used to be, but just because it's actually so much greater.

The modern man, thanks to his inventiveness, has suddenly been given a hundred arms and seven-league boots. But we can't go forward and build up this new world order, and this is our real war aim, unless we begin to think differently, and my own personal view, for what it's worth, is that we must stop thinking in terms of property and power and begin thinking in terms of community and creation.

Now, I'll explain just what I mean. First, take the change from power to creation. Now, power – whether on a large or small scale – really boils down to the ignoble pleasure of bossing and ordering other people about because you have the whip-hand of them. All these Nazi and Fascist leaders are power worshippers, they're almost drunk on it. I suspect it's simply a bad substitute for the joy of creation, which everybody understands, whether you're creating a vast educational system or a magnificent work of art, or bringing into existence a vegetable garden or a thundering good dinner. People are never so innocently happy as when they're creating something. So, we want a world that offers people not the dubious pleasures of power, but the maximum opportunities for creation. And even already, in the middle of this war, I can see that world shaping itself

And now we'll take the change from property to community.

Property is that old-fashioned way of thinking of a country as a thing, and a collection of things on that thing, all owned by certain people and constituting property; instead of thinking of a country as the home of a living society, and considering the welfare of that society, the community itself, as the first test. And I'll give you an instance of how this change should be working.

Near where I live is a house with a large garden, that's not being used at all because the owner of it has gone to America. Now, according to the property view, this is all right, and we, who haven't gone to America, must fight to protect this absentee owner's property. But on the community view, this is all wrong. There are hundreds of working men not far from here who urgently need ground for allotments so that they can produce a bit more food. Also, we may soon need more houses for billeting. Therefore, I say, that house and garden ought to be used whether the owner, who's gone to America, likes it or not. That's merely one instance, and you can easily find dozens of others.

Now, the war, because it demands a huge collective effort, is compelling us to change not only our ordinary, social and economic habits, but also our habits of thought. We're actually changing over from the property view to the sense of community, which simply means that we realise we're all in the same boat. But, and this is the point, that boat can serve not only as our defence against Nazi aggression, but as an ark in which we can all finally land in a better world. And when I say 'We', I don't mean only the British and their allied peoples, but all people everywhere, including all the Germans who haven't sold themselves body and soul to the evil Nazi idea.

I tell you, there is stirring in us now, a desire which could soon become a controlled but passionate determination to remodel and recreate this life of ours, to make it the glorious beginning of a new world order, so that we might soon be so fully and happily engrossed in our great task that if Hitler and his gang suddenly disappeared, we'd hardly notice that they'd gone. We're even now the hope of free men everywhere but soon we could be the hope and lovely dawn of the whole wide world.[190]

*In the following broadcast Priestley amplified his theme, turning a tribute to RAF aircrew into a plea for a better Britain to greet them when they came home after the war. He also highlighted the letters from right wing critics telling him to 'get off the air'. They were far outnumbered by those in praise of him, but Priestley's mention of his critics raised the temperature again and provoked a fresh flood of supportive letters, including one to the* Radio Times *saying that if Priestley were taken off the air, 'the whole BBC should be clapped in jail'.*[191]

*Priestley had an intuitive ability to assess the mood of the country and reach into the hearts of people, and they in turn wrote in large numbers to share their concerns and ideas. Like him, they were looking for a better post-war world. He was not manipulating them, but expressing simply and clearly their own feelings, in a warm and human way. His son Tom, then at boarding school, remembers 'being allowed to stay up in my dressing gown to hear my father's steady voice from the headmaster's wireless. There was something wonderfully reassuring about his measured delivery.'*[192]

## Sunday 28 July 1940

Not long ago I had the privilege of attending a little family party. This party was given to celebrate the safe return of the youngest member of his family, who's a Pilot Officer in the Royal Air Force. He and his crew – that implies a big bombing plane – had been missing for many hours; they'd spent these hours in a rubber dinghy on the North Sea, but now, with nothing worse than a bruised hand and arm, he was on leave, with his pretty young wife in attendance at this party.

He hadn't changed very much, really: it was I who stared at him with new eyes, as if I were meeting a figure from some epic – a cheerful young giant out of a saga. Before the war I used to spend an occasional Sunday playing lawn tennis with his family, and now and again he would turn up, in a battered little sports car, with this same pretty girl in attendance - a tall, casual but friendly lad, who played an enthusiastic but slapdash game of tennis with one of those terrific first services that nearly always go miles out, but when they do hit the court are winners.

I knew – for I'd heard him mention it casually – that he piloted heavy bombers, but to what kind of life he went roaring back in his little car, I'd no idea, and, to be truthful, I wasn't interested. I'd never even seen him in uniform; I saw him as a nice, long-legged, untidy lad, putting in a few years in the Air Force until he thought of something more serious to do. And then the other day we met again – and talked; though that wasn't too easy at first because he was shy and modest, and absurdly respectful to this middle-aged civilian.

To realise properly and appreciate what he'd done and where he'd been, since the beginning of last September, you have to bring out your map of Europe, then let your eye range from the Arctic Circle to the Gulf of Genoa. Norway, Denmark, Germany, Holland, Belgium, France, Italy – he'd flown over them all, and had had to find in them certain points far too small to be marked on any maps that you and I possess – an aerodrome, a railway station, one particular factory, a certain crossroads. And in the R.A.F. you have to find what you've been sent out to find – you have your target, and there is no nonsense about unloading your bombs merely in its vicinity.

Night after night – at first carrying pamphlets, then, in the dread cold of winter, making reconnaissance flights, and ever since, carrying bombs – he's gone roaring out of his aerodrome in England, over the North Sea, over strange darkened lands far to the North, far to the East, far to the South, to come circling down where coloured searchlights went wheeling and there would be a golden hail of tracer bullets, and the earth below belched and spat its anti-aircraft fire, and there was the thresh and the shudder of exploding bombs. And then he'd turn, and lift the great machine towards home, and see the pale-washed light of dawn spread over the floor of cloud or far below over the cold tumbling seas, and then see at last the familiar pattern of fields, and wonder if there were sausages or bacon for breakfast in the mess. And not all who set out would always come back. 'From these operations,' the easy, glib phrase runs, 'two of our aircraft are missing.' Empty chairs in the mess – letters in the rack which will never be claimed – shadows of eyes and dying echoes of voices - they pass and smile, the children of the sword.

So that's his life; and though I've given you not even a glimpse of what is exacting and responsible in it, the actual piloting of these great vessels of the air across thousands of miles – the intricate co-operation both on land and in the air – the response to all those severe demands made by our Royal Air Force upon all its personnel.

But let us remember now that pretty young wife. She lodges as close as regulations permit to the aerodrome, so that her husband can dash out now and again at lunchtime and see her. In the evenings she hears the Squadron take the air for its new adventure, knowing no more than you and I would know where they're going; but she counts the planes as they go roaring up. Then, hours and hours afterwards, somewhere around dawn, after a series of uneasy, broken naps, she hears the faint familiar drone of the returning bombers; sits up, and above the loud beating of her heart, counts the planes that have come safely home. One-two-three- and so on, until there's silence again; and if the total is the same as it was when she counted them going up, then it's all right – it must be all right, and at last she can go to sleep. But if it isn't the same, then there's no more chance of sleep for her. And that's her life these days.

A year ago these were just a pair of light-hearted youngsters, dashing about in their battered little car, and even now, on leave, as I met them, they're a light-hearted pair still. Nevertheless, that's their life, and it's passed in our service. And what I want to know now is this: it's all right feeling a lump in the throat, and saying 'God bless you', but what are we really going to do about it?

I will tell you what we did for such young men and their young wives at the end of the last war. We did nothing – except let them take their chance in a world in which every gangster and trickster and stupid insensitive fool or rogue was let loose to do his damnedest. After the cheering and the flag-waving were over, and all the medals were given out, somehow the young heroes disappeared, but after a year or two there were a lot of shabby, young-oldish men about who didn't seem to have been lucky in the scramble for easy jobs and quick profits, and so tried to sell us second-hand cars or office supplies we didn't want, or even trailed, round the suburbs asking to be allowed to demonstrate the latest vacuum cleaner.

No doubt it's going to be all different this time, but some of us can't help discovering, to our dismay, that the same sort of minds are still about. Among bundles of very friendly letters just lately I've been getting some very fierce and angry ones telling me to get off the air before the Government 'puts you where you belong' – the real Fascist touch. Well, obviously, it wouldn't matter much if I were taken off the air, but it would matter a great deal, even to these Blimps, if these young men of the R.A.F. were taken off the air; and so I repeat my question – in return for their skill, devotion, endurance and self-sacrifice, what are we civilians prepared to do? And surely the answer is that the least we can do is to give our minds honestly, sincerely and without immediate self-interest, to the task of preparing a world really fit for them and their kind – to arrange for them a final 'happy landing'.

Don't insult them by thinking they don't care what sort of a world they're fighting for. All the evidence contradicts that. And here's a bit of it in a letter that reached me a day or two ago. It runs as follows: 'My son was formerly a salesman; he resigned in order to join the Air Force. On a recent visit home he said: "I shall never go back to the old business life - that life of what I call the survival of the slickest; I now know a better way. Our lads in the R.A.F. would, and do, willingly give their lives for each other; the whole outlook of the force is one of 'give', not one of 'get'. If tomorrow the war ended and I returned to business, I would need to sneak, cheat and pry in order to get hold of orders which otherwise would have gone to one of my R.A.F. friends if one of them returned to commercial life with a competing firm. Instead of co-operating as we do in war, we would each use all the craft we possessed with which to confound each other. I will never do it."'

His father ends by saying: 'You, sir, will be able to adorn this tale – it's a true one – I hope you will.' But I don't think it needs any adorning.[193]

*In his 'Postscript' on the anniversary of the start of the First World War, Priestley delineated the differences he saw between the two conflicts and stressed again the importance of winning the war of ideas as well as the war of weapons.*

Sunday 4 August 1940

... Do you ever look back on your life, and see it as a road that wanders through wildly varying landscapes? I do. And now, as I look back, before August 1914 the road seems to be in a sunlit plain, coming out of the mists of early childhood. Then, for the next four or five years, the road goes through black and terrible mountains, and is sometimes almost obliterated by avalanches.

It comes out into 1919 and enters a confused landscape, with swamps and dark forests and sudden pleasant uplands. These were the years of the false peace, of the defeat of good will. There was plenty of good will about in those nineteen-twenties – it's a sad mistake to think there wasn't – but somehow it couldn't secure adequate representation. It let the old hands, the experts, the smooth gentry who assure you that your inexperience tends to make you gravely underestimate the difficulties of the situation, speak for it, and they sold it out.

Then came the Thirties, and that road descended into a stony wilderness of world depression and despair; and very soon in that desert, fantastically shaped rocks and cruel jagged ridges began to show themselves, and soon there were more and more of them, closer and closer to the road; until at last it climbed and narrowed to a track between iron-edged boulders and sometimes clinging to the edge of precipices.

These were the years when it was evident that the war had started all over again, assuming new and even more sinister forms, when we were appalled by the violence and cruelty hidden in the modern man's depths of despair. Great lie machines were installed in Central Europe, and far below them, in bloodstained basements, were official torture chambers.

We were now to be shown how men can behave when they have lost all hope of the Kingdom of Heaven, how when you have robbed men of all belief in this or any other world, the first madman who arrives can capture them with his fantasies. And so the disguised war of the Thirties became the open war of 1940.

This war is quite unlike the one that broke out twenty-six years ago. Have you ever noticed how all the attempts – and there have been many – to see this war in terms of the last, have failed? You just can't give this war a 'Tipperary', 'Keep the Home Fires Burning' flavour. It won't have it. The queer thing is that these attempts, which have been deliberate and often well organised, are frustrated by masses of people who could give no explanation of why they shrug their shoulders and turn away. I suspect that the wisest historian resides somewhere in the collective unconscious minds of whole populations. You can't deceive that mysterious fellow. He knows that this conflict is not a repetition of the last war.

I think all our people here know it, too, in their hearts, and this explains why they respond so eagerly to really new appeals to their loyalty, and don't respond to the old routine stuff, of which they've been given far too much. They notice, for example, that the old strictly nationalistic divisions don't quite fit. There are millions of Germans who are praying that Hitler will lose. There may be some Britons, of a certain psychological type, persons hungry for power at all costs, who would like Hitler to win.

The history of France in these two wars offers the most vivid and significant illustration of the profound difference between these wars. And I feel that the popular mind, though perhaps for the most part rather obscurely, understands this difference much better than many of our official minds. This isn't 1914. It isn't simply a question of Germans fighting for Germany and Britons for Britain. And- Communists here and abroad, please note - it certainly isn't a question of who shall collect the dividends of some African trading company. You couldn't get people to fight five minutes on such an issue.

Reduced to its simplest, but profoundest, terms, this is a war between despair and hope. Nazism, beneath its show of efficiency and organisation, its triumphant nationalism at home and its revolutionary propaganda talk abroad, has a basis of complete and utter despair, its one belief being that man is a contemptible creature, incapable of finding any truth anywhere, to be ruled by alternate doses of crude flattery and cruel punishment, a fool, a liar, a coward, a perpetual cheat.

It is significant that not one Nazi leader has ever been associated with any great movement to uphold and strengthen the dignity and nobility of mankind. They came, like their vile creed, from an underworld of despair and hate. To oppose these men and their evil doctrine We must not only summon our armed forces, wave our flags and sing our national anthems, but we must go deeper and, by an almost mystical act of will, hold to our faith and our hope.

We have to fight this great battle not only with guns in daylight, but alone in the night, communing with our souls, strengthening our faith that in common men everywhere there is a spring of innocent aspiration and good will that shall not be sealed. This is the real test. If we have men on our side who don't share this faith and hope, then let them leave us and join the armies of despair. But whoever shares this faith and hope, no matter to what race they belong or what language they speak, let them be welcomed as allies. And this test remains for all policies from now on. If such policies, and all the actions resulting from them, enlarge and strengthen this faith, this great hope, then they will help us to victory, the only victory worth having, the final conquest of despair. Any sly, nasty, vindictive, utterly cynical policies and actions belong not to our side but to the other despairing mind with which we are at war. And so much truth, at least, we have discovered on the long, hard road from August the Fourth 1914 to August the Fourth, 1940.[194]

*In a cold-eyed examination of Britain at war,* The Myth of the Blitz, *Angus Calder noted the difficulties of Priestley's role.*

While Churchill's matchless rhetoric could help sustain a will towards the aggression necessary to win the war, there is implicit in the developing Myth an understanding that England will be fully itself under a new, peacetime dispensation, in which qualities of friendliness and co-operative assistance, emphasised in war, will determine social relationships. So Priestley, as intimate Sunday-night broadcaster, has the difficult job of sustaining such hopes without creating frustration and yearning for peace.[195]

*Like other BBC contributors, Priestley was subject to censorship; all scripts had to be presented in advance and once approved, had to be strictly adhered to. However, his views on the sort of Britain that should emerge from the war appear to have escaped the red pen, drawing plaudits from Graham Greene – not always an admirer – for 'giving us an ideology',[196] 'for those dangerous months when the Gestapo arrived in Paris, he was unmistakably a great man'[197] but further infuriating 'hard-shell Tories'.[198]*

*Priestley's Postscripts were being heard by a third of Britain's entire adult population. 'Suddenly with these radio talks, I had millions and millions of fans. My mail arrived in bulging postbags. I couldn't ask for a drink in a bar without my voice being immediately recognised and people crowding round me.[199]*

*However, his popularity was breeding increasing disquiet in some circles. Immediately following the broadcast of 4 August, complaints about Priestley's perceived left wing bias were made to the BBC by the Government Chief Whip, Captain David Margesson, acting on behalf of a group of right wing Tories, scathingly described by Priestley as 'Captain Margesson's troupe of performing sea-lions'.[200]*

*Churchill's dislike of Priestley's constant stress on Peace Aims – made all the more potent by his huge popularity with the public – may also have been behind pressure exerted through the Ministry of Information. The ministry had been set up at the outset of the war to handle government propaganda with a remit that included liaison with the BBC. The former head of the BBC, Lord Reith, had been minister when Churchill took power in May 1940, but he at once removed Reith, replacing him with someone more reliably 'distanced' from the corporation, Duff Cooper, a close ally of Churchill since their joint opposition to Chamberlain's Munich 'piece of paper' in 1938.*

*Ironically Cooper himself admitted to Labour leader Clement Attlee that he had wanted a statement of Government peace aims to be made, but it had been vetoed by Churchill, who was willing to discuss the post-war world only in terms of international politics, not domestic issues. As a result, Cooper was obliged to block debate in the House of Commons on the issue.*[201]

*Priestley's theme for his next broadcast was a non-controversial one, but questions were already being raised within the BBC about his influence on public opinion and the debate would intensify in the following weeks, as he returned to contentious subjects.*

Sunday 1 September 1940

This is the last Sunday of the first year of the war. I want to go back tonight to the first Sunday, the very first day of the war. I'll close my eyes and then wait to discover that Sunday of a year ago. It's a queer process, this hurrying through the blackout of the closed eyes, to find at the other side of this darkness the rich wonderland of memory, reflection, imagination. We call it 'going inward', but surely the most inward world is the dense compact little world of our senses that's completely ruled by time. From that, we can only move outward; there's no other way. We can't retreat but must advance, in order to explore the vast golden globe of memory, reflection and imagination.

And now, here I am – it's that Sunday morning a year ago, and I am on my way up from the Isle of Wight, where I have been busy finishing a novel called Let the People Sing – yes, it was I who invented that phrase before the war – for it had been arranged weeks and weeks before that on Sunday the 3rd of September, I should broadcast the first chapter of my novel, and they said they still wanted it in spite of the terrible news. So there I was, and it was an exquisite calm morning; the little voyage from Cowes to Southampton was pleasanter than usual, and the London road was very quiet, even for a Sunday morning.

Nearer London, down the long hill from Bagshot, there did seem to be rather a lot of heavily loaded cars passing us, but nothing happened until we entered the long narrow street of Staines. It was then, clean out of a quiet blue, that all the sirens screamed at us. Beneath the astonished noonday sun, people in steel helmets came hurrying, shouting and gesticulating. It was then I learned that we had been at war for the last hour.

Caught by surprise in this crowded little town, jammed with people and cars, I must confess to having a moment of very real fear. As a civilian in the cheerful muddle of ordinary civilian life, surrounded by staring children and slow moving old folk, I didn't feel as I felt as a soldier; didn't know what might happen. I was for a moment terrified by the thought that it might be the worst I'd ever imagined, or, indeed, something unimaginable; a mumbling horror.

It is, of course, upon such fears, which are themselves the result of a newly won tenderness, a deepening piety, that the dictators depend for most of their power. From the beginning they've carefully taken into account other people's affections and decencies, and have struck at the places from which a growing civilisation has removed the armour. It is for this reason that no talk of treaties, or economic injustices, can ever excuse them as persons, for they and all their kind recognise the goodness in others as a weakness to be profited by; a bared breast for their daggers, and if this isn't evil, then nothing is.

But no bombs fell that morning, and we continued our journey into London, now a strange city of sandbags and shelters and first-aid posts. I knew then that the London I'd quitted so casually six weeks before had vanished for ever. Whatever might happen; I could never see that City again. It was at the end of one chapter of world history, while this strange City was at the beginning of another chapter.

Then, after packing some things I wanted at my Highgate house, in the middle of the afternoon, that hour so blank, colourless, tasteless on a hot Sunday, I rolled down through the long vacant roads of Kentish Town and Camden Town, which were as empty of life as old cities of the plague, into a Portland Place as quiet as a colour print, and then plunged, like another Alice down her rabbit hole, into Broadcasting House. There I seemed to have returned to the deep dugout life I'd once known among the chalk hills of the old French line. Down there the War was apparently in its second or third year. At any moment I felt I might be told to crawl out to a listening post, up towards Regent's Park. The tiny canteen where I had some tea was exactly like some frowsty Brigade Headquarters in the reserve line. The idea of reading my comic chapter into a microphone there now seemed more preposterous than ever. But there, gasping and wheezing a little, I read it, as many of you probably remember.

I was making my exit from London that evening by train from Paddington, and I never remember seeing streets so empty before. It was like going in a taxi through an immense deserted film set of a city, still illuminated by great yellow lights. Through this unreality I carried within me a companion feeling of unreality, not unlike that I remember having on my way to a Nursing Home for an operation; a rather chill sense of a dreamlike state. This didn't survive my entrance into Paddington, which was crowded and looked as if it had had six consecutive Bank Holidays. History was being made, and as I suspect is usual when history is being made, the place reeked of weary humanity. The platforms were thick with wastepaper, half-eaten buns and empty bottles, and everywhere mothers appeared to be feeding their young. The trains you felt had no longer the old particular destinations. They were simply going and perhaps would never return.

As soon as my train pulled out, perhaps because although the train was crowded I happened to be alone, I was back again in that dreamlike state of mind. As we moved through the western suburbs I stared up through the open window at the evening sky. Over in the west, hiding the dying sun, was the only patch of cloud to be seen, and it was shaped like a dragon. Do you remember that, any of you? Yes, a rampant dragon; etched in fire. The beast had been trapped inside the vast azure bowl. Against the exquisite fading blue, the barrage balloons glimmered like pearls, and they might have been a pattern of pearls, that had somehow been stitched on to the fabric of the evening sky. I don't ever remember seeing a nobler end to a day. It was the strings and clarinets and flutes bidding a high clear farewell to some lovely adagio. The light had grown unbelievably tender. How was it possible to believe that such a sky could spill ruin and death?

It caught at the heart – that sky; not the heart that is entirely human and can go home and be content, but that other homeless heart we all possess, which even when there's no war, is never at peace, but dimly recognises that long ago it was conscripted for a bitter campaign and nameless battles in the snow. The train gathered speed; the Bowl of Heaven paled and expanded, and the dragon smouldered and then utterly faded.

There's no time to tell you now by what adventures I came that night to occupy the last bed in Basingstoke. But little good it did me I remember, for all the night the army lorries went roaring beneath my window, and sometimes I heard men singing, just as I'd gone singing through an autumn night five and twenty years before. I'd time enough that night to wonder what was in store for us all; whether soon all our cities would be blazing, or there would be a long stalemate of huge entrenched armies. I never imagined then that before the next summer was over, Nazis would have swarmed like locusts, and have devoured like locusts, from Norway to the Pyrenees. And that the British Commonwealth alone would be defying both the Nazis and the Fascists, and not only defying them but answering blows with stouter blows. All that, and much more, was unforeseen, as I turned and wondered throughout that first night of the War.

But there was something that wasn't unforeseen, for I'd already written it down, and it has all come gloriously true. I guessed then what I have seen for myself since, and what I have told my overseas listeners more than once. The true heroes and heroines of this war, whose courage, patience and good humour stand like a rock above the dark morass of treachery, cowardice and panic, are the ordinary British folk.

Talk about giving courage and confidence – you've given me more than I could ever give you; not only courage and confidence in the outcome of this war, but also faith in what we can all achieve after this war. Not only for ourselves but for decent men and women throughout the world, who all await the hour when the dragons will fade from the sky.[202]

*Within a week of that broadcast, the Blitz had broken upon London. At first the Priestley family endured the bombing with their fellow-Londoners, as Jane Priestley related in a letter to the Davisons in America.*

11 September 1940

If you could see us this minute, I think you'd have to laugh. I am sitting on a mattress in the basement of my house in Highgate. Two mattresses are opposite and one on either side. Opposite are the cook and parlourmaid, on my left the housemaid, on my right the Master of the house. There is just room for our five mattresses.

Our ceiling is shored up with heavy timber held up by ten heavy beams, covered with fire proof paint. Our windows which only lead into the pantries, which in turn look on to a basement area, are covered with double wire netting. Every window is blacked out with thick black curtains so that down here we can have a bright light. We have our brightest Navajo rugs about which give a note of gaiety.

It is now 10.30 pm. The air raid sirens went just as we were finishing our early dinner at 8 pm and ever since the anti-aircraft guns have been banging away like huge muffled drums ..

We are all quite cheerful, the maids are flushed and rather excited. They chat and laugh and read. Jack keeps going into the next room where there is a typewriter – he has a half-written article. Every time he sits down to the typewriter our nearest guns start and make a terrific noise. At the moment he has given it up and is back on his mattress. Tonight we've heard more anti-aircraft fire than usual and not so much on consequence of the droning German planes. Last night when I slept alone under the kitchen stairs the enemy planes seemed to be over the house for hours. Jack was broadcasting to you and couldn't get home till 6 am.

I went to Bond St. this morning to have a suit tried on. My taxi had to make several detours to avoid streets roped off where bombs had fallen. I can't tell you how absolutely grand Londoners are. They seem to me to be much more calm and confident than I remember them in the last war. And already there is far more damage done than there was then...

We are shutting this house up for a few weeks as it is too difficult for Jack to get to and from the BBC. I am going with the maids to the country where we've volunteered to look after mothers and babies from London. If raids are less we shall be able to return.[203]

Priestley at the microphone, giving a Postscript broadcast.

Priestley playing Ludo with his children in a
service flat that the family occupied early in the
war at Whitehall Court, central London.

Playing piano accompaniment for daughter Mary on the violin – a photograph taken in 1941 at the Whitehall Court flat.

The first bombs fell on London on 24 August 1940, heralding the launch of The Blitz that soon spread to other cities.

Priestley's Postscript broadcasts celebrated the indomitable spirit of the unsung heroes who lived through the Blitz and came to terms with the immense damage it caused.

Unsung heroes give the thumbs up to the Queen Mother as she visits properties devastated by The Blitz.

Sheffield city centre in flames, dramatically captured by an intrepid photographer following a bombing raid in December 1940.

Homes reduced to rubble in Wakefield. It is small wonder that ordinary Britons faced with such devastation drew great strength from Priestley's warm and uplifting broadcasts.

Even small towns such as Bridlington did not escape from bomb damage. The after-effects bred a sense of common purpose among his fellow citizens that Priestley dreamed of translating into peacetime.

Family portrait of Priestley, Jane, Rachel and Tom, thought to have been taken in the Lake District about 1942.

Churchill touring ruined Berlin. Behind him in the Jeep is Anthony Eden. Priestley admired Churchill, but the feeling was probably not mutual; his repeated calls for a statement of 'Peace Aims' to ensure a land fit for heroes infuriated Churchill and probably led to the termination of the Postscripts.

Churchill, Roosevelt and Stalin at the Three Powers Conference in February 1945. Priestley's hatred of Fascism was matched by his dislike of Communism, but his criticisms of Stalin did not diminish his liking for the Russian people.

Churchill gives his famous 'V' salute while campaigning in the 1945 General Election, in which Priestley unsuccessfully stood as an Independent.

Churchill arriving at Leeds Civic Hall on 27 June 1945, shortly after the VE Day celebrations. Less than two weeks later he was defeated in Labour's election landslide, when voters opted for a vision that Priestley had articulated in his wartime broadcasts.

Priestley on the balcony of his Moscow hotel during his visit to the Soviet Union in the autumn of 1945.

In typical pose at the typewriter, pipe in hand. This photograph was taken at the National Hotel, Moscow, during Priestley's 1945 visit.

Anti-nuclear protesters gather in Trafalgar Square at the start of the first CND Aldermaston March in April 1958. Although Priestley helped to found the movement, he felt he had done more than enough marching in the Great War and remained at his typewriter.

Michael Foot, who along with Priestley was one of the keynote speakers at the launch of the Campaign for Nuclear Disarmament on 17 February 1958.

The philosopher, Lord Bertrand Russell, who became the CND's first president with Priestley as vice-president.

Priestley in October 1975, arriving at Bradford University.

The classic Priestley pose captured in 1972 – the year he wrote a devastating critique of modern society.

A 1980 photograph of Priestley, age 86, in his library.

*Later the Priestleys took a house in Herefordshire to escape the bombing. Jane and the children remained in the country while Priestley travelled up to London to make his broadcasts from the BBC, staying in hotels, or with friends, or sometimes even sleeping in Broadcasting House. If his family were relatively safe, Priestley was very much in the danger zone – a fact brought home to him when twice in three days, he had hair's-breadth escapes.*

It was an extra broadcast to Canada, which I undertook with much grumbling, that probably saved my life. This was in September 1940. I had just moved into the Langham Hotel, to be close to Broadcasting House and the late-night job. I had done two broadcasts on the Sunday, and would be up late again on Tuesday, so, being free on Monday night, I decided to go to bed early for the sleep I badly needed. But then a message came from across the road begging me to do an extra broadcast on the Blitz specially for Canada. Growling and cursing, I agreed to do it, and left the Langham for Broadcasting House while the going was still good.

I never returned to the Langham. That was the night when bombs fell all round Broadcasting House. The room in which I had planned to enjoy an early night was in that part of the hotel which was sliced off by a bomb. Probably that early night would have lasted for ever. Two days later I ran into Edward Hulton, who invited me to spend my first free night in the shelter bedroom he had had constructed below the basement of his house in Mayfair. The prospect was delightful – at last I could get out of my clothes (I said at the time that I had always looked as if I slept in my clothes and that now I actually did), and huddle luxuriously between clean sheets. This I prepared to do, slowly and with satisfaction, disregarding the remote sounds from the mad world above. But it was a night of incendiaries. I was just about to enjoy those clean sheets when I had to jump into my clothes again. The house was on fire.

The bright eyes of danger have never fascinated me. If I am not quite a coward, I am much closer to being one than I am to being any sort of hero. Yet I can honestly declare that on the whole I enjoyed that time, those splintered nights, those mornings when the air was the freshest ever tasted. Even later, during the buzz-bomb time, when I appeared to be firewatching every night in Albany, where I lived, and had to make do with about two hours' sleep, so that afterwards exhaustion struck me down and I was hurried into an operating theatre, I liked living in a West End that suddenly seemed to be empty. We were all an improvement on our unendangered selves. No longer suspicious of gaiety, we almost sparkled. What more than half the English fear and detest is not threatened disaster, material insecurity, sacrifice or danger, but boredom. They should be offered crises, not guarantees of prosperity and security. There is of course among us, too widely reflected in our legislation, a minority of life-haters, enemies of everything sensuous and generous, adventurous and creative.[204]

# Chapter 9
# Survival as a free people

*Despite his popularity with the public, pressure from Priestley's right wing critics was intensifying, fuelling debate within the BBC about the desirability of continuing with him. Although the* Radio Times *had described him as 'the prince of Postscripters, the voice of Britain, the apostle of sturdy common sense', the Director of Talks, Sir Richard Maconachie, raised the question 'whether any single person should be given the opportunity of acquiring such an influence, to the exclusion of others.'* [205] *Meanwhile, Priestley carried on, undaunted.*

Sunday 8 September 1940

There are people who really enjoy being in danger. They fall in love with what seems to them its beautiful bright face. An immediate threat of destruction and death makes them feel more alive than they are at ordinary times. Danger wakes them up and gives the mere act of living a fine flavour. Now I'm not one of those people myself. I don't like being in danger. I've too much imagination, thank you. You can't live for years by using and developing your imagination without also becoming a rather apprehensive type of person.

In my time I've been to a doctor to have some test or other, and in three seconds of his silence I've promptly given myself some frightful incurable disease, kept myself dying by inches, and then buried myself, to learn then that there was nothing the matter with me. Which ought to remind us, by the way, that we're always in danger, and that once past the age of twenty or so we know that the deaths we call violent, coming straight out of the blue, are the most merciful. But I'll admit that these noble reflections don't reconcile me to being in danger. I lived dangerously for long spells in the last war, and when that war was over I decided from then on I would be a comfortable pipe-and-slippers man and keep as close to cowardice as possible.

I mention these facts so that you'll understand, in what follows, that you're listening to a frail fellow citizen and not to one of these fire-eating heroes who occasionally find their way to the microphone. So when I talk of danger, I mean just what most of you mean, and I don't enjoy it. But like you, I try to carry on as cheerfully as I can, and don't do badly at it.

The fact that now we are nearly all at least within reach of danger seems to me one of the better and not one of the worse features of this war. I consider this an improvement on the last war, in which civilians, who developed some most unpleasant characteristics, lived in security while young men were mown down by the million. Twenty-five years ago we were preparing for the Battle of Loos, where on a six-mile front we had between fifty and sixty thousand casualties. This was good going but the following summer we did much better. On the 1st of July, 1916, there were whole towns in the north - my own amongst them - that lost at a stroke the fine flower of their young manhood. Almost every companion of my schooldays perished that morning. There never was such sudden terrible reaping. To have been a civilian then, sitting at ease while the telegrams arrived at every other house and the casualty lists grew and grew, must have been unendurable.

We are much better off now. At least we are sharing such danger as there is, and are not leaning back watching all our young men wither away. Strictly speaking, we're no longer civilians, and I think it was a pity that in the earlier months of this war the authorities were so emphatic that we were civilians, a helpless passive lot, so many skins to save, so much weight of tax-paying stuff to be huddled out of harm's way. We see now, when the enemy bombers come roaring at us at all hours, and it's our nerve versus his, that we're not really civilians any longer but a mixed lot of soldiers – machine-minding soldiers, milkmen and postmen soldiers, housewife and mother soldiers – and what a gallant corps that is – and even broadcasting soldiers. Now and then, I feel, we ought to be paraded, and perhaps a few medals handed out.

Two days ago, an oldish man came to see me about an inventory, for he was employed by an estate agent, and he mentioned mildly at the end of the meeting that he was still feeling rather disturbed because a few days before a bomb had arrived in his front garden and brought the whole house down on the little sitting-room where he and his wife were taking shelter, and they had had to be taken out of the wreckage. And there he was, homeless himself, coolly going through our inventory. Yes, I think a few medals would do no harm.

We haven't, of course, quite settled down yet to this soldier-civilian life; we haven't all adopted the same technique, and there are wild differences of opinion. I've been noticing these differences all this last week because some workmen have been doing a very necessary job outside my house, and I haven't been able to avoid overhearing their heated arguments. These chaps represented all the familiar attitudes. One man insisted on working on during the alarms and roundly declared, in my hearing, that anybody who went off to a shelter was no better than a Fifth Columnist – in fact, was a so-and-so Fifth Columnist, which seemed to me a bit severe. Another, at the opposite extreme of opinion, legged it for a shelter as soon as he heard the sirens. The other two, like most of us, avoided these extremes, and now tried this way and now tried that.

It's a good thing, by the way, during these weeks of battle – for that is what they are, and we're all in it – to take a very tolerant line about differences of opinion, to remember that we're all fellow soldiers, to make more and not less allowance than usual for the astonishing queerness of other folk, to be more polite and considerate and, indeed downright friendly than ever before, just because we are sharing a battle. It would do us no harm to imagine that everybody we meet during the day, even if it is only to buy or sell some little thing, has been encountered in the smoke and fury of the battlefield.

After all, you know, just now we're not really obscure persons tucked away in our offices and factories, villas and back streets; we're the British people being attacked and fighting back; we're in the great battle for the future of our civilisation; and so instead of being obscure and tucked away, we're bang in the middle of the world's stage with all the spotlights focused on us; we're historical personages, and it's possible that distant generations will find inspiration, when their time of trouble comes, in the report in their history books of our conduct at this hour; just as it is certain that our airmen have already found a shining place for ever in the world's imagination, becoming one of those bands of young heroes, creating a saga that men can never forget.[206]

Sunday 15 September 1940

There is no evidence to suggest that Herr Hitler and Marshal Goering are well-read in English literature, and I should doubt if they ever spent much time with Pickwick Papers. But their attention ought to be drawn to Chapter Ten of that immortal work, in which chapter Samuel Weller makes his first appearance.

He was, if you remember, cleaning boots in the yard of the White Hart Inn, when a smart chambermaid called over the balustrade of the gallery, 'Sam.'

'Hello', replied Sam.

'No. 22 wants his boots.'

Sam replied: 'Ask 22 whether he'll have them now or wait till he gets 'em.''

'Come, don't be a fool, Sam,' said the girl coaxingly, 'the gentleman wants his boots directly.'

'Well, you are a nice young 'ooman for a musical party, you are,' said Sam. 'Look at these 'ere boots; eleven pair of boots, and one shoe as belongs to No.6 with a wooden leg. The eleven boots is to be called at half-past eight and the shoe at nine. Who's No. 22 that's to put all the others out. No, no, "regular rotation," as Jack Ketch said when he tied the man up. "Sorry to keep you a-waiting, Sir, but I'll attend to you directly".'

That's Sam Weller, and there seems to me nearly all the true cockney spirit, independence, ironic humour, cheek and charm shown in that tiny bit of dialogue. A lot of us, especially if we are from the North, and thought we knew everything, imagined that that old cockney spirit was dead and gone. We thought the Londoner of today, catching his tubes and electric trains, was a different kind of fellow altogether, with too many of his corners rubbed off, too gullible, easily pleased, too soft;

and we were wrong. This last grim week has shown us how wrong we were. The Londoners, as the Americans are saying, can take it, and London itself – this grey sea of a city – can take it.

The fact that the savage indiscriminate bombing of the city has seized the world's imagination is itself a tribute to the might and majesty of London. There was a time when, like many north-countrymen who came South, I thought I disliked London; it had vast colourless suburbs that seemed to us even drearier than the ones we had left behind. We hated the extremes of wealth and poverty that we found, cheek by jowl in the West End, where at night the great purring motorcars filled with glittering women passed the shadowy rows of the homeless, the destitute, the down-and-out.

The life here in London seemed to us to have less colour, less gaiety then life in capitals abroad, and at the same time to have less character and flavour than the life we remembered in our provincial cities. And so on and so forth. But on these recent nights, when I have gone up to high roofs and have seen the fires like open wounds on the vast body of the city, I've realised, like many another settler here, how deeply I've come to love London, with its misty, twilit charm, its hidden cosiness and companionship, its smoky magic.

The other night, when a few fires were burning so fiercely, that half the sky was aglow, and the tall terraces around Portland Place were like pink palaces in the Arabian Nights, I saw the Dome and Cross of St. Paul's, silhouetted in sharpest black against the red flames and orange fumes, and it looked like an enduring symbol of reason and Christian ethics seen against the crimson glare of unreason and savagery. 'Though giant rains put out the sun, here stand I for a sign.'

In a supreme battle for the world's freedom, there can be no doubt that you and I are now in the midst of such a battle, there are only two capital cities in the world that are worthy of figuring in its portrait – one of them is Paris, city of quick barricades and revolutions, now temporarily out of the fight, not because its brave people lost heart but rather because they lost interest and so allowed banal men, intriguers greedy for wealth and power and all the enemies of a people on the march, to deceive and betray them.

The other city is great London, which during the last thousand years – and what are the wobblings and timidities of the last ten years compared with the nine hundred and ninety that went before – has many a time given itself a shake and risen to strike a blow for freedom, and not only its own freedom but that of men everywhere. In this capacity, as any European history book will show you, it is in sharp contrast to Berlin which has never yet been regarded as a beacon light by the free spirit of mankind. But London has often been seen as such a beacon light. Even the chief revolutionaries of our time lived here in their day and were nourished on books paid for by London citizens. And now, in the darkest hour, it blazes again; yes, because the incendiary bombs have been rained upon it but also because its proud defiance and unconquerable spirit have brought to men and women all over the world renewed hope and courage.

This, then, is a wonderful moment for us who are here in London, now in the roaring centre of the battlefield, the strangest army the world has ever seen, an army in drab civilian clothes, doing quite ordinary things, an army of all shapes and sizes and ages of folk, but nevertheless a real army, upon whose continuing high and defiant spirit the world's future depends.

Much has been made, both here and overseas, of the fine courage and resolution of the London citizen, and especially of all the people in the various air-raid services, and our most inspiring voice, that of the Prime Minister, has told us of our high destiny. But I venture to think that not enough has been made of two facts. First, that we are not civilians who have happened to stray into a kind of hell on earth, but that we are soldiers fighting a battle. And this isn't a mere figure of speech and shouldn't be regarded as such, because I am certain it would be wiser to treat persons doing essential work in certain areas on a military basis, removing all people not doing essential work from such areas and providing the rest, the front-line troops of our battle of London, with all necessary shelter, food and transport.

Some of us said long before this blitzkrieg began that the pretence that life was more or less normal for everybody was a very dangerous one. It's better to say outright, now we're all going to have a jolly good shake up, but only in order to carry on all the better. Most people don't mind that - they rather like it, but, of course, nobody likes being bombed at all odd hours; to go home as I did the other morning at dawn and notice that a large bus has been flattened like a tin toy against the second storey of a building, is to feel, to say the least of it, that things are becoming most rum and peculiar.

Which brings me to the second fact that's been understressed. It is that we have not suddenly entered upon a new and quite lunatic way of living with the prospect of months and months and months of sirens and shelters and bombs before us (which is what some authorities appear to imagine), but that we have been flung into a battle – a real terrific honest-to-God battle – perhaps the most important this war will see, and that, therefore, we must summon up all the courage and resolution and cheerfulness we possess and stick it out until the battle is over. As a kind of civilian life this is hellish, but as battles go, it is not at all bad – with some shelter, meals arriving fairly regularly and a quick rescue of the wounded. But I am not giving this advice to the cockneys – they don't need any from me, only an apology for ever imagining their old spirit had left them, and a stare of admiration. They can say to Herr Hitler and Marshal Goering (who really will have to read Pickwick) what Sam Weller said: 'Sorry to keep you waiting, Sir, but I'll attend to you directly.'[207]

*Although in those early months of the war, Priestley's broadcasts often reflected the thoughts and concerns of ordinary Britons better than any other public figure, in some areas, not least his attitude to the role of women, he was far in advance of most of his countrymen.*

Sunday 22 September 1940

... There's a familiar type of masculine mind that believes that women should have nothing to do with political and public life. Woman's place, they tell us, is in the home. It's largely the same mind, I believe, that then muddles away so that the home is put on short rations and then bombed.

Privately I've believed for years the opposite of this – that a great deal of political and public life is nothing but large-scale common-sense housekeeping, and that as women have an almost terrifying amount of common-sense and the ones who are good at housekeeping are very good at it, then the sooner some of our communal and national affairs are managed by women the better. The same kind of man would say at once that women would make a mess of it; to which we can retort that it would be hard to make a bigger mess than men have made during the last twenty-five years, culminating in the world-wide idiocy of today.

Moreover, please notice this, that where all the worst mischief has been started women have had the least say in affairs. For example, high finance and big business have not exactly played a brilliant part in our life during these last years, and it's well known that women are entirely unfit to intervene in these matters. Then we know that the Nazis and the Fascists from the first swept aside all thought of co-operation with their womenfolk, whom they regarded as mere breeding stock or toys to amuse the tired warrior.

You can easily imagine that there weren't any women in Germany and Italy – no wondering, suffering, sorrowing mothers, wives, sisters, sweethearts – nothing but trampling, bragging, swaggering, idiotic males, silly little boys who've somehow grown to be the size of men. You'd have thought, too, that at the mere first sight of the neurotic, screaming Hitler and of his gang of toughs that all the women would have risen in instant revolt and have cried that such men were unfit to control the destiny of even one single schoolboy. That they didn't is our tragedy – resulting in a war that seems to me to hit harder at women than it does at men.

For this is total war; and total war is war right inside the home itself, emptying the clothes cupboards and the larder, screaming its threats through the radio at the hearth, burning and bombing its way from roof to cellar. It's ten times harder being a decent housewife and mother during such a war than it is being a soldier. You have to make a far greater effort to keep going, for you've no training and discipline to armour you. The soldier has his own responsibilities, but when he assumed them he was released from a great many others; whereas his womenfolk know no such release, but have more and more responsibility piled upon them. And they needn't even be wives and mothers. Nothing has impressed me more in this bombing battle of London than the continued high courage and resolution, not only of the wives and mothers but also of the crowds of nurses, secretaries, clerks, telephone girls, shop assistants, waitresses, who morning after morning have turned up for duty neat as ever – rather pink about the eyes, perhaps, and smiling rather tremulously, but still smiling.

Here's this big bully, Goering, who for six years has been given all the resources of Germany to create the most terrible and merciless weapon of oppression Europe had ever known – the German air force; and he arrives in Northern France to command it himself, and to tell it to do its worst; and there are launched all the thunderbolts of the new Teutonic fury, and the whole world holds its breath. And what happens? Why, a lot of London girls – pale-faced little creatures living on cups of tea and buns, who go tripping from tiny villas and flats with their minute attache-cases to Tubes and buses and then to offices and shops – defy this Goering and all his Luftwaffe and all their high explosives and incendiaries and machine-guns – and successfully defy them, still trotting off to work, still carrying on, still trim and smiling. Isn't that a triumph?

I've just had a message from an American friend, concluding with this cry: 'What a great race you are!' But I shall tell him that our men wouldn't be so fine if our women at this fateful hour were not so magnificent. There isn't an airman, submarine commander, or unnamed hero in a bomb squad who hasn't behind him at least one woman, and perhaps half a dozen women, as heroic as himself.

Not that everybody rises at once, of course, to the heights – there are bad gaps in the roll of honour; for instance, spending an odd night in a village where my own womenfolk were busy trying to arrange for the billeting of mothers and babies who've been bombed out of the East End, I was shocked to learn that some middle-class women in that neighbourhood, with any amount of room to spare in their houses, made every excuse to avoid receiving any of these mothers and babies.

I feel sure that if such women had been in London lately they would have soon changed their minds – which perhaps lack imagination rather than goodwill. But if they know – and still don't care – then they ought to be ashamed of themselves. It means they belong still to the world that's brought itself, and us, into this hell of senseless destruction and suffering –a world of cold narrow minds, of greed, privilege and love of power. And we're fighting not merely to keep the German jackboot off our necks but also to put an end once and for all to that world, and to bring into existence an order of society in which nobody will have far too many rooms in a house and nobody have far too few.

And all wondering, suffering women – some of them homeless, lost, with bewildered small children in their arms – should be told here and now that that is what we're all struggling and battling for. Not for some regrouping on the chessboard of money and power politics; but for new and better homes – real homes – a decent chance at last – new life. And every woman should remember that – keep the promise locked in her heart, and when the time comes, with one voice-and, if necessary, with that full feminine fury which is among the most awe-inspiring phenomenon – demand that the promise be redeemed, so that the children now hurried through the shelters can one day walk in the sunlight, and build upon our ruins a glorious new world.[208]

*Priestley's stress on the war-work of women reflected his belief that, 'I don't think most people realised, that the British called up a larger proportion of their population for war service than any other country; far more than Nazi Germany, women and all.'* [209] *Priestley also celebrated women's war work in a propaganda book,* British Women Go To War, *pointing out that their role was doubly vital because Germany's population was almost twice as large as that of Britain.*

Our survival as a free people depended up on our adequate use of manpower. Unless we made the very most of what we had, we could not hope to survive. We had seventeen million adult women in this island. It was urgently necessary that women should play their part in the war effort... agreements were reached [with the unions] relaxing existing rules and customs... doors that had been closed to women for years were now opened...

Essential industry, from shipbuilding and heavy ordnance work down to the mass production of tiny parts for time fuses, was invaded by women... Some people, who grumble loudly about idle young women in cocktail bars, forget that appearances are deceitful, and that just as able-bodied young men in civilian clothes sometimes turn out to be fighter-pilots on leave, so, too, the young women in skirts and jumpers or coats and slacks, caught gossiping in a cocktail bar, may very well have been recently ferrying planes, driving ambulances in air raids, or working among the TNT in a Filling Factory.[210]

*Priestley was prompted to write what became one of his best loved 'Postscripts', on both sides of the Atlantic, by a return visit to inspect bomb damage in his home city of Bradford. An American reporter travelled with him and described Priestley at work.*

The room looks down on to a square in the heart of a bustling Northern city. It is a square that throbs with life – a flowing stream of traffic, hurrying pedestrians; shouting newsboys, and the occasional overhead shriek of a train somewhere.

Detached from it all, yet part and parcel of that Northern scene, as he absorbs and reflects its bustle, a squarely built man in a rough blue sports jacket sits near the window tapping away at a typewriter. A pipe droops from one corner of his mouth. Half-a-dozen other pipes – all veterans – lie ready to hand. The morning's papers drape the bed and a sheaf of letters, telegrams, and manuscript crowd the hairbrushes on the dressing-table.

That was a picture I carried away with me the other day of Britain's No. 1 spokesman to the people of North America – J.B. Priestley, essayist, novelist, playwright, and now broadcaster with the biggest regular listening audience in the world.

Priestley fans in this country, and they number millions, hear him only once a week, when he gives his Sunday-night Poststript. Across the other side of the Atlantic a still larger fan army tunes in to Britain three times a week to listen to the man who is talking to them from three thousand miles away. That transatlantic audience has just finished its supper and is at uneasy peace with the world. Here it is 2.30 in the morning. As often as not bombs are dropping uncomfortably near, but Priestley talks on, unrattled and unperturbed, sane, sound, and Yorkshire homespun in accent and philosophy...

This dynamic Yorkshireman works incessantly from the moment of rising, through a long day of material-hunting, interviews, visits to factories, and script and article writing, until he says goodnight to America in the small hours.

He is often busiest when he is just mooning around the streets of the town. One delightful afternoon was spent in Bradford just roaming around, looking for the shops and the queer corners he knew as a lad. That afternoon provided the delightful story of the pie which has been steaming away in a shop window for forty-five years. Maybe you heard that story in a recent postscript. Priestley told it to America as well.

We nosed around the covered market, browsed over bookstalls, and searched out the little eating-shops where the patrons sit in pews and demolish large helpings of everything. Flaming flower-stalls with their pools of water on the stone flags evoked memories of funerals – with or without personal associations. There was always an imperishable tradition of handsome wreaths about those stalls. 'And where's that music shop got to?' asked Priestley. 'The assistants were fixtures.'

This was the spokesman of Britain, at work – noting, memorising, and building up from a dozen casual conversations with ordinary folk a picture of Britain today – a picture he will present to thousands of the ordinary folk of America. [211]

*The 'Pie Postscript' was fondly remembered by hordes of listeners, but in later years Priestley would be infuriated that despite a lifetime of literary achievement, what people would most readily remember was the homespun tale of the Bradford pie shop.*

Sunday 29 September 1940

Perhaps the only solidly real place we ever know is the place in which we spent our childhood and youth. It's there there are genuinely real streets, squares, shops and houses, and their only fault is that they have a trick, like the queer cards that conjurers sometimes use, of appearing diminished every time we go back to have another look at them.

I was thinking this when I returned the other afternoon to my native city of Bradford, where I went to see what damage had resulted from a recent air-raid. And, as I anticipated, it was far more of a shock to see a few burnt-out buildings in this town than it had been to see all the damage in London. It was astonishing to discover that the familiar large drapery store and the old chapel were no longer there, and that in their places were some blackened ruins with odd pillars and bits of walls still standing, which had an unexpectedly dignified look about them; not the now familiar ignoble and now almost obscene sight of bombed buildings, with their pitiful broken rafters and motionless cataracts of debris, but rather picturesque ruins with a hint of Pompeii or Herculaneum about them. But I think the sight made a far deeper impression upon me than all the bombing I had seen for weeks and weeks in London, because it somehow brought together two entirely different worlds; the safe and shining world of my childhood, and this insecure and lunatic world of today, so it caught and held my imagination.

I was appalled by the sheer stupidity of it; these Nazi airmen had flown hundreds and hundreds of miles in order to destroy a draper's shop, part of a cinema and a market, an old chapel, and so on; nothing that made the least difference to our war effort, nothing that couldn't be soon replaced – except, of course, the old walls of the chapel. Even already the drapers have taken other premises, the market's open, and I've no doubt that the congregation of the old chapel has found hospitality, if perhaps an inferior brand of sermon, at other places of worship.

Moreover – and now we come to the point – the pie-shop and the pie were still there. I must explain about these. Ever since I could remember there'd been just at the back of this draper's a small eating-house that specialised in meat and potato pie; one of those little Dickensy places that still survive in provincial towns. I remembered it well, though I was never one of its customers, because there'd always been on view in the window, to tempt the appetite of the passer-by, a giant, almost superhuman, meat and potato pie with a magnificently brown, crisp, artfully wrinkled, succulent looking crust. And not only that – and now we approach the marvellous, the miraculous – out of that pie there came at any and every hour when the shop was doing business, a fine rich appetising steam to make the mouth water even as the very window itself was watering

There it was, a perpetual volcano of a meat and potato pie. And that steaming giant pie was to my boyish mind and, indeed, to my adult mind, for we never forget these things – as much an essential part of my native city as the Town Hall and its chimes.

Now, I'd heard that this shop and its famous steaming pie had been destroyed in the raid, and so when I went to see what had happened, I'd made up my mind that I would stand in the ruins of that shop, catching perhaps a last faint lingering whiff of that steam, and would compose some kind of lament or elegy. But, I found that the shop hadn't finished, but was there, wide open, and doing business. True, it was showing a few scars, and instead of the window, it had been neatly boarded up, but there was a square opening in the middle of the painted boarding and there, seen through the opening, framed perhaps a little narrowly but in itself as magnificent as ever, was the great pie, still brown, crisp, succulent, and steaming away like mad. Every puff and jet of that steam defied Hitler, Goering, and the whole gang of them. It was glorious.

Now, the owner himself, an elderly man with one of those 'folded-in' Yorkshire faces, and character written all over him, was standing just inside the doorway. So I asked him, in my delight and relief, what had happened. He replied shortly, and, indeed, rather grumpily that the shop had had its front blown out but was now open, as I could see, and that the famous pie hadn't been damaged at all, because it was his habit when closing the shop to remove this noble trademark to a place of safety.

As he said this I could feel his hand on my back and a distinct sensation of being gently but firmly pushed into the street, where, the hand hinted, I belonged. Rather grieved by his suspicious reception, I went further along to have a closer look at the neighbouring ruins. I had not been there more than a minute or two before I was clapped on the shoulder, and there was the pie-man again, this time wearing his coat and not wearing his apron, holding out a hand and beaming at me.

It seems that his wife recognised my voice. I am not telling this for my own glory, though I must say it's one of the most handsome compliments I ever received. And so after doing a quick change with his apron and coat, he came round after me. He didn't admit as much; indeed, we never went into the question, but I think that he'd imagined that I was some trade rival – no doubt I have a look of the younger ambitious pie-man about me – who was anxious to discover after years of unsuccessful fifth-column work the secret of the famous steaming pie.

Now, this secret was revealed to me, without my even asking, by its owner, all smiles and friendship and confidence, but, of course, I can't pass it on to all you people, but I will say this: that suspicions I'd entertained ever since the age of fourteen about that giant pie, for ever jetting forth its fragrant steam, were now amply confirmed.

'Ai,' said the pie-man proudly, 'it's a secret, that pie is, and a rare lot 'ud like to know how it's done. I've had it five and forty years, that same pie, and luckily I'd put it away in a good safe place same as usual, so as soon as we got started again, and we wasn't long I can tell you, and I get's window boarded up, I got pie out again. There's only one thing,' he added wistfully, 'that 'ole I'd left in the centre of the boarding to see the pie through. Ai, well, it's not quite big enough.'

I wanted to tell him that that was a national fault of ours. We have the pie, and nobody's going to take it from us, but we do have a habit of boarding it up a bit too closely, and we need to open out and to give the people a better look at the pie, and give the pie a better sight of the people. And now, I suppose, all my more severe listeners are asking each other why this fellow has to go on yapping about his pies and nonsense at a time like this when the whole world is in a turmoil, the fate of empires is in the balance, and men, women and children are dying terrible violent deaths; to which I can only reply, that we must keep burnished the bright little thread of our common humanity that still runs through these iron days and black nights; and that we are fighting to preserve and, indeed, I hope to enlarge that private and all-important little world of our own reminiscence and humour and homely poetry in which a pie that steamed for forty-five years and successfully defied an air-raid to steam again has its own proper place.[212]

## Sunday 6th October 1940

The other evening I was going by car down the western side of England, on my way to do a certain job. I was being driven by an engineer in the employ of a well-known public corporation. It was an unpleasant evening, chilly, damp, with rain threatening, and dusk coming far too early. It seemed as if winter was only just round the corner. This may explain why our talk along the road was more grim than gay.

The engineer grumbled because his subsistence allowance was now less than it had been before the war, having been reduced by some strange officials who imagined that prices would be less in wartime. I grumbled at the evening and said I'd rather be faced with a desperate war in summer than any kind of war in winter. He said that travelling, which he had to do continually, was a wearing game these days for sometimes it took him an hour or two at the end of a long day to find any sort of bed. I replied, with my eye on the sad, early dusk, conjuring up thoughts of a 4.30 blackout, that now was the time for our leaders to use a little imagination, to light beacons in this gathering darkness, to warm our hearts and set fire to our minds, by proclaiming noble and universal aims; by so ordering affairs in this country that we might serve as an example to the world, not merely in courage and endurance, but in bold and hopeful planning for the future, releasing in us great creative forces. Just a little imagination, that's all, I added.

My companion, a sceptic, said he hoped we'd see it. I said that I hoped we would, too; and by this time the last glimmer of daylight had vanished, and we were crawling through a rainy darkness. I said we'd better stop at the next town and put up for the night. The engineer said that it would be a good idea to start trying to find beds at the next town.

We arrived there – nothing to be seen, of course – but I knew which it was and remembered it as being a pretty little place. We were told that of the three hotels, there only one had been left open to the public, so we went to that one, where I enquired for two rooms; or at least two beds. This seemed to amuse them; no beds to be had there. I gathered, though it wasn't exactly mentioned, that there wouldn't be vacant rooms there for months. So I telephoned to other hotels further along our route and they laughed merrily, too, and hinted that they had been full for weeks and would remain full for months.

I said that there appeared to be a surprising number of people travelling in these rather out-of-the-way parts, and was told that all these guests weren't travellers, but resident guests; people who had settled in these hotels to be out of the way of sirens and anti-aircraft guns, and bombs. Well, that was all right. Nobody in their senses wants a noisy night in a shelter if a quiet night in bed is to be had at all; though this arrangement did seem rather tough luck on all those people who have to be travelling about the country on what might be urgent business. Eventually, through the personal attention of one landlord, we did manage to obtain a room and a couple of beds, and were able to say good-bye to the black, dripping road.

It was after that, and after comparing notes with several knowledgeable persons, that I began to meditate, sombrely, perhaps being influenced by the night, on one of the smaller ironies of this war here; and it's this, that a large proportion of the people who are able to live in comparative peace, security and quiet, consists, not of persons recovering from overwork, strain or shock, but those persons who don't know what to do with themselves. I don't say for a moment that it's their fault. Many of them no doubt have tried, over and over again, to find some useful wartime occupation before settling into these remote and charming places; and, so far as this is the case, they are to be pitied and not envied. Some of them have been made to feel useless, first by stupid parents, and afterwards by a badly organised community, all their lives.

This has, for a long time now, been a country in which there are far too many pleasant, able-bodied persons who, because of some system of private incomes or pensions and all kinds of snobbish nonsense, are condemned to yawn away their lives, forever wondering what to do between meals; in startling contrast to the other people who wonder how to get it all done between meals.

This is undoubtedly true of certain types of women, who have been made so comfortably secure by timid parents that they have been shut out of the whole adventure of living. The bitterest letters I have received during these past few months, have not been from men, piloting fighters or bombers, or stoking minesweepers, or from women nursing under fire, or looking after evacuated babies, but from ladies doing nothing in inland resorts, where their energy is all turned inward instead of outward, turning into hostility instead of into helpfulness and fun.

So don't think I'm blaming anybody personally. But the situation is, you must admit, rather peculiar. It's as if you went to one hospital in a town and found most of the beds occupied by people who had nothing to do and thought they would have an afternoon's snooze. And if at the same time in this town you found scores of injured persons lying about the pavement, you might reasonably come to the conclusion that things were badly managed in that town.

Well, of course, we don't have injured persons lying about the pavement for long. But, on the other hand, I do seem to have heard of and, indeed, to have seen, a great many mothers and children from badly bombed areas who have been got away but not, so to speak, anywhere in particular, certainly not to nice, quiet rooms in pretty places where they might quickly recover from recent shocks. And some of them I am afraid have been regarded as a nuisance, which is just like treating a trainload of wounded soldiers as a nuisance.

I am not blaming anybody – I really don't know if anybody is to blame; but all this, with many more unpleasant little ironies besides, does suggest that, for all our grand, vague talk, we are at present floundering between two stools. One of them is our old acquaintance labelled 'Every man for himself, and the devil take the hindmost', which can't really represent us or else why should young men, for whom you and I have done little or nothing, tear up and down the sky in their Spitfires to protect us, or why should our whole community pledge itself to fight until Europe is freed.

The other stool, on which millions are already perched without knowing it, has some lettering round it that hints that free men could combine, without losing what's essential to their free development, to see that each gives according to his ability, and receives according to his need. That aspiration, which might have come from the merest and mildest sermon, used to shock our fathers and grandfathers, but we – who've seen a thousand things that would have shocked them still more, who've seen all hell let loose because men refuse to think properly and feel decently – are now being hammered into sterner stuff, and may even consider, before we've done, letting Sunday's sentiments spill over into Monday's arrangements, and acting out a mild sermon or two; and so prove that not only when we say we'll fight, we'll fight – which we have already done to the great astonishment of the Nazi leaders – but also that what we say we are fighting for is the very thing for which we are fighting; that here, at least, is no mere propaganda but blazing truth of the mind and heart.[213]

*Priestley's criticism of those on 'private incomes or pensions and all kinds of snobbish nonsense... condemned to yawn away their lives', provoked fresh outrage on the Right. The next day two senior civil servants at the Ministry of Information, Lord Davidson and Colonel Scorgie, complained that the latest 'Postscript' might have been 'calculated to set rich against poor and to annoy country districts'.[214]*

*Priestley was also open to a charge of hypocrisy in criticising those who had taken long-term occupancy of hotel rooms to escape the bombing, when he and Jane had also left Highgate for a cottage in rural Herefordshire, though Priestley was still in Central London several nights a week for his broadcasts from the BBC.*

*More seriously it was already known that Nazi propagandists had seized on the 'Postscript' and quoted it in a broadcast to Denmark to demonstrate that the British middle and upper classes were evading wartime dangers while leaving the lower classes to endure them. However the BBC Controller (Home), Patrick Ryan, offered at least a partial defence of Priestley in a meeting that afternoon, pointing out that, like Priestley's other broadcasts, his latest script had been passed by the MoI. He also warned that Priestley would not accept censorship and had the potential to 'raise Cain' if taken off the air.*

*Whether in response to the criticism from some quarters, or purely on his own initiative, Priestley informed Ryan later that week that he wanted 'a complete rest from broadcasting quite soon', arguing that he was tired after five months of late night overseas broadcasts in addition to his 'Postscripts', though he then went on to rail against 'silly little censorships of my script and the lack of any real co-operation with the authorities'.*[215]

*The BBC did not demur from his plan to take a break and two weeks later, on Sunday 20 October, he delivered the last of his first series of 'Postscripts'. He used it, defiantly, to have one further snipe at his critics and to restate his belief in the promise of a transformation of British society, not merely as a desirable result of the war but as the very key to victory.*

Sunday 20th October 1940

This is my last Sunday postscript for some time, perhaps the last I shall ever do. The decision was mine and was in no way forced upon me by the B.B.C. My relations with the B.B.C. are excellent. But I had some good reasons for wanting to stop; in the first place people get tired of hearing the same voice at exactly the same time each week, and I'd be the last man to want to add to the boredom and tedium of this war. I've always pleaded for more imagination in the handling of the war; more flags and less red tape; more music and fun, hard work and high jinks, and the least I can do when I am in danger of becoming one of the war bores myself, is to get out and so make a little change for you even if it's only on Sundays at 9.15...

Stupid persons have frequently accused me in public of – I use their own words – taking advantage of my position to bring party politics into my talks. This is extremely ironical because I am not a member of any political party. I've no close personal relations with any prominent members of any party, and no expectations from the success of any particular party, whereas it is obvious that these critics of mine are members of a political party and that their criticism comes from taking a narrow party line. It's not I, but they, who put party before country, for I've never even learnt to think in terms of a political party.

And the most I've asked for in these talks is that we should mean what we say; be really democratic, for example, while fighting for democracy; and that we should make some attempt to discover the deeper causes of this war and to try and find a remedy for them, thus making this a colossal battle, not only against something, but also for something positive and good. If all this, together with certain obvious elements of social justice and decency seems to you Socialism, Communism or Anarchy, then you are at liberty to call me a Socialist, a Communist or an Anarchist, though I would implore you to stop merely pasting on labels and instead to think a little.

There's a danger that as this high mood passes, apathy will return to some sections of the community and selfishness and stupidity to some other sections. Bear with me, those of you who disagree, for a last minute or two, while I try and explain as briefly as possible what I feel about this country and this war. I think it's true to say that at the present time this country of ours, because of its courage and its proud defiance, its determination to put an end to this international brigandage and racketeering of the Hitlers and Mussolinis and their riff-raff is the hope of all that is best in the world, which watches us with admiration. But our greatest potential ally is not this power or that, but the growing hope in decent folk everywhere that civilisation can be saved, or, should I say, the seeds of civilisation could be saved to take root and to flower afterwards; that a reasonable liberty along with a reasonable security can be achieved; that democracy is not an experiment that was tried and that failed, but a great creative force that must now be released again.

If we can make all these things plain to the world by the way in which we now order our lives here, then I don't believe this will even be a long war – the daylight will come soon and all these evil apparitions from the night of men's bewilderment and despair will vanish, but if apathy and stupidity return to reign once more; if the privileges of a few are seen to be regarded as more important than the happiness of many; if a sterile obstruction is preferred to creation; if our faces are still turned towards the past instead of towards the future; if too many of us will simply not trouble to know, or if we do know, will not care, then the great opportunity will pass us by, and soon the light will be going out again.

For this reason I make no apology to those listeners who, out of their impregnable fortresses of stupidity, have assured me of their hostility. I can only assure them that I propose to go on disliking more and more everything they stand for. To all the other listeners – a very large majority – I can offer whichever they prefer, apologies or thanks; apologies if they found a North-country accent is irritating or wearying, as some of us find other accents; if they wearied of me talking about myself, though sometimes the most honest way of discussing general topics is to be personal about them; if they became impatient because I couldn't – as I obviously couldn't convert a ten minutes postscript into a six hour political and economic lecture, and if they wrote letters, many of which I am afraid are still strewn all up and down the country, to which they expected a reply; and thanks, well, thanks for the thousands of pleasant letters, for all manner of little kindnesses and expressions of gratitude and, for listening.

I'll always be proud to remember how many times I caught your ear as we all marched through the blitzkrieg together. It might have been worse, mightn't it?[216]

*Although Priestley was at pains to absolve the BBC of any blame for his departure from the 'Postscripts' slot – 'it was at my own request, for I felt I had had my share of this peak hour and other men ought to be given a chance' – many of his listeners suspected he had been 'silenced', a view*

*expressed in numerous letters to Priestley himself and to the BBC, and in*
*Home Intelligence's Weekly Report No. 5, for 11 November 1940: 'From a*
*great number of sources there are reports of strong feelings because J.B.*
*Priestley's broadcasts have stopped. His views on social reform appear to be*
*shared by the great majority.'* [217]

*Writing soon after the event, Priestley took pride in the way his*
*broadcasts had touched so many people's hearts and lifted morale during the*
*darkest days of the war.*

Two important conclusions emerge from my experience of
broadcasting these Postscripts. The first, and less important is the
immense, the staggering power of broadcasting... Unfortunately the
only persons here who do not seem aware of this terrific power of the
broadcast word are the members of our War Cabinet, who still do not
realise that in the B.B.C. we have something as important to us in this
war, which is quite unlike previous wars, as an army or navy or air
force. The official under-valuation of this great medium of
communication and persuasion is to my mind one of the most serious
weaknesses of our war effort...

The second and more important conclusion that emerges from this
short chapter of broadcasting experience is that the British listening
public as a whole, and that means a gigantic cross-section of all our
people, responds immediately to any sincere attempt to use a little
insight and to penetrate beneath the surface of this conflict. The tricks
of the writing trade and some fortunate accidents of voice and manner
are all very well, but what really holds the attention of most decent folk
is a genuine sharing of feelings and views on the part of the broadcaster.
He must talk as if he were among serious friends, and not as if he had
suddenly been appointed head of an infants' school. People may be
almost inarticulate themselves and yet recognise in an instant when
something that is at least trying to be real and true is being said to
them. Thus it is useless handing out to most of them a lot of dope left
over from the last war. They may not understand this present war, but
unlike many official persons, they do know that it is not the last war,
that a simple, almost idiotic nationalism will not do, that either we are

fighting to bring a better world into existence or we are merely assisting at the destruction of such civilisation as we possess.

A final word. Many listeners, writing appreciative letters to which I am sorry I have never had time to reply, seem to have imagined from certain remarks of mine that most of my correspondents have been hostile and abusive. I apologise – if it was my fault – for conveying this impression, for the truth is that of the thousands of letters that these Postscripts brought me, only a very tiny minority were anything but warmly appreciative. And even most of these appeared to be in such a hurry to denounce what I said that they had not time to listen to what I said. But here... is what I actually did say, upstairs and downstairs in Broadcasting House and elsewhere, Sunday after Sunday, during those strange months when first the world wondered if each week would see the end of us, then afterwards drew a long breath of relief and admiration, as the common folk of this island rose to meet the challenge and not only saved what we have that is good but began to dream of something much better.[218]

*In later years Priestley was much more ambivalent about the huge popularity that the 'Postscripts' had brought him and the mere mention of them could be enough to provoke an irritable outburst from him.*

One of my activities was ridiculously overpraised, so much so that I dislike hearing it even mentioned... Those Sunday night Postscripts ... took about ten minutes to deliver, usually between half an hour and an hour to write. They were nothing more than spoken essays, designed to have a very broad and classless appeal. I meant what I said in them of course: a man is a fool if he tries to cheat the microphone. (Add television cameras, and an artful experienced performer can risk some insincerity.)

No doubt I had the right voice and manner, but then so had plenty of other men. I didn't see then – and I don't see now – what all the fuss was about. To this day middle-aged or elderly men shake my hand and tell me what a ten-minute talk about ducks on a pond or a pie in a shop window meant to them, as if I had given them King Lear or the

Eroica. I found myself tied, like a man to a gigantic balloon, to one of those bogus reputations that only the mass media know how to inflate. I never asked for it, didn't want it. This sudden tremendous popularity, which vanished in a few years and indeed was put into reverse by the same mass media, gave me no pleasure, merely made me feel a mountebank.

Voices cannot be disguised, and if I went into a crowded shop or bar all the people not only had to talk to me but also had to touch me – I had thousands of hands laid on me – as if to prove to themselves I was more than a disembodied voice. There are people who open out like flowers in such an atmosphere, gracefully and smilingly accepting all popular tributes. I have never pretended to be one of them.[219]

# Chapter 10
# Fitness to govern

*Whatever the right wing view of Priestley's domestic Postscripts, they had struck a chord with millions of Britons. His overseas broadcasts 'Britain Speaks' – aired 'several times a week, always very late at night, to America, the Dominions, and in fact, through recordings transmitted every hour or so, to all parts of the world where English was understood',[220] were also hugely popular, especially in Australia and Canada – though, as Priestley later sourly noted, 'when I visited these Dominions, all traces of this enthusiasm appeared to have vanished with victory'.[221] The broadcasts to the United States also arguably played a significant role in altering public sentiment about the war and support for Britain, aiding Churchill's principle diplomatic aim of securing America's participation in the war.*

*A succession of people were tried in Priestley's place in the domestic 'Postscripts' slot, including Emlyn Williams, Leslie Howard and AP Herbert, but none was anywhere near as popular with the public. Herbert began his reign with a snipe at his predecessor: 'There's a type of restless mind that must be forever shifting the furniture. It is the restless type of mind that allows itself to be teased by Hitler's chatter about the "new order in Europe" into insisting that we must offer a new order in Europe ourselves.' His message was not welcomed by his audience and he was little short of a disaster, drawing the lowest ever audience figures and attracting a barrage of criticism.*

*Whether on its own initiative or at Government prompting, BBC officials took steps to mollify Priestley and woo him back, sending him a series of flattering letters and offering him greatly increased fees and much better travel and accommodation arrangements for any future broadcasts. In January 1941, after high-level negotiations between BBC Controller, Home, Patrick Ryan, and Sir Walter Monckton, who was both Director-General of the MoI and an Under-Secretary at the Foreign Office, agreement was reached for a new series of Priestley 'Postscripts'.*

*He was initially booked to do six broadcasts but more would be 'considered' – he later wrote that it never occurred to him that an agreement to continue the series beyond those initial six was anything other than a formality. 'Popular clamour brought me back early in 1941. Now I made the talks rather larger and gave them more bite; they were more aggressively democratic in feeling and tone, and I soon ran into trouble with sections of the Tory Press and the Ministry of Information.'* [222]

*His first broadcast, on 26 January 1941, returned to the necessity of 'Peace Aims' and demanded social justice and a guarantee that there would be no repeat of the betrayal of the hopes and aspirations of returning servicemen that had occurred after the Great War.*

Sunday 26 January 1941

I'm sorry for the delay! Whenever possible during the last three months, I've listened to the Sunday night Postscripts, and like you I've been delighted by the charm and persuasiveness of the various speakers, no matter whether they'd learnt the trick of it in the law courts or in Shaftesbury Avenue.

The matter could be more easily criticised than the manner, but three statements seem to emerge from all these talks: ONE: that the ordinary common folk of this country, who so far have had more to withstand than anybody else in this war, are brave, patient, humorous, wonderful people; TWO: that Hitler and his associates are bad and dangerous men; THREE: that we shall win the war.

Three excellent statements, of course, but they don't seem to take us very far. There are people who feel such statements are taking us quite far enough, like the anonymous man who took the trouble to find me by telephone across country, the other day, to inform me, pretty sharply, that if I wanted to please him and his friends, I would concentrate entirely upon statement Number Two, and spend quarter of an hour each week telling you that Hitler was a very bad man. But many of us feel that three statements don't take us very far, that they could easily and profitably be enlarged upon, and that the result of this enlargement would only confirm a view of this war for which some of us have been rather unscrupulously attacked.

We who take this view – this broader view of the war – are accused of 'dragging red herrings' across the trail, of confusing the issue, of using a terrible national emergency for our own ends. So I propose tonight to show how completely false this charge is, simply by examining these three statements, to which nobody can object because they are the purest cream of our official doctrine, and discovering where the briefest consideration of them will take us.

First, then, that the ordinary common folk of this country are heroic grand people, who can take all that's coming to them. Now, I made this point, both to you and to American listeners, before the heavy bombing began. I took the risk of prophesying what would happen, because I felt I knew these people. I didn't suddenly discover them and their good qualities, as some persons have done, just as if they hadn't been living in this same little island all these years.

By all means praise them because they 'can take it', but at the same time tell them exactly for what they are taking it; swear by all the gods that this country will never go to sleep again; and if you are a public man then stand up in public and solemnly pledge your word to these same people that you will never rest until you have created for them an infinitely better Britain, and to show that you mean it, do something now, give a sign that a new democratic order is on the way.

The eyes of the world are on this country. One clear signal that such a new Britain is rapidly emerging, and a beacon will be lit that will soon be seen round the world. All Europe, even those countries on which the hand of the Gestapo lies heaviest, even Germany itself outside the Nazi party, will instantly take hope. Nazi propaganda, with its artful sneering references to 'the plutocracies' and its false talk about its own New Order, will have to start all over again, having had the bottom clean knocked out of it. Our own war effort, now backed by the rising faith and enthusiasm of all the people, will rapidly reach new heights of achievement. I ask you is this a red herring across the trail? Or isn't it the trail itself?

We'll now take statement Number Two: that Hitler and his associates are bad and dangerous men. With this, of course, I agree, and indeed, to be frank, I have no respect for any public men who have only recently made this discovery about Hitler and his gang. They ought to have made it years ago, when it was just as obvious as it is now. Bit in any event, it seems to me that this statement about Hitler and his gang, when left to stand by itself, not only tends to be misleading but actually plays the Nazis' own game for them. Because, if you say that Hitler and his associates are bad and dangerous men and leave it at that, it suggests that there is something darkly magical about them, that we are dealing with some evil magicians and sorcerers, which is precisely the effect that Nazi propaganda itself has often aimed at.

What you really do is to overestimate them, taking them almost at their own sense of their importance. Now let's look coolly at the situation. Here you have gang of clever and desperate adventurers who first succeed in capturing one state and then go on to hold up the whole world. Now there have always been clever and desperate adventurers, but it's not until our own time that a gang of them have been able to operate on this gigantic scale. Thirty years ago, even, they wouldn't have had a dog's chance.

Then why have they been able to pull it off now? Because the world after the last war simply played into their hands. Their rottenness flourished in a rotten world, a world of mess and muddle and intrigue, of crumbling codes and vanished values, in which men would close their eyes even to torture and murder so long as it suited their pocket and prestige. It's only in such a world that a Hitler, a Goering, a Goebbels, would rise to control the destinies of a hundred million people.

Therefore, it's ridiculous to pretend that everything in the garden would have been lovely if it hadn't been for Hitler. No garden that ever had a chance of being lovely could ever have produced a Hitler. To see him as a solitary evil giant is to flatter him. What he really is, is a wicked dwarf perched on top of a gigantic toadstool of mess and misery, thrown up because the world, after the plain warning of the last war, refused to reform itself. The Nazis and their like are the festering sores on the diseased body of our world. Fight them? Of course we must fight them, but at the same time we must fight the diseased condition that produced them; otherwise we shall simply go on and on, battling with neurotics and crooks and brigands until civilisation disappears.

We've said goodbye to our ordinary lives in order to make a real fight of it, so while we're at it, let's make a real fight of it, and not only banish Hitler and his gang from the scene but also all the conditions that made Hitler possible. It's just as if we were called upon to set aside everything to battle against a plague of typhoid, due to bad drains, and those of us who said that while we were at it we might as well attend to the drains were rebuked for not taking sufficient interest in fighting the plague. But, some people will say, though I agree with your general argument, I say you must do one thing at a time, and that the first thing we must do – never mind all our fancy reforms – is to defeat Hitler. That we must defeat Hitler, I absolutely agree. But it seems to me that this one-thing-at-a-time method is the very worst way to set about defeating him.

Which brings me to the third statement I said I'd examine, namely that we shall win the war, but the question now is, when and how shall we win it? And here, it must be admitted, the one-thing-at-a-time school of thought seems to me depressingly vague. Sooner or later, they murmur, we shall have scores of thousands of bombing planes, millions and millions of heavily armed men, and then everything would be set going at once, and we shall batter our way through to victory, all rather in the style of 1918.

There is somewhere about all this too great a suggestion of the last war. We don't want to fight the last war all over again. We want to fight this one, and even the dullest blockhead can see that there are vast differences between the two wars. So now we ought to ask ourselves if it's possible, by recognising these differences and making the most of them, to turn this into a relatively short war instead of allowing it to become an agonisingly long-drawn-out affair, terrifyingly destructive to human life and property.

My own view is that it is possible, but not if we bring 1914 minds to the task and talk about one thing at a time. Because whatever this present war may be, it is simply not one thing at a time. It is twenty or a hundred different things at a time. And about fifty per cent of it, in my opinion, is not concerned at all with conventional military operations but with propaganda and morale and prestige. Thus, when the Nazi propagandists suddenly stopped saying that they were after more living room for the master race and announced that they were trying to establish a new European order, what they were really doing was occupying a new and highly important strategic position, as significant perhaps as their position along the French coast. We should never have let them occupy this New Order position, and cannot drive them out too quickly, instead of talking nonsense about one thing at a time.

If we fight with ideas as well as weapons, we shall not only help to construct a world worth living in, but also shorten this war perhaps by years. For here, in spite of their years of effort and their vast machinery of propaganda, the Nazis are in the weaker position. Most of their own people are apathetic and sullen, and the people they have recently conquered are mostly hostile. (Notice, by the way, how the Nazis, as in Poland, always try to win over or exterminate the men of ideas first — the scholars, the scientists, the artists. They know where the danger lies.) And try as they will, the Nazis can't make people enthusiastic about a New Order based on the Gestapo and wholesale looting. Thus their position is weak. But unfortunately our attack upon it so far has been feeble. We talk too often as if we'd learnt nothing from the last ten years. We have no programme to arouse enthusiasm and moral fervour everywhere.

Nobody outside Germany wants Hitler, but when you have seen the destruction of whole states and have felt yourself at the end of an epoch, a mere vague anti-Hitlerism is not enough to set you – and by you I don't mean us but the typical inhabitant of the Nazi-occupied territories — risking everything.

What we want is a short, clear creed, acceptable to the decent common man everywhere, that will act like a trumpet-call; and then we must proclaim it every hour of the day and night, sending it thundering through the ether, showering it down in millions of pamphlets, painting it indelibly on walls, until at last even the Nazis themselves see it written in letters of fire everywhere and their huge crazy empire of blood and terror suddenly cracks and totters and crashes to its doom.

It might fall like Jericho, but not if we merely mutter dreary old political platitudes at it; but as in the Book of Joshua: 'When ye hear the sound of the trumpet, all the people shall shout with a great shout; and the wall of the city shall fall down flat, and the people shall ascend up every man straight before him...'

It was, you see, the People who gave the great shout.[223]

*The Tory right wing was infuriated that he had again been given a platform to air his views and outraged by the content of his first broadcast; a deputation from the Tory 1922 Committee lobbied Duff Cooper, still Minister of Information, on the following Wednesday.*

*There were other, more powerful critics. Whatever his feelings about Priestley – and as a committed socialist, the writer would never have been high in Winston Churchill's estimation – to make one of many speeches urging Britons to abandon thoughts of everything but winning the war, and then hear Priestley effectively telling listeners to ignore that, drove Churchill into a fury. He fired off a memo to Duff Cooper, expressing regret that 'you have got Mr JB Priestley back' and went on to complain that Priestley was advancing 'an argument utterly contrary to my known views... is far from friendly to the government, and I should not be too sure about him on larger issues.'[224]*

*Cooper tried to soothe Churchill by – inaccurately – claiming that Priestley's popularity was declining and agreed to 'give Priestley a rest' once his current series of six talks had been concluded.[225] Churchill grudgingly agreed that Priestley could complete the series of talks, 'providing that no fee is paid' – Cooper replied that a fee had already been agreed for the series and the BBC could not renege on that agreement.*

*It is inconceivable that Priestley was not made aware of the Prime Ministerial displeasure and whether by coincidence or not, the following broadcasts were less confrontational in tone and dealt with 'safer' topics like the national diet, though once more, his call for Britons to eat more home-grown fruit and vegetables and less imported food items, strikes a curiously modern chord.*

Sunday 2 February 1941

I need hardly tell you that this is a most peculiar war; it breaks all the rules; thus while millions of trained and heavily armed young men have hardly heard a shot fired, short-sighted middle-aged men with a perpetual cough and flat feet earn medals for valour, and old ladies turn aside from feeding the canary to put out fire-bombs.

It's a war that can be won or lost in the strangest ways; just by the way we think and talk, for example. It might even be won or lost in the kitchen, for there's a food front on which we are all fighting. We have desperate hand-to-hand fights with strange malignant sausages; we are lured, perhaps to ultimate destruction, by the will-of-the-wisp rumours of lemons and onions. We become contrary to our tastes. Stout men who would never touch chocolate when the country was crammed with it, now plot and intrigue to obtain a slab or two, and may be seen in railway carriages smearing their faces with it as if they were schoolboys again. Ladies who had never been seen with a lemon in peacetime now swear they can't live without them, just as if they were football teams. A smell of onions is now regarded as a sign of power and privilege.

Let's consider this food problem. Now half our foodstuffs and especially those very things most people prefer, have to be imported. There's no difficulty about obtaining them and paying for them, but the trouble is they have to be brought here in ships and men have to risk their lives, which they are willing to do with a cool courage that's not sufficiently admired, to steer those cargoes past the torpedoes, mines and bombs. Moreover, some things need special ships. Meat, for instance, has to be brought in special cold-storage ships and there are only a limited number of these ships, some of which are being used to supply our troops in the Near East. Those soldiers at home, I think, could do with less meat than they are actually being given. Soldiers on active service, as I know from experience, need plenty of meat. On the other hand, middle-aged men who work in offices – the very fellows who are always roaring for fat chops and big steaks – need very little meat, and wouldn't suffer so often from acidosis and high blood pressure if they had less meat.

Again, some stuff just isn't worth the shipping space it takes up. Tinned fruit, for instance, is very bulky cargo and sometimes mostly consists of sweetish coloured water. If you and I were climbing a mountain and had to carry some emergency rations, I don't think we'd include among them many whacking great tins of apricots and pineapple.

The fact is, these wartime restrictions give us a chance of doing what we ought to have done years ago, namely, of improving our ordinary diet, which for years now has been both monotonous and rather unhealthy, using too much tea and bread and meat and tinned fruit, and not enough milk, fresh fruit, green vegetables, stuff that we could produce ourselves. For some time we English – and when I say English, I mean English, not British, as I'm not sure about the Scots or the Welsh or the Irish – haven't been very satisfactory civilised feeders, and in this matter the war may do us more good than harm. We have two bad uncivilised prejudices that sheer necessity may now compel us to abandon. The first is that both as cooks and diners we're desperately afraid of experiments. We go on dishing up and eating the same old stuff week after week, year after year.

I've never known a visitor from abroad who didn't complain of the heartbreaking monotony of our diet. It is as if we had voluntarily put ourselves into prison. We've any amount of enterprise, courage and imagination, but not in the kitchen and the dining-room, where we're almost as dull and unimaginative as cows and sheep. Some of Wodehouse's characters talk of 'putting on the nosebag' when they're going to dine, and really often we didn't seem to do much more than put on the nosebag.

It's just as if we made exactly the same remarks every day or read the same book very night. Some of us having known countries where the food was not so timid and unimaginative, have grumbled for years, but nothing much happened except that we got the name of being stuck-up fancy fellows. Apparently it takes torpedoes, mines and bombs to blast us out of this dreary round of monotonous feeding, and I say that if they succeed in doing that, at least something will have been gained.

The other prejudice that we may soon be compelled to discard is our national dislike of eating in public. I suppose we have fewer restaurants per head of population than any other civilised people in the world. This has always seemed to me a pity; for it's often very pleasant to enjoy the main meal of the day with other people in a public place.

Now the Ministry of Food is rapidly establishing a number of 'communal feeding centres', as it calls them, in various cities. After telling the Ministry that if it wished to make these places popular the sooner it stopped calling them 'communal feeding centres' the better; nobody wants to dine in a communal feeding centre – that grim official title with its suggestion that we're really livestock on a vast farm, puts us off.

I'd said that I'd visit one of these places, and they recommended me to try the Byrom Restaurant, just off Scotland Road in Liverpool. So there I went, the other day – and a foul sleety day it was too – and Scotland Road, Liverpool looked more Godforsaken than ever. I was pleasantly surprised, however, by the communal restaurant, which had been made out of four empty shops. It was clean, bright, sensible, and had some excellent mural paintings on the walls.

I took my place in the queue, which was composed of many different types of people, young and old, rough and smooth. I bought a sixpenny ticket for the meat and vegetable dish, a twopenny one for the sweet, and a penny one for coffee. Young women in spotless white, working quickly and deftly, handed me a plate of meat stew and vegetables, some apple pie and custard, and finally a cup of coffee.

The beef stew was very nicely cooked, though I could have done with a little more beef in it. The apple pie was quite good. The coffee, which I had expected to be hot and wet and nothing more, was surprisingly good. You are not expected to clear your dirty plates away and wash them up or anything of that kind. Once you've eaten your lunch, you can relax over your coffee, light a pipe, and enjoy a little table talk, though most people there didn't seem to linger long.

I was told some of them occasionally bring portable wireless sets, and I wondered why the management, having gone so far and done so well, didn't go further and do still better, and install not-too-loud loud speakers. Indeed, I began to wonder why, if we are to have more of this communal feeding – and we ought to have, to save waste and to obtain the maximum value out of our foodstuffs – why we shouldn't have bigger and jollier places, with rather more cosiness about them too, and introduce into them a few of the hundreds of musicians who are now out of work, turning more communal feeding into jolly dining. At the same time, drop the official titles and call them 'The Lion at Bay', 'The Winston Tavern', 'The Blitz Arms', 'The Victory Inn', and restaurant proprietors, ready to protest against unfair competition should be invited to assist in the movement.

Now – I'm quite serious. Communal feeding, for at least one good meal a day, may soon be necessary on a large scale. All right. Instead of being dreary about it, let's make even more than a virtue out of this necessity, let's use it to add fun and adventure and colour to our lives. And let the Colonel's lady and Judy O'Grady sit at the same table – it'll do them both good.

After this meal, I was taken to see the pride and joy of civic Liverpool – it's vast Central Kitchen, designed to send out hot meals to schoolchildren and now sending out equally hot meals to A.R.P. workers and others. It's the largest kitchen I've ever seen. At a pinch it can dish you up sixteen thousand meals. I saw steaming smallholdings of Irish stew, and rice pudding by the acre. Wherever we went there, machines magically began doing their tricks for us. I saw everything except the inside of the refrigerating room, Liverpool in winter being refrigerator enough for me. All the women working there seemed to be fat and jolly, rosy with nourishment.

Now a kitchen like that, I felt, ought to be working now twenty-four hours a day, its colossal vats steaming and bubbling like mad, so that not one single human being for miles doesn't have at least one sensibly-planned, nourishing meal a day, a meal too in which not the tiniest scrap of essential foodstuff has been wasted. I wish we'd hundreds of such kitchens. Not that I have any particular passion for large-scale cooking and equally large-scale dining. Indeed, my own preference is for nice little dishes done especially for me – or at least for my family and friends and me – and eaten in a cosy corner. But then I also have a decided preference for cities that are lit up and not blacked out; for airplanes carrying mails instead of bombs; for ships going in safety to their destinations instead of being torpedoed and bombed, in short, for a world at peace instead of a world at war. But our only chance of reaching again a world at peace is to make sure that we succeed in the war, and our best way – perhaps our only way – of doing that is to make the best possible use of every tiny particle of our resources.

My own private opinion, for what it's worth – and it is only fair to add that to the Glasgow Unionist Association, that group of bold thinkers, it's worth nothing – is that on the whole the Minister of Food is doing a good job, and that much of the grumbling shows a lack of adaptability and imagination on the part of the grumblers, many of whom seem to think that Hitler's conquest of Europe had been overshadowed by their own tragic want of chocolate creams and tinned pears.

I believe too that if, as a nation, we really make the best of this wartime necessity, adapting our diet and eating habits sensibly to these various temporary shortages, experimenting not only because we have to but also for fun, taking pleasure if necessary in dining outside our own homes and in the company of neighbours, we may come out of this war a healthier and more civilised community.

Now, to have destroyed the Gestapo and at the same time to have improved our digestion, to have shattered the storm troops and to have found ten new soups and fifteen new salads – why, that would be an achievement that would earn the gratitude of the world twice over.[226]

*There was a one-week interruption to Priestley's 'Postscripts' as Churchill himself claimed the post-news slot on Sunday 9 February to make his famous 'Give us the tools and we will finish the job' broadcast, with Priestley resuming the following week.*

Sunday 16 February 1941

I have to spend a lot of my time now in trains. I don't like them. They seem quite different from the pleasant trains of peacetime. Now they are either as cold as a fishmonger's slab or very stuffy and a jungle of germs and bacteria. Hours and hours and hours I seem to spend each week sitting hunched-up in railway carriages, while the iron landscape of winter goes clanking by – or, as too often happens, refuses to go by and stays still, breathing hoarsely. There I am, covered with crumbs and tobacco and newspapers, not quite asleep, not quite awake, with my middle-age, which ought to have been glorious, crammed into this dustbin of existence.

During these times in trains I think a great deal in a dreamy sort of fashion. It's anything but a sharp-edged, purposeful sort of thinking, but perhaps it's none the worse for that, because the dreaminess and loose edges allow images to rise from that mysterious deep ocean of unconscious mental life. And today in the train, sunk inside myself, I was thinking of all the trains I have been on in my time that I can't take any more; the high swaying expresses of the P.L.M. in France; the stuffy wagons-lits to Switzerland; that train, on which you breakfast far too early, which left the Hook for Germany; the majestic Rome express; the train from Wadi-Haifa to Khartoum with the desert glaring even through the greeny-blue windows; a train in Costa Rica where I travelled with a bullfighter across rickety bridges above steaming gulfs; the magnificent American trains, such as the thundering Twentieth Century Limited, or the Chief out of Chicago, where the second morning out you see the amethyst peaks of New Mexico; or the Cascade Express that goes roaring parallel with the Pacific Coast, surrounded by the giant trees; or the glorious Canadian Pacific train that climbs from Vancouver up among the salmon rivers and green firs to Kicking Horse Pass.... yes, I remembered all these and many other trains, almost as a man might remember the friends of his boyhood, the girls of his youth.

For a moment, simply because I could no longer take a ticket on any of them, I thought of all these trains as having ceased to exist; but then I remembered that they're nearly all running as usual, and there flashed through my mind a confused composite image of all these trains, in Europe, America, Africa, filled with men like myself. We middle-aged men – you must have noticed it – are the great train travellers. Younger men have fewer opportunities, and older men have had enough of it, and refuse to go. It is we men in middle life who are for ever taking trains and settling down in our corners to worry out our problems, each one of us balancing a vast invisible pagoda of responsibilities, professional, domestic; financial, and the rest.

At this very moment, I thought, there are hundreds and hundreds of thousands of us, lumped in our jolting comers, staring through the steamy windows at nothing in particular, wondering about this, worrying about that... and there we go, all over Europe or America, or even in Asia, where they ought to have more sense. Warning voices still echo in our ears. Small round-faced Japanese gentlemen can still hear their political leader saying 'Sterner sacrifices will be demanded of you this year...' Italian merchants, wondering what on earth to do with their lemons and vermouth, stare at leading articles in the newspaper that ask for a larger and more united effort these coming months. In fifteen assorted countries in fifteen assorted languages but in railway carriages that look pretty much alike, these passengers, solid family men who wish no harm to anybody, are being warned to have a care, to tighten their belts, to make greater sacrifices.

As for the German variety of our middle-aged train-travelling species, he's had years and years of it, doing without this and accepting a substitute for that, filling in forms and paying up and saluting, so that now he sits huddled in his suit made out of wood, in an unheated railway carriage, glumly glancing at news he has long ceased to believe in, being carried from one part to another of a vast prison-house in which colossal victories have come to mean much less, as indeed they ought, than the wistful hope of yet one more evening of good beer and sausage and music and fun. And, last irony, the man who keeps the key of this vast prison-house, whose evil dream is being realised, has to be saluted with almost divine honours. And as soon as night falls over the western half of this worried Europe, the darkened trains drop down to a crawl because somewhere overhead are the bombers, ready to deal with the cities like some giant idiot child knocking down a pile of bricks.

All this, I reflected, is of course merely the final stage in a long process of idiotic frustration, an insane obstacle race that we moderns have set ourselves. Some things, such as the speedy production of goods or rapid transport, have become so easy for us that we have made up our minds to make everything as difficult as possible. We began to set iron bars between ourselves and all possible happiness.

What men need to do easily and quickly, to live with any satisfaction, that must be done with difficulty, or not at all. Frontiers were so fixed and so severely guarded that you'd think that blue men with eight legs lived on one side and scarlet men with wings lived on the other. The sensible convenience of money, the mere arrangement of tokens for goods and services, was turned into a nightmare labyrinth.

Lightning communication having been established round the world it was decided that less and less of importance should be communicated. Just when knowledge was accessible to everybody, it was agreed that it should be severely rationed. The national economies were so planned that every good harvest was a further step towards bankruptcy and starvation. Great scientists, acknowledged benefactors of the whole human race, were chased and pelted because their noses were curved and they had grandfathers called Isaac. High diplomacy, which too often consists of behaving like a common cheat for your country's good but to the ultimate disadvantage of everybody in your country, was in full flower. Never before were there such diplomatic comings and goings, such conferences, such gatherings of foreign and special correspondents, such expense sheets. And semi-lunatics and crooks, the kind of men that no sensible woman would leave in charge of village post office for half an hour, went about in special trains and were received with guards of honour, and could be observed afterwards moving jerkily and noisily across the screens of the news theatres. There, for instance, smirking darkly, was the face of that worthy man, apparently trusted by more than one nation, Pierre Laval – a typical figure of the period.

It was a period, I told myself, when democracy was sinking rapidly. The trouble was that it was being abandoned even in the countries where officially it was supposed to flourish. There was a decline of that sharp, critical, vocal public spirit without which a true democracy can't exist. One of the safest tests of the health of any democracy is its power of showing derision, of instantly replying to some obvious piece of humbug and chicanery with a gigantic spontaneous 'Gert-cha!' But this power was rapidly vanishing. The 'Gert-cha!' was becoming fainter and fainter, and more and more humbug and chicanery were being allowed to pass without protest.

Even Mussolini, thumping his chest and talking about his eight million Italian bayonets, was accepted at his own valuation as a terrible war lord, another Caesar, another Napoleon, and the democracies he taunted muttered that it was really all right because he made the trains run on time. We train-travellers like our trains to be punctual, but we have other and more important values. What was becoming of them? What, indeed, was happening to our world?

Foolish as I sound – and I must sound foolish because so many people, who don't seem to me intellectual giants themselves, write to say that I have a kind heart but no head – foolish then as I may sound, I know all the usual answers to this question about what was wrong with our world. I could give you a neat list of them, economic, political, social, with a dash or two of the philosophical thrown in. But I was thinking today, as I sat in the train and thought of us all over the world sitting in our trains, worried, bewildered, brooding, that one reason, underlying many of the other reasons, is rarely mentioned. It is this, that in these major affairs of life, as distinct from the minor ones, we are rarely in the hands of disinterested men.

It is as if, to come back to trains for a moment, the man who sold us our railway ticket was really in the pay of another company, or a small group of shareholders, or about to work for himself, so that he might sell you a genuine ticket or any bit of nonsensical pasteboard; as if the stationmaster and the guard have a strong but secret reason for keeping the train in the station, perhaps having an arrangement with the firm that supplies the buns to the refreshment room; as if the signalmen don't worry too much about giving the right signals because they happen to be enthusiastic members of the train-wreckers league;

as if the engine driver is not, as you innocently imagine, going to take you to Paddington, because it happens that he is extremely interested in a young woman who lives in Birmingham, and hopes to be able to work it so that the train arrives there.

Or take another example. It is as if, when diphtheria broke out in your village, there arrived, not some competent businesslike doctors and nurses, but an astonishing gang, consisting of two commercial travellers for a firm of wholesale chemists, three undertakers' touts, a student of witchcraft, several wild-eyed hoarse-voiced gentlemen who specialised on lengthy rhetoric and on nothing else. The outlook for your village would be as grim as the outlook for the world has been during these last ten years. I suggest then that the first test for fitness to govern should be the possession of a pure passion for the welfare of our species, and outside that the complete disinterestedness of a man of science.

Now I take it that the least disinterested persons in power today are the leaders of the Nazi party, who to my mind are motivated by nothing but a personal lust for power and wealth, for I find it hard to believe they're even moved by any love for the country they have looted and swindled and whose good name they have destroyed. Therefore, our first task is to rid the world of them and their bodyguards, and then to go straight on, smashing one racket after another, until at last the world's affairs are in the hands of disinterested men, and stout chaps in trains everywhere are all smiles again.[227]

# Chapter 11
# Commanders from the Carlton Club

*Despite the less contentious nature of his last two 'Postscripts', Priestley's critics continued to snipe from the sidelines and demand his removal, and in his next broadcast he hit back at the 'commanders from the Carlton Club'.*

Sunday 23 February 1941

With all this talk of invasion ringing in my ears, I decided the other morning to have a look at Dover. We were lucky in the day, which was like Spring, being clear and soft and sunny. Midway across Kent we stopped the car to look up, for the whole blue was throbbing with an angry drone. There, in exact formation, were war planes flying north. But they were our planes - not theirs.

This was a most welcome sight, especially after reading so many newspaper articles about invasion. Most of these articles are irritating. Their writers tell us that if Hitler doesn't try this, then he might try that, but gradually lose their air of being in the know and finally admit they have no real information. The trouble about these articles is that behind their screen of 'ifs' and 'buts' and 'whens', they do suggest a darkly magical idea of Hitler and the Nazis – almost present them as mysterious powerful wizards conjuring up new spells of doom; and to my mind, this darkly magical idea of Nazi power – which all their propaganda encourages – has done them more good so far than all their dive bombers and armoured divisions, and so it should be sharply discouraged here.

The great Nazi trick is by cheating, treachery and propaganda to take away at least fifty per cent of your power of resistance, and then to wade into you with everything they've got – which is never quite as much as they say they've got – making a terrifying noise. In spite of their vast organisation, they remain half-gangsters, half-showmen – a fact we'd do well to remember. Thus, it's about time we had a few articles hinting at the strange unpleasant things we've prepared for Hitler's dejected mooncalf louts scattered between the Arctic Sea and the Pyrenees if they should attempt the conquest of this island. How many young men with blonde empty faces will drown in the cold seas or rot in chalk pits, all to satisfy the vanity, envy and spite of a little man who will not even be with them?

Dover itself, the other day, was an immense surprise – and for this reason – that it simply looked like Dover. I don't know quite what I expected – something fantastic, no doubt, something in keeping with the notion that here was the last outpost of the free world. But what I did see was Dover – women doing their shopping, elderly men smoking their pipes over the newspaper, errand boys loitering together, offers of bargains in the shop windows, chaps popping in for haifa pint of bitter, and numerous posters announcing firmly on behalf of the Royal Hippodrome music-hall 'the return of old and new favourites'. You might have been almost anywhere in the southern half of Britain.

If you were in search of the sensational, it was all rather disappointing; but if you like a quiet sensible life, it was comforting. I admit that on the front itself it was not quite the old Dover – all those charming Georgian and Regency houses had a vacant look. They had, for the time being, done with us. The sea was a dark blue with an occasional twinkle and sparkle about it, and with faint mist far away. It looked enchanting, and I suddenly realised I hadn't seen the sea for a long time. Here I'd been for months and months on this island, and hadn't caught a glimpse of the sea – I mean the real open sea, not the flowing mud and grease you get off Liverpool and such places. So I stared at this dark blue water, which now and then gave me a wink, almost as if I'd just arrived from the middle of Siberia. But, of course, this was no ordinary bit of sea. It was the frontier – the barrier – the great moat. Somewhere at the other side of it, only just out of sight, began the crazy rickety empire of the crooked cross with its vast bustling organisation and its equally vast inner hopelessness – the mad kingdom of man's despair.

Looking at the familiar harbour, from which I had sailed so many times, I had another surprise – but this time of the opposite kind, because now I was astonished that all was not as it used to be – that the cross-Channel steamers weren't there as they'd always been before – that all the hurrying passengers and porters had completely vanished. Silly, of course, but somehow I'd vaguely thought of all that cross-Channel traffic going on as usual. In the good honoured old wars of our great-grandfathers it probably would have been going on, for in the old days you left wars to professional armies and didn't allow them to interfere too much with commerce, travel, science and art. It was Napoleon – a thoroughly bad influence – who began widening the gulf between nations at war. The Nazis, of course, have carried this policy to an extreme that even Napoleon would have regarded as simply barbaric. Thus the Nazis have not yet conquered Poland as states used to be conquered, but they've swarmed into that unhappy country like man-sized ants, devouring and exterminating or enslaving.

All this bears no relation to what used to be called war, and shouldn't be discussed as such. The world struggling towards order and civilisation could survive half a hundred of the old wars, with their neat campaigns among the professional soldiery and with their civilians leading their ordinary lives. But it is certain that the civilised world won't survive much of this new wholesale lunacy, in which the production of expensive instruments of destruction becomes a major – if not the chief – activity. After this we must all co-operate or perish.

A tiny group here, much encouraged by the enemy, says in effect, 'But why not co-operate now?' The answer to that is easy: we have tried it already and failed. It can't be done because even the most elementary co-operation demands that the parties concerned must have some primary values in common. How can you come to any working agreement with a man who regards the signing of a solemn document as no more than a trick to gain time, who wouldn't hesitate as soon as your back were turned to jump on it and knife you, who thinks that ordinary decency is a sign of weakness? Where can you begin with him? The answer is – Nowhere. Therefore you must oppose him with force, about which he makes no mistake.

So far I am in agreement with commanders from the Carlton Club and other gentlemen who tell me in public to stick to my business of writing books and plays, forgetting that they have made such a mournful hash of their business of running the world that I can no longer attend to mine, even if I wanted to. But now I leave them again – so let them switch off – by declaring that while you're opposing the Nazis with force you must at the same time make it clear that they are outlaws – for we're not merely one gang fighting another gang to decide which shall have the loot – you must make it clear that there is a system of law, a possibility of world order, respect and co-operation, which these men have rejected; and the more obvious you make this to everybody, the more obvious it is that we're fighting against outlaws.

So once again the point emerged that, though it's true we're fighting for our existence, it's not enough. For it's also true – and this is what concerns the wide world – that we're fighting for something more than our existence, for something greater than ourselves, that means as much to men at the other end of the world, men of other races and creeds and language, as it means to us. And as I thought this the other day on Dover beach I seemed to hear in the vast in-drawn breath of the sea a whisper that we should prevail, and that the world would be cleansed – perhaps by the sea – of this madness, but also a reminder that the sea circles the globe and washes all its shores.

It must have been nearly a hundred years ago when a poet – Matthew Arnold – came here and told us what he thought and felt in one of the finest of his poems – 'Dover Beach'. He heard then, as we do now:

> ...the grating roar
> Of pebbles which the waves draw back, and fling,
> At their return, up the high strand,
> Begin, and cease, and then again begin,
> With tremulous cadence slow, and bring
> The eternal note of sadness in...'

But it was of the last verse of this poem that I was thinking as I stared at Dover Beach again, and wondered when hell itself might begin to steam and spout out of the dark blue water.

This is the verse:

> Ah, love, let us be true
> To one another! For the world, which seems
> To lie before us like a land of dreams,
> So various, so beautiful, so new,
> Hath really neither joy, nor love, nor light,
> Nor certitude, nor peace, nor help for pain;
> And we are here as on a darkling plain
> Swept with confused alarms of struggle and flight,
> Where ignorant armies clash by night.

For a moment we wonder if the poet, standing there so long ago, saw round a comer in time. The minds of these poets seem to be visited by prophetic images – like that of Tennyson who could foresee 'The nations' airy navies grappling in the central blue'. But then we see that the situation is not for us as it was for Arnold, for now the world doesn't lie before us like a land of dreams. We know the worst of it, and live among the confused alarms, and have been, now or five-and-twenty years ago, where the ignorant armies clash by night. We have had all the easy illusions that he tries to dispel fairly bombed and machine-gunned out of us; we've met old men who have been tortured in cellars, and have heard little children scream among the ruins of cities.

We feel like trying to get back to Matthew Arnold as he stands on that moonlit innocent Dover beach of a hundred years ago, tapping him on the shoulder, and whispering, 'Listen! You ain't seen nothing yet!' We're at the grim far end of a journey that he with his elaborate, melancholy and rather enjoyable doubts, has only just begun. But – and this is most important – we are at the far end. We must either drop and rot – or turn back. Back to that faith in our common nature and its relation with things that compels us to affirm that some sort of security and happiness are possible to men.

We must – for we have no other choice – turn his verse round, and say, on this Dover beach that we mean to defend, that though we are here on this darkling plain swept with confused alarms of struggle and flight, the world could seem to lie before us like a land of dreams, so various, so beautiful, so new, that we can so contrive it that it shall have joy, and love, and light, and certitude, and peace, and help for pain. Not enough – never enough, perhaps, to satisfy the poet's heart. But enough for common men and women to feel they have a good life to live, and haven't been trapped by evil circumstance like rats. Then there could come a day when men could point to Dover beach and say, 'That was once the threshold of our new world'[228]

## Sunday 2 March 1941

The title tonight, if one should be needed, is New Men. It is, believe me, a very important subject. We hear a lot these days about a New Order, a New Britain, a New Europe, a New World, but not very much about New Men.

Most of you will agree with me in regarding the twenty years between 1919 and 1939 – between, in fact, the two great wars – as a melancholy period of disappointment, dwindling hope, growing fear. One reason why this period began to turn out so badly is so simple and obvious that it is often not mentioned at all. It is this: during the last war, we in this country had a million men killed. (Other countries, notably Germany and Russia, lost far more men than this, but we'll consider our own case.)

Now most of these million men who were killed were young men of good physique and health, and many of them, the ardent young volunteers who perished at Neuve Chapelle and Loos, Suvla Bay and the Somme, were youngsters of the very highest promise, the pick of the country, the salt of the earth. Those of us who were there with them and have not forgotten them can testify to this startling fact, that the best of all, the heroes of our boyhood, the fellows we looked to for leadership, vanished into the mud and dust, so that those of us who returned – none too sound in mind and body; men I think for ever a little haunted and bewildered – were nothing but a remnant of Britain's young manhood. The best were left behind, never to know the years after the war.

This was especially true of the so-called governing classes, whose losses, due to the slaughter of young officers, were truly appalling; so that the gaps in these upper ranks were heartbreakingly wide – so wide that they could never be properly closed again. And I think that in the years that followed we forgot that where there should have been men now reaching the prime of life, ready to take command, to lead the nation in politics, arts, sciences and industries, too often there were nothing but ghosts; young faces staring out of old snapshots, voices fading from the memory.

And so, often, we wondered during those years why in every department of our national life there seemed so few new men coming along, to take the reins from shaky old hands, and it wasn't until we happened to attend some regimental reunion dinner, looked round the tables in vain for the strongest, clearest faces, that we remembered that the best of our generation had been taken away from us.

Every year we bought red poppies, forgetting that the poppy is the symbol of sleep and forgetfulness and oblivion. But especially during these last ten years, when all this vanished youth would have arrived at ripe manhood and maturity, we missed the New Men. We were always having to make do with men who were rather too old and cynical, or with men who were too young but also, curiously enough, too cynical. And through the wide gaps in our ranks marched the enemies – distrust and indecision and hopelessness. Where were the New Men?

During the first three months of this war, I did a tour of the country for the Press, visiting camps, aerodromes, naval bases, aircraft and munition factories. I noticed then what I hadn't noticed for years before: that there were New Men about. One of them, typical of a whole class, comes back to mind now. He was, I imagine, in his middle thirties, and an engineer. He had created and was now in charge of a factory that produced, in colossal quantities, an article urgently necessary to us in wartime. He had evolved a system of high-speed mass production of this article that had proved very successful. He was very proud of his factory – and I call it 'his' factory not because he owned it but because he had more or less created it – and was eager to explain every wheel and belt in it.

On the other hand, he wasn't simply a man of wheels and belts. He had read widely and sensibly. He was interested in political and economic ideas. He had a quick; keen mind, though there are people – and I think they are wrong – who wouldn't call it an 'educated' mind, just as there are other people who'd tell us that he hadn't 'come out of the top drawer'. It would, I think, be truer to say of him and all his kind, that he simply hadn't come out of that particular chest of drawers at all, and so didn't care whether you imagined he came out of the top, middle or bottom drawer.

Nevertheless I felt in him a considerable amount of frustration. I gathered that this was because he felt hampered by the occasional presence and interference of superiors who were not, in the sense of knowing about the job in hand, superior at all – who were indeed, when compared with him, almost so many figureheads, but figureheads that in their huge wooden fashion would keep getting in the way.

This was, remember, at the beginning of the war. No doubt he couldn't help feeling frustrated because here he was, the necessary new man, who hadn't yet arrived in the necessary new world. But here, at least, was a new man. And of course, then and since, I found other new men in the fighting services themselves, sometimes in quite unexpected places in those services.

In this connection I'd like to quote an interesting letter of protest I received the other day from a listener, not himself a serviceman but an oil mining expert. After agreeing with something I'd said about disinterested man, he goes on to say: 'Where do you find the young ones today? In the R.A.F., and Royal Navy and Army. But when these young disinterested men become middle-aged we jeer at them as "Colonel Blimps". General Wavell in twenty years' time will be called a "Blimp". These men have character and tradition of courage and going straight ..... and are used to giving their health and lives for little pay or thanks. There is a big reservoir of character there...'

Now with some of this I for one am in agreement. I'm not sure about the little thanks, for the nation usually shows its gratitude towards its military and naval officers of high rank much more openly and profusely than it ever shows them towards its scientists, artists, thinkers, educators. However, that's a small point. Where my correspondent seems to me to be wrong is in assuming that we apply the term 'Colonel Blimp' indiscriminately to any middle-aged or oldish officer, no matter what his outlook may be. But surely Colonel Blimp, or Blimpishness, is simply applied to a certain wooden and untouchable sort of mind, which has really stopped thinking for itself and taken refuge in violent statements divorced from truth and reality and nonsensical opinions that have been expressly manufactured for it.

What's wrong with Colonel Blimp is not that he's middle-aged or elderly and has spent most of his life in one of the services, but that he will no longer use his eyes and ears and his intelligence; is simply a mass of absurd prejudices, and likes to shout down anybody who tries to correct him. In actual fact, most Blimps aren't colonels. But they are Blimps the old men – not because they are old in years but because they don't understand the realities of today – as opposed to the New Men. And it's the new men we're talking about now.

People who know more about these things than I do, and people whose judgement I respect, keep on telling me these days that this air-raid life of ours, this war brought to our own doors, is producing some genuinely first-class new men. Air-raid wardens in heavily blitzed areas, shelter marshals who take command in some of the gigantic new shelters, and the like; men whose names are quite unknown to the public in general but men who are deeply respected, trusted, admired, loved by the men, women and children brought into immediate contact with them, are now emerging as figures of some consequence, as natural leaders of the people. Here, then, are some new men.

Lightning has struck the barren rock and suddenly there has come gushing out of it the life-giving spring. We needn't be surprised. We are, if you like, a complacent people, a lazy-minded people, a muddle-headed people, but we are not by a thundering long chalk yet a decadent people, incapable of building up reserves of conscientious, responsible and courageous manhood. It was in believing that we were a decadent people that the dictators made their greatest mistake, probably because they didn't send their agents up and down the country enough, and put too much trust in reports brought back from smart cocktail parties. Therefore we can't be astonished by this recent talk of new men, whose value hasn't been discovered in examination rooms, or on platforms run by political machines, whose names haven't been searched for in Debrett or the Directory of Directors, but who have been promoted on the field of battle by the very people fighting that battle.

Now what can be done with these new men? Surely a few of them at least might be given posts of much greater responsibility, might possibly be put in charge of whole departments of our war effort. I should like to see one of these men – a man unknown to the newspapers and the wide public, yet trusted by thousands like a brother – suddenly promoted to some position of great trust. It would, to say the least of it, be a fine democratic gesture - and we have not been too free with those gestures. Possibly, shot up so suddenly, he might fail, but he could hardly fail more conspicuously and expensively than some old well-tried hands have done in the recent past.

Coming as he might do from the homely but urgently necessary organisation of our civil defences, he might easily not fit in at all with the more elaborate routine of higher government circles, but even so, the experiment would be worth trying. After all, he might suggest changing the routine. The new men might produce new methods. After all, we are fighting new men, not the kind of new men I like at all – outlawed men, lusting for power, thirsting for revenge, haters of life.

No use complaining such men break the rules; they've probably never even read them. But these are not really the creative, inventive men, these Hitlers and Goerings and Goebbels. We can show far more creative inventive men than they can. But these men have achieved power, easily brushing aside the mere men of routine, because they have been inspired – inspired by hate. They cannot be successfully opposed by routine men – that has already been tried and failed – but they can be successfully opposed and finally destroyed by people also inspired, and even more inspired, by love – every kind of love, from love of a single bit of ground to love of all decent humanity.

Now I fancy that these new men suddenly emerging from obscurity have been so inspired, have been warmed at heart, at times when the heart might well feel cold and sick, by a deep steady glow of affection for their fellow citizens, often such a nuisance, often so impossible, for ever wanting this or forgetting that, but still their fellow citizens, rowing somehow or other in the same boat, loveable in their fears and hopes. These men and women may belong to any class. We're sick of classes anyhow – let's give them a long rest. It doesn't matter tuppence whether they talk as if each word were a sugar plum, or shovel out their syllables as if they were coaling.

It's of no importance who their fathers and mothers were. What matters is that they're thoroughly alive and not half-dead in routine; that they can plan and lead, and are capable of being trusted and loved, aren't broken but inspired by the challenge of events, and that this, whether it's halfway to hell or heaven, is a new age, and that there arise to meet and mould it – New Men.[229]

*Priestley's listening figures were even larger for the second series of 'Postscripts' – one estimate put the audience at fourteen million people, forty per cent of the adult population[230] – but after the 'bite' of his first broadcast, the next few, culminating in the 'New Men' broadcast, were in general so bland and uncontroversial that many respondents to BBC audience research, while still expressing overwhelming approval, offered the belief that Priestley had been forced by the government to 'tone it down'.*

*The axes were still being ground at the Carlton Club, however, and Duff Cooper had already made the decision to remove him. Indeed on 5 March, a minute, probably from Sir Walter Monckton, acting on Cooper's instructions, called for Priestley's broadcasts to end at once, but advocated sugaring the pill by suggesting that it was the need for a diversity of speakers rather than any problem with Priestley himself that lay behind the move.[231]*

*However, Patrick Ryan had already agreed a further two talks with*

*Priestley and the axe could not fall until after those. In a telephone call to Priestley, Ryan told him frankly that Duff Cooper wanted him off the air because 'people who don't like the talks object to your having the peak time', perhaps forgetting that, as Richie Calder remarked in the* Daily Herald, *'it was Priestley himself who made it the peak time'.*[232] *Ryan offered Priestley the compromise that he should stand down after his eighth 'Postscript', but then return to the air after a gap of six or eight weeks. Priestley rejected this but told Ryan that if the series was extended to twelve weeks in total, he would then leave with a good grace. No final decision was reached and meanwhile Priestley continued.*[233]

## Sunday 9 March 1941

Dear Mrs Smith, shall we call you?

Thank you very much for your letter, Mrs Smith. I'm replying to it in this way because I believe you represent a great many listeners, and yet you strike a different line from most of my correspondents. A great many of the people who write to me – and very sensible, friendly, encouraging letters they write too – have only one complaint, and that is `– to use their own favourite phrase`– that I 'don't go far enough'. They mean by this that I keep on giving them short postscripts to the Sunday night news instead of giving them gigantic lectures on political, economic and social reconstruction, building the new world for them almost brick by brick. Many of them send me their own plans for world reconstruction – sometimes written in a close handwriting on both sides of thin foolscap sheets – and as I sometimes get fifty of these reconstructions a week, all of which I am expected to digest and then comment on at length, you can imagine the life I lead.

But you, Mrs Smith, take quite a different line. You are the mother of three small children. Your husband is away in the Army. You are, obviously, an intelligent woman, with no desire to run away from the problems we are all called upon to solve. But you find it difficult to look ahead yet. As you say: 'I must reserve all my energies to getting through this day-to-day life with all its petty little troubles, its difficulties with eggs and meat and coal. And I still need help to fight against the things that are hovering in the background – the separation from my husband, the fears for the children – so much harder to bear than any fears for myself.'

And then, after paying me some compliments I don't deserve, you ask me to stop building the new world sometimes to help you to get on with life here and now. To quote your own words, won't I 'tell us how to enjoy life still, instead of just existing through all these miserable days and months and years. I want to enjoy my life with my children but sometimes I seem to have lost the secret of it all.'

Well, there you are. Now first, let me put in a quick plea for new world-building as an essential part of our lives here and now. If we are called upon to suffer, it's better to feel that we are suffering not merely for other people's past mistakes, like tragic characters in the last chapter of a miserable story, but are enduring all this as heroic characters in the first chapter of a happy story, are doing without so many things now in order that our children soon may never do without them.

We have to make a great effort, all right then, while we're at it, let's make it a truly gigantic effort, and begin to clean the whole rotten thing up, once and for all. I suggest, humbly, that the acceptance of that point of view will help you. Now I put in 'humbly' there because I meant 'humbly'. The fact is, Mrs Smith, that your request makes me feel humble, quite inadequate. I think of myself working hard these days, but I know that if I'd your job to do, looking after those three children, in these times and with a husband away, I should probably cave in about the end of the second week. Most men would, I fancy. We'd simply pack up.

There's no doubt whatever that this War presses far more heavily on women than it does on men, for there is something deep down in the average masculine mind that doesn't altogether object to this orgy of destruction, this piling up of monstrous gadgets, this sudden fantastic adventure of war; whereas to the average feminine mind, the whole thing is nothing less than repulsive lunacy, about as sensible and satisfactory as introducing a man-eating tiger into a birthday party. And if you all said, 'Well, this comes of leaving things to men to settle, and we've had enough of this rubbish,' I for one wouldn't blame you.

But this isn't what you want from me, is it, Mrs Smith? What you want are ideas, for once, that will help our ordinary day-to-day life. Well, here's one I ask you to consider very seriously. As each new responsibility arrives – and we all have new responsibilities piled upon us now – try to get rid of an old one. Don't allow yourself to be overloaded. The trick is, accept whatever new responsibility the War brings, because we're still fighting for our lives, you know, but at the same time dump on the roadside one of the old, peacetime responsibilities. Realise, in fact, that this War can help us to set ourselves free from some old and heavy encumbrances.

For instance, people in this country used to worry themselves silly and sick about their social position, where exactly they stood on the ladder. Well, thank God, that's done with now. Anybody who bothers about that nonsense any more must enjoy worrying. So we're rid of all that. Then a great many people used to scheme all day and worry half the night about what we can call long-range security – how to be financially independent by 1955. Well, that's out too. I wouldn't give it a thought. It's like wondering if you're going to catch a cold during a shipwreck.

Worry about the world of 1955 if you like but not about your own standing in 1955. By that time there'll be security for none of us or for all of us. So that's another headache gone. And don't tell me the load isn't getting lighter. By taking away those two great worries – and, mind you, they assume a thousand different shapes, and are always popping up in various menacing disguises – we begin to simplify our lives where we can do with some simplification. We release mental energy hitherto bound to these treadmills. You can go out and listen to the birds or stare at the spring flowers now breaking through magically under the trees, without wondering if the vicar's wife will call or doing a lot of mental arithmetic for an endowment policy.

Then again, though we don't want the children to look shabby or to look shabby ourselves, let's admit that appearances don't matter as much as they did two years ago – all kinds of appearances, in fact; and that saves time and attention and worry, and means that you can have more fun when there's any fun going. But, you may complain, there isn't any fun going. Then you must try and make some. Having some fun, when we've done our duty, is one way of defeating Hitler. He can never have had much. Any set of people who have to organise a monstrous thing called 'Strength through Joy' are not my idea of uproarious playmates.

> For the good are always the merry,
> Save by an evil chance,
> And the merry love the fiddle,
> And the merry love to dance...'

But, I admit, opportunities for fun may be rare. But what you can do when time allows, is to knock off wondering and worrying about the War, and read Jane Austen. Hitler and Goering can't knock off and read Jane Austen. Or try to listen, with an easy mind, to some Mozart on the gramophone. Mussolini can't listen to some Mozart with an easy mind. Now I said this once before, last summer, but it's worth repeating. What we all ought to do is at times to think hard and if possible constructively about the War, try and obtain some insight into it; but when we're not doing that, we mustn't simply go on wondering and worrying and nagging ourselves about it, with our minds dragging round in a circle. Knock off and forget about it for an hour or two.

But of course there are times, in peace as well as in war, when all such heavy advice means nothing. These are the times when we feel that the unbearable moment is rushing on its way to meet us. We imagine that a few more steps will take us straight into hell. And sometimes when we think of what maybe in store for us, we are very much afraid, though not perhaps so much afraid of the monstrous thing itself as afraid of ourselves and what we might do when we have to meet the challenge.

Those of us who have vivid imaginations meet horrors more than halfway. We can people the darkness with terrible approaching shapes. How shall we meet the frightful moment? Well, it's worth remembering that nearly always at such moments a curious and comforting thing happens: life suddenly becomes like a dream. It's as if at such times we become aware of the strange fact that there's a deeper and profounder reality underlying what we call reality, our ordinary life, which now seems to bear the same relation to this deeper reality that our dreams do to our waking life. So that the terrible moment, which was to be more blastingly real than anything we'd ever known, suddenly takes on this removed and dreamlike quality, and almost before we know where we are, we are through and out at the other side. Now this isn't going to make heroes out of us. Probably heroes don't need to comfort themselves in this fashion. But if, like me, you don't pretend to be heroes – well, then it's worth remembering.

Another thing, Mrs Smith – don't you find any compensations? Is it really all extra worry and fuss and brooding with no little gains of any kind? Because I must say – and I understand all about the worry and fuss and brooding – that I find myself enjoying moments of exceptional and quite unexpected happiness, a sudden rush of joy. Perhaps after broadcasting to America very late and only snatching an hour or two's sleep afterwards, I wander out into the streets, and there I am, still alive, and suddenly the whole early morning sparkles and everything is fresh and new, and for a few moments I feel as I used to do as a small boy when we arrived at the seaside, and there, smelling of Paradise, was the whole miraculous glittering ocean.

And isn't there, somewhere behind that, not always working, of course, but ready to sustain us, a sense that, bad though all this may be, we are at last getting on with something? It depends perhaps on what you felt in the years immediately before the War. I know that I began to feel gloomier and gloomier deep down, because I felt that we were all drifting to disaster, that there was a vast creeping tide of evil over the world, and that our bright lights and good dinners and parties and games – all the things we miss now, if you like – were more and more an awful sham, because just behind this pretty enamelled screen of life was an ever widening and deepening pit of rottenness.

Whereas now - and Lord knows I don't pretend all this is any picnic – we've at least taken a stand; we've built stout walls against that vast creeping tide, and though we may be trudging through a dark rocky place, that's preferable to the false painted screen and the stinking pit.

So far, I believe, we're better people than we were before the War, except when some of us scream for every alien to be put behind bars, as if it wasn't better for Britain to risk a few spies rather than behave hysterically and ignobly. But except for a few screamers and snarlers, we're a more admirable people than we were before. There's more sense and friendliness about, more real fellow-feeling, more knowledge of other people, more promise of good.

Here's a passage from a quaint old text that somebody sent me: The world is so large, and we people are so small that not everything can concern us alone. If we get hurt and have to suffer, who knows that it is not to the advantage of all mankind. Goodnight, Mrs Smith. Goodnight, everybody.[234]

*Although the 'Mrs Smith' broadcast was the last of the original six, Priestley also completed the two further ones agreed with Patrick Ryan, the first of which, at government request, was devoted to the men of the merchant marine. If its subject was government-ordained, however, its treatment was pure Priestley, and once more, he found a way to turn his discourse to the familiar themes of Peace Aims and a transformation of British society.*

Sunday 16 March 1941

The other Saturday night, in an attempt to entertain twenty mothers evacuated into the country, I got out our old Kodascope film projector and ran through some of the family films we'd taken in what looked like another world. Among these films – indeed, the most vivid of them – was one taken on a cargo boat that had magically transported the family from the coal-dust and fog of the Manchester Ship Canal to the bright coast of California.

There, on the screen, all as sharp as a new coin, was the ceremony of Crossing the Line, the revels on the equator at the Court of King Neptune, who could be seen presiding in a stupendous beard while his attendant mermaids in the swimming pool below – creatures who in spite of their flowing locks looked uncommonly like engineers and stewards – ducked the passengers and made a colossal splashing.

And then, as one grinning face after another came into that tiny patch of bright, vanished sunlight on the screen, and I found myself putting a name or a ship's rating to each, I remembered that this ship, which once seemed like a home to us, was now somewhere at the bottom of the sea. And where now were those shipmates and old friends of ours? Where was the short, broad, smiling skipper with his soft Welsh voice? Where was the First Officer, who knew about Mohamedism and claimed to have second sight? Where was Number Two, with his brick-red face and his devastating cut-drive at ping-pong? Where were the three engineer officers, with whom I used to play such ferocious deck-tennis on the for'ard hatch? Where was Sparks, who was so long and thin and had literary ambitions? Where were they all? There was only one answer I could give myself. These were good men of the British Merchant Service – they were either dead, or still doing their duty somewhere.

Then something happened that's always happening to me, as it probably is to you too, to hint to us that what may appear chance events have their place in some mysterious pattern. For by the very next post there arrived, quite unasked for, a large registered envelope containing a number of typewritten documents, and a short letter which said among other things; 'I think it may interest and help you to read through, confidentially, some intimate papers concerning ships and seamen in wartime.'

That night, the day's work done, I went through all these documents, which were mostly copies of formal statements by masters of ships or senior officers, describing accurately but very tersely, with no attempt at drama or atmosphere, what had happened to their ships, to themselves and their shipmates. As I read on and on, the curt conventional phrases came to life, and it seemed to me that not Conrad himself, nor my friend H.M. Tomlinson who writes about ships and the sea like an angel, could have done it better.

There was unfolded a vast panorama, stretching from Liverpool and the Clyde to the Cape and the waters off Singapore. There was played before my inward eye the terrific drama of the Merchant Marine in this wartime. Somehow it made everything else in this war – yes, even the

two-mile-high combats above the Channel, the bombing of London, the evacuation of Dunkirk, or the desert thunderbolt of Wavell's Army – seem like tuppence. I don't know why, unless it's because these men had to meet their dangers just trying to do their ordinary job, without any special uniforms or training. They signed on for a voyage, and would find
themselves in roaring hell.

Then those who after the most astounding adventures came back again, just took a week or two's leave, went back home where nobody paid them any special attention, and then quietly signed on for another voyage. There isn't one touch of heroics in all these statements, not the ghost of a suggestion anywhere that the writer is a fine fellow. Mussolini can do more in this line in two minutes than all these men could do in fifty years. Just quiet, sensible men of the sea, explaining in curt, professional terms exactly what happened.

One phrase recurs like a refrain throughout: 'The behaviour of the officers and crew was excellent.' Just that. And the trouble is, that's all I dare quote from all these fascinating documents. If I could give you their words and not mine, I would like a shot. But even if the censorship would allow it, I can't because I'd be breaking a private confidence. So that's all you get of the original – 'the behaviour of the officers and crew was excellent.'

Sometimes these captains describe how they themselves returned to their ships, when these were now helpless, in a sinking condition, and perhaps liable to be bombed, raked with machine-gun fire, or shelled again, just to 'have a last look round' to see that nobody, perhaps trapped in a damaged cabin, had been forgotten, that all papers had been either taken off or destroyed, that all was done that could be done.

Imagine the cold courage demanded by some of those 'last looks round'. And not only that, but the sudden anguish of feeling your ship, now beyond help, reeling and shuddering before taking the last plunge! For ships are more like people than like mere things. As Tomlinson, who ought to be doing this talk, once wrote:

I learned why a ship has a name. It's for the same reason that you and I have names. She has happenings according to her own weird. She shows perversities and virtues her parents never dreamed into the plans they laid for her. Her heredity can't be explained by the general chemics of iron and steel and the principles of the steam engine; but something counts in her of the moods of her creators, both of the happy men and the sullen men whose bright or dark energies poured into her rivets and plates as they hammered, and now suffuse her body...

Our officials, and those of the enemy, merely lump these half-living creatures of the sea together, for ever making different totals, and call it so-much tonnage: sixty-thousand tons this week, fifty-five thousand tons last week, and so on. But to the men of the sea, ships with names, with familiar tricks and devilries and graces, have been wounded and murdered. And men have been wounded and murdered with them. Reading these statements you realise that there's apparently no direction from which destruction and death can't spring. Mines and torpedoes in the sea; shells across the water; bombs and machine-gun bullets from the sky; and you have to add those to a formidable list of peacetime perils – storm and fog, icebergs and shoal.

Merely to be one member of a great convoy, zigzagging through the dark, trying to keep in position and at a uniform speed, perhaps with fog coming on, is enough to test any master and his ship's company. And that's only the beginning, though fortunately for us it's also for many ships the end of danger, too. But going through these documents, one little window after another suddenly opened for me. It might be on a ship grounded on an unsuspected sand-bank; before she can get off, and now in full daylight, an enemy raiding plane swoops down to bomb her and then sweeps her decks with machine-gun fire, often continuing even after the men have taken to the boats. It might be on another ship, heading south for blue water, with the men off watch having a smoke and enjoying the sun – and suddenly there's a great hole in her side and she's listing so badly it's hard to lower the boats. Or further away still, in the distant tropics, a far smudge of smoke suddenly hurls great shells; and before you know where you are and what's hitting you, half the bridge has gone and all the wireless room, and No. 2 hold's on fire. It might be rafts then, as it was more than once in these narratives. But – 'the behaviour of the officers and crew was excellent.'

Now it's no secret that during the next few months the Nazis will probably produce their maximum possible attack upon our shipping, and a glance at a map of Western Europe will show that they're favourably situated to make such an attack, whether by U-boats, operating as we are told in swarms, or by big bombing planes. To arrive at or depart from this island of ours will be a very tricky and sometimes a very nasty business. Yet, of course, it's essential that our ships come and go freely, that this counter-blockade is defeated, as we are certain it will be. But the strain put upon the men of the Merchant Service will be greater than ever. By all means let us be grateful to them, let us salute and honour them. But that isn't enough. 'The behaviour of the officers and crew was excellent.'

It's high time now that the behaviour of the nation served by such officers and crew should be equally excellent. We owe them something more than sentimental speeches, made at a time when our lives depend on their skill and courage and sense of duty. We owe these men a square deal. In the last war, when they served us so well we praised them to the skies, clapped them on the back, stood 'em drinks. What we didn't stand them, though, were better conditions and a reasonably secure future. We've no right to be praising men one year and then ignoring them a year or two afterwards.

Do you remember what Kipling said about the soldiers of his day? 'For it's Tommy this and Tommy that, and chuck him out the brute. But it's "saviour of his country" when the guns begin to shoot!'

If we're proud of the Merchant Service now, then let's see to it that we remain proud of it, and that it's something to be proud of, in the years to come. And as we have time to give out honours and decorations and medals while the war is on, why shouldn't a grateful nation honour and decorate the whole Merchant Marine by making it a solemn promise that the old neglect will never be allowed again to let ships and men rust in idleness. Of course, it isn't really honouring and decorating them; it's merely giving them a square deal. It's all right, of course, they'll go on doing their job, bringing us the food and planes and supplies we need, even if the Nazis throw everything they've got at the Western sea lanes.

The behaviour of officers and crew will still be excellent. Masters of doomed ships will still go back to 'take a last look round'. They are that kind of men. But it's about time we stopped being the other kind of people, cheering them one minute, forgetting them the next. That's why there ought to be a great national gesture towards this service. Not to encourage these men to do their duty, because they don't need it; but to encourage the rest of us to do our duty by them, because we do need it.[235]

*On Tuesday, 18 March, Duff Cooper made a final, irreversible decision to terminate Priestley's broadcasts. However, Ryan was still trying to broker a compromise and after a telephone call to Priestley, was convinced that he had accepted the original offer to take a break and then return. However, Priestley had already berated an audience at the National Trades Union Club for failing to come to his defence and was now claiming that, contrary to what he had said at the time, he had also been forced off the air the previous October. He kept his powder dry until a lunch with Duff Cooper the day before the final broadcast. At the lunch, Priestley remained insistent on wanting to complete twelve broadcasts, but Cooper rejected that and told him that AP Herbert had already been signed to replace him, to which Priestley 'responded dismissively'.*

*His final 'Postscript' was broadcast the next day, Sunday 23 March. If ostensibly on the relatively uncontroversial subject of adult education, it did allow him to again air his 'desire to see some plan for a reconstructed world' and his refusal to accept that it would be 'a hindrance to our War effort'.*

Sunday 23 March 1941

In five hour's time, if spared, I shall be broadcasting as usual to America and the Dominions, and tonight I shall tell them something about a meeting we had, last Saturday afternoon, in Galgate. Galgate is a village in North Lancashire, one of those grey stone villages in the shadow of the Pennines that always make me feel that I'm coming home again; and it has a men's discussion group, organised by the county authorities for adult education in rural areas.

They're very keen in Galgate, and every year they hold a rally, attended by representatives of other village discussion groups, and they ask somebody to give them an address. This year they flung scholarship to the winds and asked me to go, and I'm very glad they did. I'll admit that when the actual time came I wasn't glad, because I'd had several broken nights and it was a warmish afternoon and I felt sleepy and rather cross.

If it was warmish outside the village hall, it was tropical inside, where more large-boned Lancashire men were packed into small spaces than I would have thought conceivable. And everybody seemed to be smoking but me. Nevertheless I hadn't been inside the place five minutes before I lost all trace of sleepiness and crossness. This audience was the real thing. There's a story of an actor who, strolling past a fishmonger's shop and noticing a row of open-mouthed, glassy-eyed, unstirring codfish, suddenly cried to his companion, 'Good lord, that reminds me – I have a matinee!' Nothing like that about the men's discussion group in Galgate. They were all alive, and never missed a point.

You know what it's usually like at question time after a lecture: an awful anti-climax. The sensible people are too shy, and the few people who do get up merely want to hear their own voices and just blather on, and then the whole thing flops and fizzles out. But it wasn't at all like that up there. They'd got some good questions and knew how to put them, and we could have gone on for hours and hours, only we had to close the meeting, for some of us had a distance to go and others had to do a bit of milking.

I tried to tell them something of what I thought and felt about the future of democracy, which has a future, a very vital and rewarding future, if we only stand up and work for it. But these men had shown me the very foundation stones of such a democracy, for there he was, rows of him, the plain man who after a long hard day's work is yet eager to learn, and to bring his mind, sincerely and critically, to bear on the great problems of our time.

Hard work, clear thinking, free speech – you can begin to build on them, just as surely as anything you've built will go rotten once too many people want money for nothing, refuse to learn and to think, and repression takes the place of discussion. It's a great thing, and something we ought to be proud of, that in the middle of a war, and in spite of long hours of work, raids and the blackout, that men should be willing, even eager, to attend these classes and discussion groups, should demand more knowledge. And all this intellectual activity isn't peculiar to North Lancashire – though North Lancashire is doing very well indeed – but can be found everywhere in this country. In Cambridgeshire there is even a kind of rural university system in which villages have their own colleges.

There is something inspiring in the thought that during these black nights, only lit by the flashes of gunfire and the glare of incendiaries, hardworking men and women are going out to teach and to learn, and in little groups are earnestly considering their problems, our problems. This too is an answer to Nazism and Fascism, which hate knowledge and have been busy for years trying to destroy it.

Even the Army has been given an ambitious scheme of adult education, though as yet the reports on how it's working seem to be confused and contradictory, some saying that the men don't want to learn, others declaring that the men are eager but that the organisation is faulty. It's too early yet to decide whether this education in the Army will succeed, but it's my belief that if it's operated intelligently and liberally, it will succeed. And for this reason: that these citizen soldiers of ours aren't strange young men, though as they thunder past in their monstrous armed vehicles they may seem strange enough – but they're the ordinary young Britons of our time.

Now I believe that most of them want to learn, though it doesn't follow that they want to learn what those of us who are older would like them to learn, because I fancy that a great deal of what seems to educated members of older generations necessary knowledge and culture seems to these youngsters a lot of dusty lumber. They have, I think, simpler, more direct, more impatient minds than many of us had at their age. A profound change in the spirit of the time has moulded their minds, far more than we are willing to allow. That's why many of the semi-official appeals to these young minds have little effect, because the wrong words are used.

If, for example, you happen to have grown up in a world that appears to be in a perpetual state of upheaval, a world in which nothing seems stable, you don't respond, as older people do, to words like 'heritage', 'tradition' and 'loyalty'. Your mind doesn't look back, simply because it has nothing very pleasant to look back to, but it wants to reach forward. But this impatience doesn't mean an unwillingness to learn anything. On the contrary there is among many of these young men in uniform, as among a great section of the civilian population, a hunger of the mind.

If I were called upon to single out the most surprising fact of this War, it would, I think, be this: that in spite of every possible obstacle and deterrent – hard work, long hours, the constant threat of air raids, the engrossing drama of the War itself – we are now a people who want to discuss, to theorise, to debate, to plan. We are no longer a lazy-minded people. We may not know exactly what we want or how to get it; we may suffer from a lack of accurate information; we may be unable to take sagacious broad views; but our minds are no longer asleep, perhaps because some of our most powerful opiates, such as highly organised sport and commercial amusements, are no longer to hand.

Now this awakening would be a very dangerous thing if we were a Fascist State, whose one object is to keep its people drilling by day and drugged by night; but as we are a Democracy, the gain is obvious, for it is impossible to have a true democracy without an enlightened, informed, critical public opinion. Without that kind of public opinion you merely have a sham democracy, and nobody has ventured to tell us yet that we are fighting for a sham democracy.

It's true that some people show a certain impatience with these views, but that arises from another cause. These people are anxious – as indeed we all are – to get on with the War. They know that if we lost this War, that would be the end of us. And let me say very plainly that that is my own view, for in the event of defeat, all the political, intellectual and cultural life of this country would be blotted out, a large proportion of the people here would starve to death, and the rest would find themselves no better than slaves. Those who died fighting, before the final catastrophe overwhelmed us, would be the lucky ones. Yes, it would be as bad as that.

Where some of us quarrel with those who cry, 'Get on with the War' and don't appear to have any other idea in their heads, is not about the urgency of the task but about the way in which it should be carried out. We can't agree, for example, that all these signs of an intellectual awakening, the growth of an informed and critical public opinion, the spread of education, the desire to see some plan for a reconstructed world, are a hindrance to our War effort.

I have heard all the usual arguments to the contrary, about the folly of arguing and planning when there is a burglar or a tiger in the room or the house is on fire. But these are false comparisons, if only because you don't spend several years and change your whole mode of living, trying to deal with a burglar or a tiger or a house on fire. Crises of this kind demand instantaneous action, during which it would be impossible to think of anything else. But during a long war most people, who don't happen to be chiefs of staffs, have ample time to think; indeed many people feel they've got too much time to think, and fear their thoughts.

Now the Germans have called themselves – and this is significant – a 'sleep-walking people'. They won't be beaten, as they are going to be beaten, by another 'sleep-walking people'. They will go down in defeat to a people who aren't wandering in their sleep, but are wide awake, purposeful, vital. And such people haven't put their minds into cold storage. They are fighting, and - thinking. They won't fight better if they feel they're like ants in an anthill that some huge careless boot has kicked open. When every bullet that's fired is felt to be a rivet in the structure of a better future, men will take better aim.

Hitler's best weapon isn't his heavily armed robots, formidable as they are, but, on his own admission, the ruined morale of his opponents, and nothing destroys morale better than a general feeling of dreariness and hopelessness, and minds that wonder and suffer without faith and hope. Therefore I say, not only for the sake of the Peace but also for the War that must bring us a lasting peace, you and I should welcome and encourage and do all in our power to assist this spread of ideas among all our people, these lectures and classes and discussion groups, the sensible books and pamphlets that still pour from the presses. They too accept the challenge of the black magic of Fascism, and for every book that's burned produce another one; for every wise man who's hunted down and murdered they produce another one; for every liberal and noble idea that is booted out of the empire of slavery and death, they produce another one, to flourish in the kingdom of freedom and life.

We don't know how or where this War may be won; it may be won in the Atlantic, in the Mediterranean, in Africa or Central Europe. But some of it may also be won – and the Peace with it – in the village hall of Galgate, where men come down from the Pennines, after the day's toil, to listen, to ask, to discuss – and to learn.[236]

*Priestley's Postscripts were over but he was still 'blazing with sense of injustice' about the way they had been terminated.*

I was taken off the air. This annoyed me, not because I was anxious to continue these home broadcasts – I was still busy with the overseas talks – but because I dislike being pushed around, especially when I can't discover who is doing the pushing. I received two letters – I kept them for years but may have lost them now – and one was from the Ministry of Information telling me that the B.B.C. was responsible for the decision to take me off the air, and the other was from the B.B.C., saying that a directive had come from the Ministry of Information to end my broadcasts. While blaming each other, I think both of them were concealing the essential fact – that the order to shut me up had come from elsewhere.

I don't know how other people feel about this stealthy hocus-pocus, but to my mind it is one of the most contemptible features of British public life. Power is exercised in such a way – a nod here, a wink there – that it can't be challenged. We are democratic and free in theory but not in practice. Work may be censored as it is elsewhere, but not openly, through a censor's office everybody knows about; it is quietly shuffled and conjured away. Men are squeezed out of public jobs, not for political reasons – oh dear no! – but because they are discovered to be not quite the right type, not sound, old boy. This is the British way, slimy with self-deception and cant, and the older I get the more I dislike it.

With the Ministry of Information I was never on cordial terms. As a writer who made too much noise and didn't seem to know his place, I was regarded with suspicion. There were plenty of writers, innocently anxious to serve their country, working there in Malet Street. Not one of them was given a position of any importance and authority: lawyers, advertising and newspaper men came first.

When Duff Cooper, whom I liked as a man, was Minister, we had a few sharp differences of opinion. For example, when I agreed to broadcast about the men of the Merchant Marine, I felt we had no right to praise them in wartime without assuring them that we would improve their working and living conditions in peacetime. To thank a man publicly, tears in your eyes and voice, while conveniently forgetting that his fo'castle was a hell-hole and his wife and children lived in a slum, seemed to me a job for Pecksniff. I know, because they told me, that a lot of people were fighting the war to keep Britain exactly as it had been – not possible, anyhow – but none of them had lived in. back-to-back houses mostly on tea, bread and margarine.

When Brendan Bracken was Minister of Information, he asked me to go and see him. He put a hand on my shoulder and said I was a wonderful writer and broadcaster but that I ought to keep off politics and social criticism. I ought to be like Dickens. Of all writers – Dickens! (Shaw once said that reading Little Dorrit had made a revolutionary out of him.) And this from a Minister of Information! Telling writers what to do!

My relations with the B.B.C. were pleasant enough, though I never felt that its senior administrators, men who wanted a quiet life and an hour or two in the garden, were on my side. To them I looked – and perhaps still look – like trouble. Following me would be nasty comments in the press, questions in the House, angry telephone calls from retired admirals. So a legend grew that as a broadcaster I was 'difficult' – 'better not risk him, my dear fellow' – and this was entirely false, for if I undertook to give a thirteen-minute talk, that is what I gave, and I was punctual and reasonably clean and sober. I have arrived in provincial studios and been made to feel I was a bomb with a trembling detonator. When I left, the sigh of relief followed me down the street.[237]

*Subsequent suggestions from Duff Cooper that Priestley was 'getting tired' and had 'turned the 'Postscripts' into cock-fights' did nothing to douse Priestley's anger. A final BBC attempt at some sort of compromise, holding out the olive branch of an offer for him to 'assist us occasionally with a Postscript' was rejected out of hand.[238] There was controversy for years, in part fuelled by Priestley himself, about how and why he was taken off the air, and he made no secret of his conviction that Churchill had been behind it. He also claimed that the BBC and the MoI tried to blame each other and 'one of them must be lying'.[239]*

I had to stop – not this time because I wanted to, for I was anxious to keep on. I appealed to the BBC, only to be referred to the Ministry of Information. I went to the Ministry and was told that it was the responsibility of the BBC. I knew then it was neither of them; it was somebody higher up... I had no direct evidence but I soon came to believe – and friends more in the know than I was agreed with me – that it was Churchill who had me taken off the air.[240]

*Priestley's stepson, Nicholas Hawkes, carried out extensive research on the 'Postscripts' controversy and concluded that there is no hard evidence that Churchill intervened, but the lack of a paper trail leading to the Prime Minister does not necessarily tell the whole story. Churchill's memo to Duff Cooper, expressing regret that 'you have got Mr JB Priestley back' and complaining of Priestley's 'argument utterly contrary to my known views,' might have been the only intervention necessary. If word did come down from on high to get rid of Priestley, as he himself later claimed, it was as likely to have been in a quiet word from one of Churchill's aides, among the wood-panelling and leather armchairs of a London club, as in an official letter or memo.*

*Indeed, the mere knowledge that Churchill and a number of other leading Tories were infuriated by Priestley's broadcasts and accusing the BBC of 'left wing bias' – a charge that has routinely been levelled against the Corporation from its inception to the present day – might well have been enough to ensure the termination of the broadcasts.*

*A senior BBC official privately conceded that 'political issues are involved',[241] and Priestley's suspicion that the hand of Churchill lay behind his dismissal was given indirect confirmation by a comment by AP Herbert a quarter of a century later. Commenting on his knighthood 'for political and public services' in Churchill's honours list of 1945, Herbert wrote that the only public service he could recall on Churchill's behalf was that he had 'at his [Churchill's] request reluctantly done four or five of those difficult Sunday radio Epilogues in the wake of JB Priestley'.[242] He had earlier suggested that the request had come from Duff Cooper, but whoever the intermediary, it seems naive to imagine that Churchill's clearly stated view did not play at least some part in Priestley's exit from the Sunday night 'Postscripts'.*

*Throughout the remainder of the war, Priestley continued to broadcast, though primarily for overseas consumption. 'I was not prevented from broadcasting to anybody and everybody, only to my fellow countrymen. I was not only allowed but encouraged to talk on the air to the rest of the world.'[243]*

*Although he was deliberately passed over by the Talks Department for one series,[244] it is not true to say that Priestley was banned from the domestic airwaves altogether. In late 1941 he wrote, produced and presented the series 'Listen to My Notebook', and in 1943 'Make It Monday', though neither matched the quality or the audience figures of his 'Postscripts' and 'he appears to have antagonised both cast and production staff'.[245] His determination to continue the debate about 'Peace Aims' was reflected in his many newspaper and magazine articles and in his novel*

Daylight on Saturday, *published in 1943.*

They smoked for a few moments in a comfortable silence. Then Cheviot patted his companion on the shoulder. 'What's the matter with us all, Sammy?'

'Who d'yer mean, Mr Cheviot?'

'The whole lot of us - the human race, if you like – or at least the human race as it is now.'

'It might be a kind of growing pains,' said Sammy thoughtfully.

'I've sometimes thought that myself – but I don't know.' And Cheviot's voice died away.

'People do a lot of things they oughtn't to, of course,' said Sammy. 'In fact, if you count in what these young Nazis an' Japs 'as been up to lately, yer can say there's more damned wickedness about now than there ever was. But I've got a fancy even most of them's got to be worked up to it, that it doesn't come quite natural any more.'

'That may be, but they let themselves be worked up to it, and then there are the people who do the working up – a pretty gang they are. And we can't even get together to save ourselves from these devils without quarrelling among ourselves every five minutes. We're doing a useful job here – an urgent job – as you know – and yet look at us. So I say again – what's the matter with us all?'

'My feeling is,' said Sammy, slowly, struggling with his thought, 'my feeling is, Mr Cheviot, that people haven't much to get 'old of. They feel a bit empty inside. They don't know where they're goin' or what it's all about. An' nobody an' nothin' tells 'em. Wireless doesn't tell 'em. The films don't tell 'em. The pint or the gin-an' -what's-it they 'ave at the local doesn't tell 'em. The papers don't tell 'em. They're just goin' round in a circle, you might say. You listen to 'em, Mr Cheviot. They're always sayin': "So what?" An' it frightens me – that "So what?"'

'I think it frightens me too. But surely, Sam, there are plenty of chaps ready to tell them where they're going or what it's all about – parsons, professors, writers and so on.'

'But I fancy most o' them don't know either. If they did an' were certain, they'd come runnin' wi' the good news. An' people listen all right if a proper message comes through.'

'You sound religious, Sam. Didn't know you were religious.'

'An' I'm not, Mr Cheviot, as least so far as I know. I'm thinking now about other people, not myself. I'm a bit different i' some ways.'..[246]

'We can't start from scratch. We can't expect nothing. We're men – that's the point, Sammy – and because we're men and there have been millions and millions of us for the last million years, all nosing round and scraping and digging and sweating for a bit of something extra, hoping and dreaming and getting all excited when the sun came bouncing up again, it's born in us, part of our blood and guts now, to expect something, to cry out for something better than the old man had, to tell ourselves that the job can be finished right, that your pals won't rat on you, that there's a woman somewhere who's waiting for you to come home, that you'll have kids who'll start where you left off. I tell you, Sammy, it's part of us. You may have cut it out, just as some people have had half their insides cut out to save the rest, but that's not the same thing. But I'm not blaming you, Sammy. I know what you've had to put up with. Good luck to you, Sammy.'

'Ere. Mr Elrick, what are you saying that for? You're not leavin' us, are you?'

'Yes, I am. This might be my last day.'

'But – but –' cried Sammy, distressed now, 'that's not good enough, Mr Elrick. None of us wants yer to go.'

'Thanks, Sammy. But that's how it is, you see. That's what I'm trying to tell you. You see, you've left that contented line of yours already. You're telling me it's not good enough. Of course it isn't good enough. But then nothing's good enough – not for what we've got inside us, Sammy, burning us up. And then you say that none of you want me to go. But God save us! – what's that got to do with it? We don't begin to get what we want. We don't want Hitler. We don't want the black-out and the bombing.

'We don't want to spend all our time making planes and guns and shells and camps and aerodromes when we're all short of towns and decent houses and furniture and pots and pans and wireless sets. We don't want a lot of rich old crooks sitting round on their fat bottoms working out how to keep their hold over us when the war's over. But, you see, instead of blowing that fire inside us into a blaze we try to damp it down, we try to make the best of what we've got instead of turning what we've got into the best we can imagine. I know I've no room to talk. I've played the clown all right in my time. But at least I knew I was playing the clown. Well, so long, Sammy – and I needn't tell you to keep smiling.'[247]

*Now free from the restraints of censorship and control by the BBC and the MoI, Priestley found the space to expand his vision of a better, more equitable society to the kind of fuller exposition many of his listeners had been asking for. He also set up and chaired the '1941 Committee', a forum bringing together like-minded politicians, public figures and intellectuals, including Edward Hulton, Richard Acland, Michael Foot, Thomas Balogh, Richie Calder, Violet Bonham Carter, Tom Driberg, Victor Gollancz, David Low, David Astor and Christopher Mayhew. Its succinct motto was: 'The people must be worthy of victory; the peace must be worthy of the people.'[248]*

*The Committee published a report in December 1941 calling for the public control of the railways, mines and docks and a national wages policy, and in May 1942 a further report urged the setting up of works councils and the publication of 'post-war plans for the provision of full and free education, employment and a civilised standard of living for everyone'. If that sounded utopian, Priestley insisted that there was 'no magic formula' to make this happen, and warned that 'You do not get rid of false values by substituting state ownership for private enterprise... we must not let envy convince us that redistribution of the swag will do the trick. We must change the game.'[249]*

*In the same year, Priestley and Acland took leading roles in establishing the Common Wealth Party, advocating 'Common Ownership, Vital Democracy and Morality in Politics' and the public ownership of land. To back his principles, Acland gave his 8,000 hectare family estate in Devon to the National Trust.*

*The party defeated Conservative candidates at by-elections in*

*Eddisbury, Skipton and Chelmsford. However, in the 1945 General Election only one of its twenty-three candidates was successful – at Chelmsford, where there was no Labour candidate. Common Wealth was dissolved that year and most of its members joined the Labour Party.*

*Priestley had been an effective campaigner for the party in its early days but became disenchanted by its leftward drift and ended his involvement with it, but he continued to set out his beliefs and hopes for the future of the country, inspired by the communal spirit engendered by the shared experience of the war. Central to his thinking was a clear vision of the People as the foundation of the country – not the State and not the Masses – the People who had woken up and were looking forward again.*

I cannot believe, and I have much evidence to support me, that ever again will these good folk announce blandly that they care nothing about politics. Never again will they believe that public affairs are none of their business. They have been taught, with bitter thoroughness, that public affairs are people's lives. They are now politically-minded, to the astonishment and dismay of many public men, as they have never been before. They no longer believe in the false security of the suburb. They have seen their bungalows ringed with fire, and have felt the evil invader shaking the very ground. They know now that all the neat little plans they once made for their children's future may be nothing but idle dreams, that we have now to find our own way through the future years like hacking a road through a jungle.

All this these householders and good citizens have learned, and among the Home Guard or at the air raid post or down in the shelter they have spent many an hour eagerly and earnestly talking about these things. These were the men and women to whom I broadcast every Sunday night for more than half a year, and I know what their thoughts are for they wrote to me by the thousand to tell me of them. And in this gigantic swing-over from indifference to eager and close attention to political affairs, in these innumerable discussions between men and women of a great civilian army, in the determination that never again shall there be this idle drifting into disaster, the new democracy has been born.[250]

# PART IV
# The Shadow of
# the Bomb

# Chapter 12
# The hope I felt

*After the end of the war, Priestley continued to advance his social agenda, speaking on behalf of Labour candidates at the 1945 General Election and standing himself as an Independent for the Cambridge University seat. Although Priestley came a distant third in that seat, the vision that he had articulated in his wartime broadcasts and writings resonated with the national electorate.*

'Priestley... appealed, in the words of the BBC Listener Research Department, to "a very large section of the population who look for a better world but have no party allegiance": which is precisely why Conservatives were so suspicious of him. His reputation for political influence rests not only on his role in boosting wartime morale but on the perception that he contributed to a mood of popular radicalism which culminated in Labour's 1945 election landslide and the social-democratic era that followed. In 1945 Labour and Priestley marched together. He went on the campaign trail, addressing "three meetings a night, sometimes five on Sundays", wrote newspaper articles and made a Party Political Broadcast, and stood himself, unsuccessfully, and not as a party candidate, for the anachronistic Cambridge University seat...

If voters in 1945 were choosing between rival ideas of the nation, it was Priestley's and not Churchill's that they voted for. Moreover, the populist construction of national identity which Priestley helped bring to the fore during the war years would dominate the meanings which the war carried in the years after 1945, when it came to be seen as a defining moment of national unity and purpose: the moment when, in the words of two of the period's earliest historians, "England had risen", and the British people "found themselves again", and in due course the Welfare State replaced the Empire as the focus of national pride. [251]

*Priestley's belief in a broad-based, genuine democracy was restated in* Out of the People.

If it could be shown that in one great country a way out, towards freedom and equality, had been discovered, then men everywhere would be hopeful again. Although pre-war Britain was admired by nobody – a fact our official propagandists would do well to bear in mind – Britain still retained some of her old prestige, and the conduct of the British people during the war has aroused wonder and admiration throughout the world. And if these were the people who found a way out, who began to banish the demons, who started to move towards and not away from freedom and equality, who proved that democracy was not ending but just beginning, then people everywhere would take heart and try to order their affairs in the same fashion.[252]

*Priestley used the medium of a* Letter to a Returning Serviceman, *published in 1945, to give the fullest statement of his hopes and aims for British society in the post-war years.*

My Dear Robert,

No doubt it is very hard for you to imagine me as anything else but a plump middle-aged author, sitting in a cosy huddle of books, pictures and pipes in my Albany study, where we last met. But I want you to remember that 1 was once a returning serviceman too. (This is important, so you will please forgive me if I rub it in a bit.) I spent nearly five years in the infantry, was three times a casualty, and saw the flower of my generation mown down among the barbed wire.

All the best fellows, as we used to say, 'went West,' and those of us who were left were a mere remnant, which explains why there has been so little genius and leadership in my generation. I think you celebrated your twenty-first birthday in the desert; I know I celebrated mine in the water-logged trenches of 1915. And I have not forgotten what I thought and felt as a soldier: one doesn't forget, as you will discover. So put out of your mind the notion that you are being got at by a comfortable old word-spinner (and it hasn't been so comfortable either, here in London in this war), and believe me when I tell you that

I can remember my own demobilisation as if it happened only a day or two ago.

I hope you will agree with me when I say that the citizen-soldier, as distinct from the professional, finds himself at the end of a modern war a sharply divided man. He faces two ways. There is a conflict in him, and I suspect that it is this conflict that makes him appear less radiantly happy, far more weary and wary, than people expect him to be. One half of him wants to settle up, the other half wants to settle down. Sharing the same billet in his mind are an earnest revolutionary and a tired and cynical Tory. Both of them cry incessantly 'Never again!' but one of them means that never again will he allow the world to drift into the vast lunacy of war, whereas the other means that never again will he quit the safe old shelter of home for any communal adventure.

One wants to reorganise society, and the other wants privacy and a domestic life. The red half cries: 'It's your duty now to fight for security and social justice for all'; and the blue half retorts: 'You've done enough. Find a job, keep quiet, and try growing tomatoes.' One demands real democracy and the end of economic brigandage, while the other asks for a bungalow, a car and a good wireless set. The reformer shouts at the cynic, and the cynic sneers at the reformer. And both are performing inside the mind of a tired man, who is homesick and wants to wear his own clothes, to eat what he fancies and to do no more parades.

Now last time, Bob, the reformer, the revolutionary, the one who said there must be no more of this murderous nonsense, lost completely. He never really had a chance. The politicians and most of the Press told him he was a hero and that everything would be all right if he took it easy. His women, who still believed they were living in a nice settled world that happened to have had a nasty accident, told him to dig the garden or take the baby out and not talk so much. The pubs and sports grounds and racetracks were ready to welcome him. Living was dear, but there seemed to be plenty of decent jobs about at good wages. Now and again he would exchange a few drinks with chaps he had served with, and they would grow reminiscent and a trifle sentimental, remembering a comradeship that seemed difficult to fit into this civilian world of social classes and profit-and-loss relationships, with its surface softness and its queer underlying hardness.

Most of the newspapers turned out to be wrong, but they never admitted it and always found something new and exciting for him. (England was in danger again, but this time from the ruthless new Australian Test side.) Most or the politicians were wrong too of course, and they never admitted it either; and so he began to shrug his shoulders at them. A few men, not very admirable types, grew rich and succeeded at the same time in throwing hundreds of thousands of decent craftsmen – ship-builders, for example – out of work. Russia, it seemed, was a constant menace, according to the newspapers owned by very rich men. The world played power politics again. Dragon's teeth, of a new and marvellous fertility, were sown freely. And the harvest – well, you know.

They tell us that history does not repeat itself. All I can say is that history just now is trying its hardest. The 1918-19 pattern is distinctly visible. Once more you are being told to take it easy and all will be well. Anything that encourages ideas is being frowned upon, but the sports grounds and the light amusements are in full swing. The reformer, the revolutionary, the one who says there must be no more of this murderous nonsense, is being told, in a hundred different ways, not to be an ass and a bore. (Notice how, once the threat of a Nazi invasion was passed, the 'Better World' idea was a favourite target for the millionaires' hack writers)...

There was a time, round about 1940, when we were able to convince a lot of people that only a diseased and rotten society could have thrown up a Hitler, but since then there has been a huge campaign telling us day and night that it was Hitler who somehow produced, presumably from his box of watercolours, any disease and rottenness there may be in our society. Tory gentlemen who have clearly not learnt anything, and now never will, confidently offer themselves as our guardians again, assuming that because they choose to forget the sickening muddle, darkening to tragedy, of the Twenties and Thirties, we shall have forgotten too. Men who, when they were in danger in 1940, made haste to enforce government control and asked us to cheer our communal war effort, now thunder on platforms against such controls and denounce all communal cohorts. Industrialists who spent years building up vast monopolies and wrecking 'little men' now assure us, almost with tears in their eyes, that what they care most about arc competition and the economic welfare of the little man. If we had no children and disliked human beings, what a tremendous roaring farce this would be!

Now before I take up the main argument, my dear Robert, I want to dispose of two tricks that are always being worked against me, and will probably be tried on you soon: The first is: 'Ah, but you're an idealist.' This is usually said to me by some pleasant but completely muddle-headed oldish businessman, who has been wrong about everything for years. He is quite ready even now to go bumbling along in the same old way, hoping vaguely that some miracle will protect him from the disaster that has always followed this line of conduct. This he calls 'realism,' and he believes himself to be a hard-headed man. When I remonstrate with him, and point out that he is proposing to go wobbling the same old way to ruin and misery, he says complacently 'Ah, but you're an idealist,' and usually tells me that I don't understand ordinary human nature. It is no use my retorting that ordinary human nature is just what I do understand, and that I earn my living by that understanding. I waste my time if I try to tell him that, compared with him and his muddle and his vague hopes of an intervening miracle, I am a realist with a head of teak, and that on every important public issue for the last fifteen years I have been right and he has been wrong.

He contrives to forget everything that it is convenient to forget, which explains why his favourite newspapers are so blithely inconsistent and self-contradictory. He protects himself by declaring that I am an idealist, a little Johnny head-in-air, and that when I know as much about human nature as he does then I will change my views. It is he who refused to call Mussolini's bluff, would not intervene in Spain, and allowed Hitler to make himself so strong that we were only saved from slavery and Buchenwald at the last minute; who thought Churchill a nuisance in June 1939 and a demi-god in June 1945; who believes that all countries should export more than they import; who still assumes that it is only mysterious 'agitators' that prevent working folk from wanting to toil until they drop for debenture-holders they have never seen; who will vote billions of credit in wartime but thinks we cannot afford to do anything in peacetime; who is bewildered by the failure of investors and producers, clamped into a system that compels them to put profit first, to provide people with what they most badly need; who supports policies that inevitably lead to war and then wonders why further wars should threaten us.

This is the British middle-class 'realist', the man who likes to keep his feet on the ground, who has what he calls a 'healthy mistrust' of anybody with ideas, who knows all about human nature (unlike the poets and novelists and social philosophers), and who when you try to talk sense to him will smilingly dismiss you as 'an idealist'. A nice old boy, but more dangerous than dynamite.

The other trick that will be worked against you, just as it has often been worked against me, belongs to the type of man who imagines himself to be progressive, claims to be with you in denouncing the bad old world, but artfully escapes from making any positive move. He does this by asking you exactly what you want to put in place of the present political, economic and social system, and then points out a few flaws. It is he who detects the crumpled rose petal beneath the seven mattresses. And that is enough for him. 'No, no, my boy, you'll have to do better than that,' he tells you, and then dozes off again.

He imagines – or pretends for his comfort to imagine – that you and he are not trying to find some way out of a nasty mess that threatens to get much worse, but are airily designing Utopias, Islands of the Blessed, Earthly Paradises, Avalon of the unfading apple blossom. He is like a man on a sinking ship who refuses to enter a lifeboat because he does not approve the exact shade of its paint or has taken a dislike to the third mate's nose. I am not being fanciful: he really is as silly as that.

Our business now is to save ourselves, as best we can, from even worse disasters than we have known during the last thirty years. We are not choosing perfect holiday resorts but are trying to escape from shipwreck and earthquake. For example, if we cannot prevent a third world war then very soon we shall find ourselves living underground, half-starved, manufacturing nothing but gigantic rockets. If millions are thrown out of employment again, there will soon be terrible social upheavals, and bloody revolution or counter-revolution will follow.

If we cannot educate people properly and if we allow them to remain the victims of any catchpenny tactics of mass suggestion, then values will drop to even lower levels, civilisation will decay, and the world will swarm with barbarians and robots. And unless the conscious mind and the unconscious mind of modern man can be brought into harmony, then there is a danger that destruction, inspired by deep unconscious drives, will overtake construction, and that violence and cruelty will rage throughout whole communities. And there isn't much time. So let us have no nonsense from the man who leans back in his armchair, points out a flaw here, a hard case there, and demands nothing less than a complete Utopia delivered in cellophane.

Now for that main argument, Bob, that I promised you after disposing of those two familiar tricks. What is the root cause of all the mischief'! No, don't worry I'm not going to tell you that the world is as it is simply because people are not perfect. Clearly that will get us nowhere. Of course people arc selfish, greedy, lazy-minded, intolerant, illogical, timid, and wanting in faith and steadfastness. I am myself, and so are you. But people are also unselfish, compassionate, reasonable, brave, faithful and steadfast. There is enough variety in human beings to prove any argument. We are not at the moment discussing the problem of how to fill the world with shining saints.

What you and I – and at least a thousand million others – want to know is how we can avoid more gigantic disasters, how we can live together, as ordinary weak sinful creatures, without starving and bullying and murdering each other, and how we can best use all the new knowledge and skills to give men and women not an Earthly Paradise but at least some semblance of a decent life. What is it that continually frustrates us? What goes wrong? What is the matter with us? Those are the questions that both your generation and mine keep asking. And my answer is this: that we are trying to live in two different kinds of worlds at one and the same time. Or put it this way, that we try to make old patterns of behaviour fit new conditions of living, and it can't be done. One half of us forges ahead while the other half lingers behind, and the result is an intolerable strain. If we don't catch up with ourselves soon, then wc shall burst...

People are apt to think that they are standing outside history, instead of moving along in it. This leads to a view, still common among oldish people, that there is a kind of normality, a safe and settled style of life, to which sooner or later we can return. It is easy to see why oldish people should think along these lines. Their most formative years came in the period before the First World War, towards the end of what seemed a long and comparatively settled era, and that war seemed to them a mere distressing interruption. Hence the mistakes made after the war.

The years that followed didn't settle down as they ought to have done, and then, to so many people's indignation or bewilderment, they got worse instead of better, until in the end there was Hitler and hell-on-earth. But there still persisted, like a ghost from some Edwardian garden party, the notion that there would be a return to the good old settled days, plus a few more recent comforts and conveniences. And this of course is an illusion, and a very dangerous illusion. We are not only moving away from any such return, but we are also moving away at a very great speed.... If we are not moving towards the Socialism of Morris or Robert Blatchford, it is even more certain that we shall not discover, in any possible hard Corporate-State Toryism of 1950, any way back to the sleepy Tory Britain of Lord Salisbury or Balfour.

Most of the Tories I know, muddled sentimentalists, talk as if Disraeli had just walked off the platform. They are three-quarters of a century out of date. But these are not the important Tories, the ones who keep the Central Office going and initiate the big propaganda campaigns. The important Tories don't live in Disraeli's world, even if at times they talk in public as if they did. They are the tough fellows behind the huge monopolies and cartels, the secret emperors and warlords of finance and industry. And they live in our world.

They are... determined to go their way and not ours. They are often as ruthless as they are realistic. Their reaction, when alarmed, frequently takes on an ugly shape. Hitler, Mussolini, Franco, found allies among them. A group of them in France did all they could to undermine their country's resistance to the Nazis. I suspect that one of two of them here subsidised Mosley and his guard of bruisers. In America they hire strike-breakers, letting loose armed thugs among their employees. And a Britain they controlled would bear no resemblance to a Primrose League rally addressed by A. J. Balfour. It would soon be an industrial despotism, an iron oligarchy, a Venetian Republic without the art and beauty and long golden afternoons of Venice.

Modern industry is no admirer of those 'little men' about whom all politicians talk such vote-catching nonsense. It is an affair of giant organisations, with a few technical generals deploying whole armies of work people. A political democracy that stays outside these organisations is a mere shadow show. Its committees and elections would soon be of less importance than the entertainments in the canteens. Genuine power would remain in a few hands. Gigantic state machinery could soon be erected to compel the masses – and I use the term deliberately, for soon the rootless, powerless and doped folk could rightly be described as 'masses' – to toil for these fortunate and powerful few. This was of course the Nazi idea, when you add a few pseudo-mystical German trimmings, and we must not assume yet that we are rid of it. You see, my dear Robert, modern industry does not really lend itself to the cosy compromises, so dear to the average English mind, of Tory Reformers and Liberals...

Either we must completely socialise these giant industries or we must be ready to see people being enslaved by them. If we socialise them, then perhaps five hundred persons may enjoy less freedom than they did, but on the other hand perhaps about five million persons will be started on their way towards a little more freedom... When Hitler's mad empire threatened our world, the real hard core of resistance to it was found not among peasants, not among landed aristocrats and their fine ladies and priests, not among the barons or big business, but among the industrial workers. Such inheritance as we have was saved for us by the disinherited.

I said earlier that our root trouble was that our political and economic ideas belonged to one age and our inventions and industry belonged to another and newer age. But I have another notion about our trouble, and it is one that I would not mention in a newspaper article or on a public platform but that I will risk dropping into this letter to you. Suppose every age of mankind were given a task to perform, what do you imagine the task of this age to be? Is it not to lift some of the load of want, ignorance, fear and misery, that vast burden older than history, from the shoulders of men and women everywhere? That is what I believe.

Ours is the day when uncommon men must plan and toil for common men. It is the time at last when the world must reject the age-old belief that life for most men must necessarily be brief, brutish and sad. I am not talking now of full sunlight but of a glimmer of daylight in the old darkness. It is not Utopia we are planning – that is a long way off – but only the relief of the desperately besieged human family, the man beaten down by hard circumstance, the woman haggard and old long before her proper time, the children for ever hoping when there is no hope. There is no Kingdom of Heaven for us, but we can obtain a brief glimpse of it when we discover that our rescue party, deep in the thickest jungle, has taken a step or two forward in the right direction. At last we have our fellow creatures on our conscience, and from that, I most firmly believe, there is no escape... We cannot be indifferent any longer. There is in us a broad social sympathy that must either be accepted or deliberately stifled...

I have a rather irrational conviction, which no study of our contemporary history does anything to remove, that whenever our age refuses to undertake this great primary task, tries to wriggle out of it, denies being any brother's keeper, then promptly, as if a judge passed sentence on us in some invisible court, our age is punished, and once again the blood and tears flow. It is as if we were being driven back, by furious angels, to the highroad we were meant to travel. And the faces of the Nazi leaders, the foulest gang in European history, were like monstrous reflections of our own faces in our worst moments. We could still think in terms of individual power, of greed and cunning, of lies and violence, could we? Then here were Hitler, Himmler, Goebbels and Goering, our worst selves with the lid off. And they would blast and burn us, and we should have to blast and burn them, before this next lesson would be ended.

Again, glance back over the last twenty-five years and notice how much mischief, deepening to tragedy, has come to us from the fear of the Soviet Union and the ceaseless plotting, by industrial barons working with the Hitlers, Mussolinis and Francos, against the Soviet Union. We have poured enough manpower and materials into this war, into the business of destruction, to have laid the foundations of a world civilisation, and we should not have had this war if in the early Twenties we had stopped besieging and baiting Russia and instead had frankly welcomed the experiment she was making.

Whatever their faults, the Bolsheviks had put a hand to the great task and were trying to lift the load of want, ignorance, fear and misery from their dumb millions, while the Americans-as they freely admit now-were living in a fool's paradise of money-for-nothing and Martinis, and we were shuffling and shambling along, listening to our Tory politicians talking their old twaddle and being deceived at election times by any Red letter or red herring. It was at the end of this period that I visited depressed areas and found there whole towns far gone in decay and men and youths who had the grey faces of prisoners of war. So the stick had to come down on our knuckles again. The lesson was still waiting to be learned. It is waiting yet...

Modern man is essentially a communal and co-operating man. What he does best – as I have told you before, Bob – is what he does by working with a great many other men. The Italians of the Renaissance or the Elizabethans threw up individuals who cannot be matched today, when we have no Leonardo da Vinci or Shakespeare. But we accomplish what would seem miracles to our forefathers – for example, our vast feats of civil engineering, the broadcasting of a symphony concert, even our films at their best – by our new pooling of knowledge and our superb team work.

When the American O.W.I. [Office of War Information] here, with understandable pride, showed us the film they had made about the Tennessee Valley Authority, and I saw how a huge countryside had been transformed and a flood of new life poured into it, I felt as deeply moved as I would have been by a noble work of art. Here at last was the lifting of the burden. (And there never was a better argument for Socialism than this documentary film, although it was made by men who would be instantly alarmed or offended if you called them Socialists.)

Here, in this fruitful transformation of a whole countryside, not for any man's profit but for the general good, modern man was at last beginning to fulfil his destiny. Here we were doing what God intended this generation of men to do. (And the Russians of course had shown us the way too, with their great dams and electrification schemes.) And the lesson now is plain. We shall cease doing this noble work only at the risk or destroying ourselves by war. The vast communal energies of modern man must find equally vast tasks to perform, and if they are not used constructively then they will be used destructively; so that we have the choice of watching old cities burn and crumble or or watching new cities lift their towers to the sun.

It is, I declare to you, as simple as that. But if you want it put into the language of leading articles and political platforms, then what about this? Unless the great industrial powers, with their production geared up by war, can solve their marketing problems in a new way, then soon we shall all be fighting again. But if we can begin to raise the standard of living in the world's huge depressed areas, notably India and China, then these marketing problems will shortly solve themselves and the danger of war can be safely passed. And it is here that idealism and the noblest altruism, on the one side, and the plainest realism and self-interest, on the other, come together and find a common plan of action...

During this war I noticed, as you must have done, how so many people, suddenly plunged into Civil Defence duties, seemed younger and livelier, in spite of long hours of work and much anxiety, than they had been for years before the war. They had left their back gardens and armchairs and wireless sets and made common cause at last with their neighbours. Again, just before writing these pages I made an electioneering tour, to speak for Labour candidates I knew, in the Midlands, the North East and in the neighbourhood of Glasgow. In many of these constituencies the Labour organisation had had to be improvised, with helpers – often young men and girls who sacrificed their holidays – discovered at the last moment. And candidate after candidate, men and women of very different types and backgrounds, spoke to me with the same glowing enthusiasm of these helpers and of the eager and comradely spirit that seemed to light up their committee rooms. One could see too in the faces of the girls who came running with messages, in the faces of the young men who acted as stewards at our packed meetings, the same glowing enthusiasm; and because they had given so readily, they had also received much in return; and life had now both more meaning and more fun in it, was altogether a richer and more satisfying adventure.

So what? Just this, Bob. Don't, I implore you, sink too deep, too far, into that famous English privacy. You feel at the moment that you can only save your soul by boiling your door and then pottering or brooding in the most delicious seclusion. All right; go and enjoy the secret sweets of our civvy life. Fleet the time carelessly, like Shakespeare's folk in Arden, with your flower beds and bookshelves, your slippers and armchair, your comfortable jokes and tunes on the wireless ... But beware. We can keep ourselves to ourselves too long. We can do it until we go stale and dim, like the apathetic herd we were in the Baldwin and Chamberlain era, when we messed about in our back gardens, ran about in our little cars, listened to the crooners and the comics, while the terrible shadows crept nearer.

I think we make too much of our separateness in this country. We hurry home too quickly. We are too apt to imagine that life really begins where all broad human relationships end. This is no attack upon the family; and it is significant that in those pre-war years of middle-class seclusion, when whole suburbs were like tree-lined concentration camps, when to be a young wife was often to be sentenced to a term of solitary confinement, there was not more family life but less than there had been before, and the birth-rate dwindled. It is the growing family that keeps our doors open. And that is good, but it is not enough. Beware again the charmed cosy circle. Don't stay too long in that armchair-and be suspicious of all those publicity experts who tell you that you need never move out of it – but get out and about, compel yourself to come to terms with strangers (who will not be strangers long), make one of a team or a group, be both worker and audience, and put a hand to the great tasks.

I know, my dear lad, that all this is just what you don't want to do. You've had it. All right, go off with the girl and enjoy the loneliest possible holiday, among the mountains, on top of the widest moor, with

> The silence that is in the starry sky,
> The sleep that is among the lonely hills.

But when you come back, be a real citizen and not a hermit in a bungalow. Remember that even if you are not interested in politics, the fact remains that politics are interested in you, and indeed are busy already shaping your future. Remember that we are in history and are not merely watching it stream past us, as if we were sitting in the balcony of the Odeon. If we do not control our lives, then somebody else, probably a rascal, will do it for us. Remember too – and this is hard for the English, who arc at once lazy and romantic – that it is much better to create than to inherit and to possess.

I am no fusser, am soon wearied by noise and glare and confusion, am as likely as the next man to seek a quiet corner for a smoke, but I declare to you that I would rather see this whole island turned inside out and upside down every ten years, with whole cities pulled down and rebuilt as if they came out of a child's box of bricks, than I would see these grand folks of ours sinking into apathy again, lulled by the murmurs of fools and rogues. Refuse with scorn the great dope-dreams of the economic emperors and their sorcerers and Hollywood sirens. Don't allow them to inject you with Glamour, Sport, Sensational News, and all the Deluxe nonsense, as if they were filling you with an anaesthetic.

Books are good - and they still offer the widest channel of communication for an honest thinker - but perhaps better still, for the modern man with his sense of strain and feeling of separation, are the great communal arts that compel him, in order to enjoy them at all, to become one of an audience, to laugh and weep and wonder in company with his fellow citizens. Remember that we are never so lonely, so detached, so separate, as we imagine ourselves to be, and cannot escape, even if we go and bleed to death trying to escape, being members of the great human family. And because of the vast powers that are now at our command, only a little way ahead of us is either universal construction or destruction.

Every day you will meet quiet capable men and women, who will argue calmly and acutely, proving that all is well, and there will be nothing about them at first to tell you that in fact they arc at heart merely haters of life and secret worshippers of death. But you, I know, love life, and have fought hard for it - so now, my dear Robert, come out and live it, and keep on fighting for it.

Listen – there goes the last high trembling note of the Last Post – and now, listen again, here comes the Reveille.

Yours ever, J.B.P.

P.S. Stop Press – the atomic bomb has arrived. So I repeat – There isn't much time.[253]

*Almost alone among his countrymen, Priestley had been to the Soviet Union in the aftermath of the war, visiting the country in 1945 and 1946 as a guest of Voks – the society for cultural relations with foreign countries. His work was very popular there –* An Inspector Calls *actually had its world premiere in Moscow – and his wartime novel* Blackout in Gretley *had been publicly read aloud in Leningrad during the siege 'as a way of helping the city through its long, dreadful nightmare'.[254]*

*Priestley was feted and given a freedom to travel that few other Westerners would have enjoyed and spent seven weeks touring the country by plane, car and train, and walking the streets and talking to people without any feeling that he was under surveillance.[255] He saw for himself the devastated state of the country; the Ukraine, Belorussia and the entire country west of Moscow had been laid waste by the retreating Nazis.*

*If American industry and manufacturing power had been one of the engines of Allied victory, Soviet manpower had been the other, bearing almost the full brunt of the Nazi war-machine. 190 German divisions were deployed on the Eastern Front, and thirty million people were killed there, including millions of civilians – 1.2 million died in the Siege of Leningrad alone – and property damage was estimated to total almost 700 billion roubles. Over 1,700 towns and cities and 70,000 villages were completely or partially destroyed, over 30,000 factories, 40,000 miles of railroad, 4,000 stations, 40,000 hospitals, 84,000 schools, and 43,000 public libraries were destroyed. The future East European Soviet 'satellites' were equally devastated.*

*After the war, the industry of the aggressors – Germany and Japan – was rebuilt with American funding on a lavish scale, but there was no Marshall Plan to aid the Soviet Union's recovery; it had to finance its own reconstruction. As Priestley clearly saw, it had neither the energy, nor the resources, nor the appetite for aggression against the West, but the threatening posture of the bellicose Churchill and the nuclear-armed US President Harry Truman, fuelled Soviet paranoia about Western intentions – they had not forgotten the Western military intervention in an attempt to overthrow the Bolshevik regime after the First World War – and, to Priestley's despair, an escalating arms race between East and West rapidly developed.*

*Priestley felt that all Britain's social gains from the Labour landslide in 1945, including the National Health Service, were threatened by massive military spending and the menace of nuclear arms, and on 16 September 1946, he confided some of his fears in a letter to a friend.*

I suspect that the atom bomb is on the American conscience, and that many American minds are busy projecting the guilty-feeling on to Russia, Britain, anything. The Russians are irritating – and I ought to know, having had plenty of dealings with them – but they want war about as much as I want ten rounds with Joe Louis. One wonders what the American Press would say if the Russians sent a large fleet to prowl just off Panama.

I sometimes wonder if half or more of the mischief isn't caused by Foreign Offices, foreign affairs experts and the Press. If Molotov and Bevin, two vain tired elderly men, can't get on, then we don't like the Russians, all the hundred and fifty million of them! It's lunacy.[256]

*Priestley's heart must have sunk at the 'Iron Curtain' rhetoric of that old warrior Churchill, who – just as after the First World War, when he was the most enthusiastic advocate of armed intervention against the Bolsheviks – had no sooner finished one war than he was eager for the next. Priestley was no admirer of Stalin, but he empathised with the Soviet dictator's subjects.*

His sympathies did not lie with the Soviet regime but with the Russian people, whom he found 'warm-hearted, impulsive and expansive,' uncorrupted by western commercialism, and eager for culture... Beneath the regime, beneath Marxism, he found 'an intense feeling of fraternity, a conviction that men are brothers needing each other's help'... In the end, Priestley's view of Russia parallels his view of Britain. It was from the people, not from their rulers, that the true character of a nation arose; and as in wartime Britain he warmed to the prospect of a nation finally pulling together, so he found in the instinctive collectivism of the Russian people some hope for the future of humankind; and valuing that unity, he wanted the wartime alliance to remain in place after the war was over.[257]

*The optimism with which Priestley had anticipated the post-war era was dented by the harsh reality that, freed from the threat of invasion, most Britons appeared willing to abandon the community cohesion of the war years and return to insular pursuits, self-interest and the 'opiates' of sport, entertainment, film and television.*

*As early as 1946 Priestley had detected a souring of the postwar mood. People had grown selfish and cynical. 'They are trying to take as much as they can and give as little as possible in return. They are cutting themselves off from the welfare of the community. They are losing all pride and interest in the job. They are not behaving like good citizens... They believe this to be a rotten world and they do not propose to do anything themselves to improve it.' To Priestley, the reasons were plain:*

*'For five years our people were made to feel that they were all engaged in one huge communal task, the defeat of the common enemy. The emotional drive was terrific. We all had parts in a national drama, played on a world stage. There, in the spotlight, was the super-villain, and here were we, so many heroes and heroines. And then suddenly the curtain came down.'*

*People had been told that a great national effort was now needed to restore things to normal. But what they should have been told was that 'the vast drama continues, with ourselves still the heroes and heroines of it.' So 'all the nuisances and little hardships of the journey are here, but not the sustaining vision of the destination'. The left had become so preoccupied with means that they had lost sight of the end: 'a new creative Britain, hard-working but also full of fun, liveliness, colour and intelligence'. 'They fail to understand that political and economic changes are themselves only so much machinery that will help to create a finer quality of living. And it is this quality of living that really matters'...*

*The war had created – or rather revived – a radical understanding of national character and identity, rooted in the people, and based on social cohesion and common purpose. Priestley saw this as an opportunity which must be seized: we had done great things, he told the readers of* Picture Post *just before VE Day, and "now we must live up to ourselves". From the outset, however, he suspected that the opportunity was being let slip. With the coming of the Cold War, the idealistic internationalism of the early 1940s was in retreat. The postwar boom of the 1950s accelerated the cultural process of Americanisation, while leaving intact the structures of power in British society. The global culture of 'Admass' seemed to overwhelm both the social ideals of 1945 and the sense of national identity which the war had created. By the late 1950s, Priestley complained, 'we no longer appeared to know who we were'... Throughout this period, though no longer at the centre of the historical stage as he had been in the early 1940s, he remained a notable public figure and a trenchant observer from the wings, feeling 'sometimes ... a depth of sadness, sometimes a new hope for England, the country I no longer much like yet still must love.'* [258]

*Despairing of the crass materialism of the post-war capitalist West, Priestley had coined the term 'Admass' to describe the 'whole system of an increasing productivity, plus inflation, plus a rising standard of material living, plus high-pressure advertising and salesmanship, plus mass communications, plus cultural democracy and the creation of the mass mind, the mass man.' But he was equally dismissive of the Soviet equivalent which he named 'Propmass, official propaganda taking the place of advertising, but with all the same aims and objects'.* [259]

*His pamphlet,* The Secret Dream, *had seen the wartime allies Britain, America and Russia, as the embodiment of the French Revolutionary ideals: liberty, equality and fraternity. The British preferred individual liberty above everything, though they showed little sign of knowing what to do with it; America was built on the principle of equality; Russia embodied fraternity. Learning from each other and drawing on each other's strengths, Priestley argued, they could 'create a broad highway for a world civilisation', but only if the Soviet Union was embraced as a partner in a better world, not shunned and demonised. He can have had little genuine hope that his message would be heeded. Modern man was now 'in the grip of huge political and social collectives.'*

It is an age of deepening inner despair and appalling catastrophes, an age when society says one thing and does something entirely different, when everybody talks about peace and prepares for more and worse wars... The stammering helplessness of the Churches during this age of war and more war and now, the final horror, a nuclear arms race, is proof that whatever they may do for this man or that woman, they are now among the institutions contained by our society, compelled to follow every lunatic course it takes. [260]

*Priestley had been carrying on an affair with Jacquetta Hawkes since the end of the war, and in 1953 they divorced their previous partners and married; they remained together for the rest of Priestley's life. She shared his views on nuclear weapons and the folly of Britain's huge investment in an 'independent deterrent' which was, at bottom, neither of those things.*

*In 1954 Priestley wrote an article lambasting the follies, falsehoods and surrealism of the nuclear arms race, in which an announcement by the Conservative Defence Minister, Duncan Sandys – 'We have taken a very bold step in deciding not to do the impossible. We have decided not to defend the whole country, but to defend only our bomber bases' – could be regarded as a sane defence policy. Priestley placed the Western and Eastern blocs in the dock together.*

That such societies should be piling up atom bombs should surprise nobody… Soviet propaganda and American advertisements often seem to speak with almost the same voice: the management is different but the enterprise is broadly the same.[261]

*Britain's first nuclear Test had taken place on 3 October 1952 and the first British hydrogen bomb was detonated on 15 May 1957 – the first of the 'Grapple' series of tests, at Kiritimati (Christmas Island), that continued until 19 June 1957. Priestley returned to the attack in November of that year, infuriated this time not by a Conservative Defence Minister, but a Labour Shadow Foreign Secretary, Aneurin 'Nye' Bevan. Labour's support for the H-bomb, re-emphasised by Bevan's Labour Party conference speech in 1957, stunned his left wing colleagues and supporters and, said Priestley 'seemed to many of us to slam the door in our faces'. His response was an article, 'Britain and the Bombs', published in the New Statesman on 2 November 1957. 'Before he began to write, Priestley had asked the magazine to supply him with all the arguments it could muster in favour of the bombs. He then sat down at his typewriter to demolish them.'[262]*

Two events of this autumn should compel us to reconsider the question of Britain and the nuclear bombs. The first of these events was Mr Aneurin Bevan's speech at the Labour Party conference, which seemed to many of us to slam a door in our faces. It was not dishonest but it was very much a party conference speech, and its use of terms like 'unilateral' and 'polarisation', lent it a suggestion of the 'Foreign Office spokesman'.

Delegates asked not to confuse 'an emotional spasm' with 'statesmanship' might have retorted that the statesmanship of the last ten years has produced little else but emotional spasms. And though it is true, as Mr Bevan argued, that independent action by this country to ban nuclear bombs, would involve our foreign minister in many difficulties, most of us would rather have a bewildered and overworked Foreign Office than a country about to be turned into a radioactive cemetery. Getting out of the water may be difficult but it is better than drowning.

The second event was the successful launching of the Soviet satellite, followed by an immediate outbreak of what may fairly be called 'satellitis', producing a rise in temperature and signs of delirium. In the poker game, where Britain still sits, nervously fingering a few remaining chips, like a Treasury official playing with two drunk oil millionaires, the stakes have been doubled again. Disarmament talks must now take place in an atmosphere properly belonging to boys' papers and science fiction, though already charged with far more hysterical competitiveness. If statesmanship is to see us through, it will have to break the familiar and dubious pattern of the last few years. Perhaps what we need now, before it is too late, is not statesmanship but lifemanship.

One 'ultimate weapon', the final deterrent, succeeds another. After the bombs, the intercontinental rockets; and after the rockets, according to the First Lord of the Admiralty, the guided-missile submarine, which will 'carry a guided missile with a nuclear warhead and appear off the coasts of any country in the world with a capability of penetrating to the centre of any continent'. The prospect now is not of countries without navies but of navies without countries. And we have arrived at an insane regress of ultimate weapons that are not ultimate.

But all this is to the good; and we cannot have too much of it, we are told, because no men in their right minds would let loose such powers of destruction. Here is the realistic view. Any criticism of it is presumed to be based on wild idealism. But surely it is the wildest idealism, at the furthest remove from a sober realism, to assume that men will always behave reasonably and in line with their best interests? Yet this is precisely what we are asked to believe, and to stake our all on it.

For that matter, why should it be assumed that the men who create and control such monstrous devices are in their right minds? They live in an unhealthy mental climate, an atmosphere dangerous to sanity. They are responsible to no large body of ordinary sensible men and women, who pay for these weapons without ever having ordered them, who have never been asked anywhere yet if they wanted them.

When and where have these preparations for nuclear warfare ever been put to the test of public opinion? We cannot even follow the example of the young man in the limerick and ask 'Who does what and with which and to whom?' The whole proceedings take place in the stifling secrecy of an expensive lunatic asylum. And as one ultimate weapon after another is added to the pile, the mental climate deteriorates, the atmosphere thickens, and the tension is such that soon something may snap.

The more elaborately involved and hair-triggered the machinery of destruction, the more likely it is that this machinery will be set in motion, if only by accident. Three glasses too many of vodka or bourbon-on-the-rocks, and the wrong button may be pushed. Combine this stockpiling of nuclear weapons with a crazy competitiveness, boastful confidence in public and a mounting fear in private, and what was unthinkable a few years ago now at the best only seems unlikely and very soon may seem inevitable. Then western impatience cries 'Let's get the damned thing over!' and eastern fatalism mutters 'If this has to be, then we must accept it'. And people in general are now in a worse position every year, further away from intervention; they have less and less freedom of action, they are deafened and blinded by propaganda and giant headlines; they are robbed of decision by fear or apathy.

It is possible, as some thinkers hold, that our civilisation is bent on self-destruction, hurriedly planning its own doomsday. This may explain, better than any wearisome recital of plot and counter-plot in terms of world power, the curious and sinister air of somnambulism there is about our major international affairs, the steady drift from bad to worse, the speeches that begin to sound meaningless, the conferences that achieve nothing, all the persons of great consequence who somehow seem like puppets.

We have all known people in whom was sown the fatal seed of self-destruction, people who would sit with us making sensible plans and then go off and quietly bring them to nothing, never really looking for anything but death. Our industrial civilisation, behaving in a similar fashion, may be under the same kind of spell, hell-bent on murdering itself. But it is possible that the spell can be broken. If it can, then it will only be by an immensely decisive gesture, a clear act of will. Instead, of endless bargaining for a little of this in exchange for a little of that, while all the time the bargainers are being hurried down a road that gets steeper and narrower, somebody will have to say 'I'm through with all this'.

In plain words: now that Britain has told the world she has the H-bomb, she should announce as early as possible that she has done with it, that she proposes to reject, in all circumstances, nuclear warfare. This is not pacifism. There is no suggestion here of abandoning the immediate defence of this island. Indeed, it might well be considerably strengthened, reducing the threat of actual invasion, which is the root fear in people's minds, a fear often artfully manipulated for purposes far removed from any defence of hearth and home. (This is of course the exact opposite of the views expressed at the Tory conference by Mr Sandys, who appears to believe that bigger and bigger bombs and rockets in more and more places, if necessary, thousands of miles away, will bring us peace and prosperity.) No, what should be abandoned is the idea of deterrence-by-threat-of-retaliation. There is no real security in it, no decency in it, no faith, hope, nor charity in it.

But let us take a look at our present policy entirely on its own low level. There is no standing still, no stalemates, in this idiot game; one, 'ultimate weapon' succeeds another. To stay in the race at all, except in an ignominious position, we risk bankruptcy, the disappearance of the Welfare State, a standard of living that might begin to make Communist propaganda sound more attractive than it does at present.

We could in fact be so busy, inspired by the indefatigable Mr Sandys, defending ourselves against Communism somewhere else, a long way off, that we could wake up one morning to hear it knocking on the back door. Indeed, this is Moscow's old heads-I-win-tails-you-lose-policy.

Here we might do well to consider western world strategy, first grandiloquently proclaimed by Sir Winston in those speeches he made in America just after the war. The Soviet Union was to be held in leash by nuclear power. We had the bomb and they hadn't. The race would be on but the West had a flying start. But Russia was not without physicists, and some German scientists and highly trained technicians had disappeared somewhere in eastern Europe.

For the immediate defence of West Germany, the atom bomb threat no doubt served its turn. But was this really sound long-term strategy? It created the unhealthy climate, the poisonous atmosphere of our present time. It set the Russians galloping in the nuclear race. It freed them from the immense logistic problems that must be solved if large armies are to be moved everywhere, and from some very tricky problems of morale that would soon appear once the Red Army was a long way from home. It encouraged the support of so-called people's and nationalistic and anti-colonial wars, not big enough to be settled by nuclear weapons. In spite of America's ring of advanced air bases, the race had only to be run a little longer to offer Russia at least an equally good set-up, and, in comparison with Britain alone, clearly an enormously better set-up.

We are like a man in a poker game who never dares cry 'I'll see you'. The Soviet Union came through the last war because it had vast spaces and a large population and a ruthless disregard of losses, human and material. It still has them. Matched against this overcrowded island with its intricate urban organisations, at the last dreadful pinch - and party dictators made to feel unsure of their power can pinch quicker than most democratic leaders - the other side possesses all the advantages. If there is one country that should never have gambled in this game it is Britain. Once the table stakes were being raised, the chips piling up, we were out, and though we may have been fooling ourselves, we have not been fooling anyone else.

This answers any gobbling cries about losing our national prestige. We have none, in terms of power. (The world has still respect and admiration for our culture, and we are busy reducing that respect and admiration by starving it. The cost of a few bombs might have made all the difference). We ended the war high in the world's regard. We could have taken over its moral leadership - spoken and acted for what remained of its conscience; but we chose to act otherwise with obvious and melancholy consequences both abroad, where in power politics we cut a shabby figure, and at home, where we shrug it all away or go to the theatre to applaud the latest jeers and sneers at Britannia.

It has been said we cannot send our ministers naked to the conference table. But the sight of a naked minister might bring to the conference some sense of our human situation. What we do is something much worse; we send them there half-dressed, half-smart, half-tough, half-apologetic, figures inviting contempt. That is why we are so happy and excited when we can send abroad a good-looking young woman in a pretty new dress to represent us, playing the only card we feel can take a trick – the Queen.

It is argued, as it was most vehemently by Mr Bevan at Brighton, that if we walked out of the nuclear arms race, then the world would be polarised between America and the Soviet Union, without any hope of mediation between the two fixed and bristling camps. 'Just consider for a moment,' he cried, 'all the little nations, running, one here and one there, one running to Russia, the other to the US, all once more clustering under the castle wall...'

But surely this is one of those 'realistic' arguments that are not based on reality. The idea of the Third Force was rejected by the very party Mr Bevan was addressing. The world was polarised when, without a single protest from all the noisy guardians of our national pride, parts of East Anglia ceased to be under our control and became an American air base. We cannot at one and the same time be both an independent power, bargaining on equal terms, and a minor ally or satellite. If there are little nations that do not run for shelter to the walls of the White House or the Kremlin because they are happy to accept Britain as their nuclear umbrella, we hear very little about them. If it is a question of brute power, this argument is unreal.

It is, not entirely stupid, however, because something more than brute power is involved. There is nothing unreal in the idea of a third nation, especially one like ours, old and experienced in world affairs, possessing great political traditions, to which other and smaller nations could look while the two new giants mutter and glare at each other. But it all depends what that nation is doing. If it is still in the nuclear gamble, without being able to control or put an end to the game, then that nation is useless to others, is frittering away its historical prestige, and the polarisation, which Mr Bevan sees as the worst result of our rejection of nuclear warfare, is already an accomplished fact.

And if it is, then we must ask ourselves what we can do to break this polarity, what course of action on our part might have some hope of changing the world situation. To continue doing what we are doing will not change it. Even during the few weeks since Mr Bevan made his speech, the world is becoming more rigidly and dangerously polarised than ever, just because the Russians have sent a metal football circling the globe.

What then can Britain do to de-polarise the world? The only move left that can mean anything is to go into reverse, decisively rejecting nuclear warfare. This gives the world something quite different from the polarised powers: there is now a country that can make H-bombs but decides against them. Had Britain taken this decision some years ago the world would be a safer and saner place than it is today. But it is still not too late. And such a move will have to be 'unilateral'; doomsday may arrive before the nuclear powers reach any agreement; and it is only a decisive 'unilateral' move that can achieve the moral force it needs to be effective.

It will be a hard decision to take because all habit is against it. Many persons of consequence and their entourages of experts would have to think fresh thoughts. They would have to risk losing friends and not influencing people. For example, so far as they involve nuclear warfare, our commitments to Nato, Seato and the rest, and our obligations to the Commonwealth, would have to be sharply adjusted. Anywhere from Brussels to Brisbane, reproaches would be hurled, backs would be turned. But what else have these countries to suggest, what way out, what hope for man? And if, to save our souls and this planet, we are willing to remain here and take certain risks, why should we falter because we might have complaints from Rhodesia and reproaches from Christchurch, N.Z.? And it might not be a bad idea if the Nato peoples armed themselves to defend themselves, taking their rifles to the ranges at the weekend, like the Swiss.

American official and service opinion would be dead against us, naturally. The unsinkable (but expendable) aircraft carrier would have gone. Certain Soviet bases allotted to British nuclear attack would have to be included among the targets of the American Strategic Air Service. And so on and so forth. But though service chiefs and their staffs go on examining and marking the maps and planning their logistics, having no alternative but resignation, they are as fantastic and unreal in their way as their political and diplomatic colleagues are in theirs.

What is fantastic and unreal is their assumption that they are traditionally occupied with their professional duties, attending in advance to the next war, Number Three in the world series. But what will happen – and one wrong report by a sleepy observer might start it off – will not be anything recognisable as a war, an affair of victories and defeats, something that one side can win or that you can call off when you have had enough. It will be universal catastrophe and apocalypse, the crack of doom into which Communism, western democracy, their way of life and our way of life, may disappear for ever. And it is not hard to believe that this is what some of our contemporaries really desire, that behind their photogenic smiles and cheerful patter nothing exists but the death wish.

We live in the thought of this prospect as if we existed in permanent smog. All sensible men and women – and this excludes most of those who are in the V.I.P.-Highest-Priority-Top-Secret-Top-People-Class, men now so conditioned by this atmosphere of power politics, intrigue, secrecy, insane invention, that they are more than half-barmy – have no illusions about what is happening to us, and know that those responsible have made two bad miscalculations. First, they have prostituted so much science in their preparations for war that they have completely changed the character of what they are doing, without any equivalent change in the policies of and relations between states. Foreign affairs, still conducted as if the mobilisation of a few divisions might settle something, are now backed with push-button arrangements to let loose earthquakes and pestilences and pronounce the death sentences of continents. This leaves us all in a worse dilemma than the sorcerer's apprentice.

The second miscalculation assumed that if the odds were only multiplied fast enough, your side would break through, because the other side would break down. And because this has not happened, a third illusion is being welcomed, namely, that now, with everything piling up, poker chips flung on the table by the handful, the tension obviously increasing, now at last we are arriving at an acknowledged drawn game, a not-too-stale stalemate, a cosy old balance of power. This could well be the last of our illusions.

The risk of our rejecting nuclear warfare, totally and in all circumstances, is quite clear, all too easy to understand. We lose such bargaining power as we now possess. We have no deterrent to a nuclear threat. We deliberately exchange 'security' for insecurity. (And the fact that some such exchange is recommended by the major religions, in their earlier and non-establishment phases, need not detain us here.) But the risk is clear and the arguments against running it quite irrefutable, only if we refuse, as from the first, too many of us here have refused, to take anything but short-term conventional views, only if we will not follow any thought to its conclusion. Our 'hard-headed realism' is neither hard-headed nor realistic just because it insists on our behaving in a new world as if we were still living in an old world, the one that has been replaced.

Britain runs the greatest risk by just mumbling and muddling along, never speaking out, avoiding any decisive creative act. For a world in which our deliberate 'insecurity' would prove to be our undoing is not a world in which real security could be found. As the game gets faster, the competition keener, the unthinkable will turn into the inevitable, the weapons will take command, and the deterrents will not deter.

Our bargaining power is slight; the force of our example might be great. The catastrophic antics of our time have behind them men hag-ridden by fear, which explains the neurotic irrationality of it all, the crazy disproportionality between means and ends. If we openly challenge this fear then we might break the wicked spell that all but a few uncertified lunatics desperately wish to see broken, we could begin to restore the world to sanity and lift this nation from its recent ignominy to its former grandeur. Alone we defied Hitler and alone we can defy this nuclear madness into which the spirit of Hitler seems to have passed, to poison the world. There may be other chain-reactions besides those leading to destruction; and we might start one,

The British of these times, so frequently hiding their decent, kind faces behind masks of sullen apathy or sour, cheap cynicism, often seem to be waiting for something better than party squabbles and appeals to their narrowest self-interest, something great and noble in its intention that would make them feel good again. And this might well be a declaration to the world that after a certain date, one power able to engage in nuclear warfare will reject the evil thing for ever.[263]

*Priestley's article articulated the thoughts of many of his fellow-countrymen, and the editor of the* New Statesman, *Kingsley Martin, was deluged with letters of support for Priestley's views. Martin called a meeting at his flat, with Jack and Jacquetta Priestley joined by a small group of 'eminent supporters' including George Kennan, who had just delivered the 1957 Reith Lecture: 'Russia, the Atom and the West', in which he had queried the whole basis of a nuclear strategy.[264]*

*They agreed to launch a national campaign and Martin told them that an existing small anti-nuclear group – the National Campaign against Nuclear Weapons Tests – was willing to 'sink its identity in a larger movement, and would hand over its bank balance, its new office off Fleet Street and its February booking of the Central Hall, Westminster.'265*

*Preliminary meetings of 'the great and the good' were held at the official home of a Canon of St Paul's, John Collins, and the new organisation – The Campaign for Nuclear Disarmament – was formed. The philosopher, Lord Bertrand Russell, became its first president, with Priestley as vice-*

*president.*

*CND was launched at a public meeting at Central Hall, Westminster on 17 February 1958; the main hall was packed as were five overflow halls. Priestley, Michael Foot and AJP Taylor were among the keynote speakers at an event that was almost completely ignored by the national press.*

*Priestley's wife, Jacquetta Hawkes, also formed a women's CND group, joined the executive committee of CND and took an active part in the first Aldermaston march over the Easter Weekend, from 4-7 April 1958. Her husband, perhaps feeling that he had marched enough in his army service to last him a lifetime, did not join the marches, but continued to campaign for CND in his writings and in speeches at rallies all over the country. He also drew on his contacts in theatre, film and television, to organise a fund-raising event at the Royal Festival Hall, under the title Stars In Your Eyes. He also wrote a play about a nuclear accident,* Doomsday for Dyson, *which was screened on ITV. However, Priestley and a number of other CND founders resigned from the movement in the early 1960s over the issue of 'Non-Violent Direct Action' adopted by CND's 'Committee of 100'.*

*Priestley's days of political activism were largely over, though he maintained a flow of comment from the sidelines, and his literary output continued well into his old age.     Throughout his life J.B Priestley had argued and campaigned for 'a better England in a nobler world'. At times he despaired of the state of modern Western society and wrote a devastating critique in 1972, that, like so much of his work, was well ahead of its time.*

We are now living in a society that appears – outside its propaganda and advertising – to dislike itself just as much as I dislike it. We are houseguests of the Sorcerer's Apprentice, who has let loose what he can't begin to control. What was not quite so bad yesterday will be much worse tomorrow. The past (we assume) has gone. The present is dubious and mainly unrewarding. As for the future – well, I am now an old hand at this and could be eloquent and fairly terrifying on the nightmare agenda of the world population, global pollution, vanishing natural resources, radioactive garbage, nuclear doomsday or, failing that, half-starved billions staring at endless vistas of concrete and cement – I could, but why should I? ...

Even now we have allowed ourselves to build capital cities so monstrously overgrown they are no longer manageable and civilised, wrecking human dignity and decency. Men will now plot, lie, cheat, work like demons, to buy what people used to have for nothing: quiet and a little privacy. The old are suspicious of the young; the young despise the old; and all the persons in between, at any age from thirty to sixty, are mostly busy doing something they don't particularly want to do while wondering if their life has any meaning. The happiest faces are seen in the advertiser's dreamland, inhabited by radiant beings who have just bought something.

In the West we are under the spell of Admass. (I coined this term to describe a system, not the victims of it.) We are supposed to be Consumers, and not much else; surely the lowest view mankind has ever taken of itself. We are televised and advertised out of our senses. We exist among images, not realities. And hardly anybody seems to notice that quality is disappearing, chiefly because so many small firms, which took a pride in what they were making and selling, have been taken over by large firms, which take pride only in their dividends.

While money is more and more important, what it buys is steadily getting worse. The 'Good Life' is mostly a swindle; it should be given a bouquet – or better, a wreath – of plastic flowers. In our society everybody envies the very rich – except the people who have met them. Probably for nine-tenths of our younger people their Jerusalem or Mecca, Avalon or Garden of Hesperides, is Las Vegas, one of the stupidest, ugliest, nastiest cities on earth. We have created a society whose representative figures are politicians sold like soap flakes, and men who ask questions on television, and singers who have no voices but only a lot of hair, sweat and electronic equipment, and photographers and models. We are the supreme clever-silly people of man's history.[266]

*Yet such a bleak vision was alien to Priestley, who retained his optimism, his belief in the innate qualities of his fellow Britons, and his hope for a brighter future to the end. Recognised as one of the greatest British writers of the century, he was granted the Freedom of the City of Bradford in 1973 and awarded the Order of Merit in 1977. He died on 14 August 1984, a month before his ninetieth birthday. The Times' obituary remarked that he wrote 'prose of such sinew and liveliness that it is possible to say of him that he never wrote a dull sentence'.[267] Towards the end of his life, he looked back on the Second World War as not only one of Britain's darkest hours but paradoxically as the time when:*

The British were absolutely at their best in the Second World War. They were never as good, certainly in my lifetime before it, and I'm sorry to say I think never been quite as good after it..[268]

*Yet, even in his old age, JB Priestley's optimism and belief in is fellow men still shone through.*

Though growing old, gouty and grumpy, weary of power-mania and propaganda and all their imbecilities, I have not yet abandoned the hope I felt and tried to celebrate in wartime..[269]

# Acknowledgements

Many individuals and organisations have given their time and knowledge during the preparation of this book. They include: John Baxendale; Martin Bell; Alison Cullingford and John Brooker, custodians of the JB Priestley Collection, Special Collections at the JB Priestley Library, University of Bradford; Rick Watson at the Harry Ransom Humanities Research Center, The University of Texas at Austin; Julie Green at the David Hockney Studio; Kathryn Jones at Cartwright Hall Museum & Art Gallery, Bradford; David Wilson; Barry Cox, Patricia Lennon, David Joy, David Burrill, and the other members of the team at Great Northern Books; and above all the Trustees of the Estate of JB Priestley, and to Nicholas Hawkes and Tom Priestley, who shared their memories of the great man and their intimate knowledge of his work. No one has researched the background to the abrupt termination of JB Priestley's Postscripts more thoroughly than Nicholas Hawkes and I'm grateful to him for his advice and insights, and Tom Priestley has been the wellspring of this project, an unflagging source of inspiration, ideas and encouragement. To all of them, and to the many others who have contributed to this book, my grateful thanks.

# Bibliography

## *Newspaper and Magazine Articles*

Bainton, Roy, 'Battle of the Airwaves', in Saga, February 2000, 64

Beckles, Gordon, 'The BBC Postscripts', in Strand Magazine, June 1941, 100

Elstein, D, Transcript of Thames Television interview with JB Priestley, Imperial War Museum, Sound Archive, 2805/02

Nicholas, Sian H, '"Sly Demagogues" and Wartime Radio: JB Priestley and the BBC', in Twentieth Century British History, vol. 6, No 3, 1995

Priestley, JB, 'As I See Things' The Star, 14 December 1936

'Behind the Scenes of My Broadcasts', in London Calling, 109, 9 November 1941

'Blackshirts', in, The Sunday Chronicle 22 October 1933

'Britain and the Nuclear Bombs', in New Statesman, 2 November 1957

'Do Not Underrate Nazis' Propaganda', in News Chronicle, 16 October 1939

'I'll Tell You Everything: What the World Needs Now', in The Listener, 10 May 1933

'Is Europe Finished?', in News Chronicle, 17 April 1939

'The Lost Generation: An Armistice Day Article', Friends Peace Committee 1 November 1932

'Lost Germany', in News Chronicle 24 April 1939

'Round the Hearth', in The Bradford Pioneer, 11 April 1913

'Thunder on the Left', in News Chronicle, 14 January 1939

'The Truth about the Postscripts, in News Chronicle, 6 November 1940

'We Are All Propagandists But...', in News Chronicle, 24 July 1939

'We Are Being Held to Ransom', in News Chronicle 10 July 1939

'What is Freedom?' in News Chronicle 5 June 1939

'Where England Stands', in Harper's Monthly Magazine, 178,

December 1938-January 1939

'You and Me and War', in The Star, 20 March 1935

Priestley, Tom, 'JB Priestley and the Campaign for Nuclear Disarmament', in City of Peace: Bradford's Story, Bradford Libraries, Bradford, Yorks, 1997

Reid, Robert W, 'When Priestley Talks to America', in Radio Times, 18 October 1940

## Books

Baxendale, John, Priestley's England, Manchester University Press, 2007

Braine, John, JB Priestley, Weidenfeld & Nicolson, 1979

Brome, Vincent, JB Priestley, Hamish Hamilton, 1988

Calder, Angus, The Myth of the Blitz, Cape, 1991

Collins, Diana, Time and the Priestleys, Sutton, Stroud, Glos, 1994

Cook, Judith, JB Priestley, Bloomsbury, 1997

Cooper, Susan, J.B. Priestley, Portrait of an Author, Heinemann, 1970

Cullingford, Alison, JB Priestley's Service in World War I, in Bradford in the Great War, History Press, 2007

Day, Alan, JB Priestley: An Annotated Bibliography, Garland, New York, 1980

Day, Alan, JB Priestley: An Annotated Bibliography - A Supplement, Ian Hotchkins and Co, Slad, Gloucestershire, 2001

Fyfe, Hamilton, Britain's War-Time Revolution, 1944

Hawkes, Nicholas, The Story of JB Priestley's Postscripts, JB Priestley Society, 2006

Herbert, AP, APH, His Life and Times, 1970

Holdsworth, Peter, The Rebel Tyke: Bradford and J. B. Priestley, Bradford Libraries, 1994

Hughes, David, JB Priestley, 1958

McLaine, Ian, Ministry of Morale, George Allen, 1979

Priestley, J. B.,

The Balconinny and Other Essays, 1929

Benighted, 1927

Bright Day, 1946

British Women Go To War, 1943

A Chapman of Rhymes, 1918

The Dark Hours, in Apes and Angels, 1928

Daylight on Saturday, 1943

Doomsday for Dyson, 1958

English Journey, 1934

Journey Down a Rainbow, (co-written with Jacquetta Hawkes), Heinemann, 1955

Let The People Sing, 1939

Letter to a Returning Serviceman, 1945

Literature and Western Man, Heinemann, 1960

The Long Mirror, 1940

Lost Empires, Heinemann, 1965

Margin Released, Heinemann, 1962

Out of the People, 1941

Over the Long High Wall, Heinemann, 1972

Postscripts, 1940

Postscripts, Macmillan, Toronto, 1941

The Priestley Companion, 1951

Rain upon Godshill: A Further Chapter of Autobiography, 1939

The Secret Dream, 1946

The Town Major of Miraucourt, 1929

'Underground', in The Carfitt Crisis, and Two Other Stories, Heinemann, 1975

Sevareid, Eric, All England Listened, Chilmark Press, 1967

# Footnotes

1   'Round the Hearth', in The Bradford 'Pioneer, 11 April 1913
2   JB Priestley, Margin Released, 76 -77
3   Margin Released, 75-76
4   Margin Released, 77
5   Postscript, Sunday 4 August 1940
6   Diana Collins, Time and the Priestleys, 41
7   Lost Empires, 294-295
8   Margin Released, 77-79
9   Lost Empires, 294-295
10  'Swan Arcadian' – Priestley's previous employment was
    as a clerk in Bradford's Swan Arcade
11  JB Priestley, Margin Released, 75-81
12  quoted in Peter Holdsworth, The Rebel Tyke, 64
13  Margin Released, 75-81
14  Lost Empires, 296
15  Letter, Frensham Camp, 23 September 1914
16  Letter, Frensham Camp, 2 October 1914
17  'back o't' mill' – millworkers' terraced housing built
    in the shadow of the mill
18  Margin Released, 88-89
19  Letter, Frensham Camp, 29 October 1914
20  Margin Released, 75
21  Letter, Frensham Camp, 20 October 1914
22  Margin Released, 89
23  Margin Released, 89
24  Letter, Frensham Camp, 14 October 1914
25  Margin Released, 89-90
26  Lost Empires, 296
27  Letter, Frensham Camp, 14 October 1914
28  Margin Released, 90
29  Letter, Frensham Camp, 2 November 1914
30  Letter, Frensham Camp, 11 November 1914

31   Letter, Frensham Camp, 15 November 1914
32   Postcard, Frensham Camp, 23 November 1914
33   Letter, Frensham Camp, 27 November 1914
34   Margin Released, 90
35   Letter, Camberley, 7 December 1914
36   Letter, undated (January or early February 1915)
37   Letter, Aldershot, 22 February 1915
38   Margin Released, 90
39   Letter, Folkestone, 1 March 1915
40   Margin Released, 91
41   Letter, Folkestone, 1 March 1915
42   Margin Released, 91
43   Letter, Folkestone, 1 March 1915
45   Margin Released, 92
46   Margin Released, 92
47   Letter, Folkestone, postmarked 14 May,
     but almost certainly March 1915
48   Letter, Folkestone, 10 April 1915
49   Margin Released, 92-93
50   Letter, Folkestone, 10 April 1915
51   Letter, Folkestone, 10 April 1915
52   Letter, Maidstone, 25 April 1915
53   Letter, Folkestone, 1 April 1915
54   Letter, Maidstone, 25 April 1915
55   Margin Released, 94
56   Letter, Maidstone, 25 April 1915
57   Margin Released, 94-95
58   Letter, Bramshott Camp, 25 May 1915
59   Margin Released, 96
60   Margin Released, 96
61   Letter, Bramshott Camp, 20 June 1915
62   Letter, Bramshott Camp, 3 July 1915
63   Letter, Bramshott Camp, 2 August 1915
64   Letter, Bramshott Camp, 14 August 1915
65   Margin Released, 96

66 Letter from Jonathan Priestley, 1 September 1915
67 Letter, Somewhere in France, 8 September 1915
68 Letter, Somewhere in France, undated but written between 21 and 28 August
69 Letter, Somewhere in France, 8 September 1915
70 Margin Released, 97
71 Letter, Somewhere in France, postmarked Sp 18 1915
72 Margin Released, 98-99
73 Letter, Somewhere in France, Monday 27/9/15
74 Letter, postmarked 19 Oct 15
75 Letter, The Usual Place, Oct 26th
76 Margin Released, 99
77 Letter, postmarked 8 Nov 15
78 Margin Released, 101
79 Diana Collins, Time and the Priestleys, 45
80 Letter, postmarked 4 Dec 15 passed by Censor
81 Letter, postmarked 12 Dec 15
82 Letter, postmarked 17 Dec 15
83 Letter, In the trenches 1/1/16
84 Margin Released, 99-100
85 Margin Released, 102
86 Letter, 22/1/15
87 Margin Released, 100
88 Letter, 22/1/15
89 Margin Released, 100
90 Letter, date uncertain
91 Margin Released, 102-103
92 Letter, date uncertain
93 Margin Released, 103
94 Letter, dated 13/3/15 but must have been 1916
95 Margin Released, 103-104
96 Letter, dated 13/3/15 but must have been 1916
97 Margin Released, 104
98 Letter, dated 13/3/15 but must have been 1916
99 Margin Released, 105-106

100 Letter, 29 March 1916
101 Letter, 16 April 1916
102 postmarked Mar 4 16, but almost certainly May
103 Letter, postmarked Mar 4 16, but almost certainly May
104 Letter, postmarked 20 May 1916
105 Letter, postmarked 1 Ju 16
106 Margin Released, 107
107 Underground, 87-95
108 Margin Released, 107-109
109 Margin Released, 111
110 Margin Released, 112-113
111 Margin Released, 114-116
112 Margin Released, 115-117
113 Margin Released, 118-121
114 Margin Released, 121-123
115 The Town Major of Miraucourt, 353-354
116 Margin Released, 123
117 The Town Major of Miraucourt, 354-355
118 Margin Released, 124
119 The Town Major of Miraucourt, 355
120 Margin Released, 124-125
121 The Town Major of Miraucourt, 355-366
122 Margin Released, 125-137
123 Margin Released, 85-86
124 A Chapman of Rhymes, 42-44
125 Bright Day, 184
126 Margin Released, 134-136
127 Benighted, 57
128 Benighted, 125
129 'The Dark Hours', in Apes and Angels, 67-73
130 English Journey, 158-166
131 '"I'll Tell You Everything": What the World Needs Now',
     The Listener, 10 May 1933
132 Letter to Edward Davison, 27 June 1932
133 'The Lost Generation: An Armistice Day Article',

Friends Peace Committee 1 November 1932

134 'You and Me and War', The Star, 20 March 1935

135 Diana Collins, Time and the Priestleys, 37

136 Margin Released, 227

137 Margin Released, 68

138 'Blackshirts', The Sunday Chronicle, 22 October 1933

139 'Lost Germany', News Chronicle, 24 April 1939

140 'Is Europe Finished?", News Chronicle, 17 April 1939

141 'Lost Germany', News Chronicle, 24 April 1939

142 'As I See Things', The Star, 14 December 1936

143 'Thunder on the Left', News Chronicle, 14 January 1939

144 'What is Freedom?', News Chronicle, 5 June 1939

145 Letter to Edward Davison, 17 March 1936

146 Letter to Edward Davison, 31 December 1936

147 Letter to Edward Davison, 1 February 1937

148 Letter to Edward Davison, 3 November 1937

149 Letter to Edward Davison, 10 February 1938

150 Letter to Edward Davison, 17 March 1938

151 Letter to Edward Davison, 4 December 1938

152 Letter to Edward Davison, 3 July 1939

153 Letter to Edward Davison, 2 February 1939

154 'Is Europe Finished?', News Chronicle, 17 April 1939

155 Rain Upon Godshill, 222-225, 228-229, 236-237

156 'We Are All Propogandists But…', in News Chronicle, 24 July 1939

157 Letter to Edward Davison, 2 February 1939

158 'Where England Stands', Harper's Monthly Magazine, 178, December 1938-January 1939, 580-587

159 'We Are Being Held to Ransom', News Chronicle, 10 July 1939

160 Rain Upon Godshill, 304-306

161 Preface to All England Listened

162 Letter to Edward Davison, 11 October 1939

163 Letter to Edward Davison, 27 January 1940

164 'Do Not Underrate Nazis' Propaganda', in News Chronicle, 16 October 1939

165  Nicholas Hawkes' The Story of JB Priestley's Postscripts
     is an indispensable source on the background to the
     Postscripts and their abrupt termination

166  Letter to Edward Davison, 9 April 1940

167  Angus Calder, The Myth of the Blitz, 197

168  quoted in Roy Bainton, 'Battle of the Airwaves, in Saga,
     February 2000, 64

169  Susan Cooper, JB Priestley: Portrait of an Author, 7

170  Angus Calder, The Myth of the Blitz, 197

171  D Elstein, Thames Television interview with JB Priestley, 1

172  BBC Broadcast, Wednesday 5 June 1940

173  Lilian Duff, in Eric Sevareid, All England Listened, xv - xvi

174  Gordon Beckles, 'The BBC Postscripts', in
     Strand Magazine, June 1941, 100

175  JB Priestley, in Eric Sevareid, All England Listened, xiv

176  Eric Sevareid, All England Listened,
     Chilmark Press, 1967, Introduction, vi

177  Postscript, Sunday 9 June 1940

178  Postscript, Sunday 16 June 1940

179  Postscript, Sunday 23 June 1940

180  Postscript, Sunday 30 June 1940

181  Letter from Jane Priestley to Edward Davison, 30 June 1940

182  D Elstein, Transcript of Thames Television interview
     with JB Priestley, 2

183  Postscript, Sunday 7 July 1940

184  Gordon Beckles, 'The BBC Postscripts', in
     Strand Magazine, June 1941, 98

185  Roy Bainton, 'Battle of the Airwaves, in Saga, February 2000, 65

186  JB Priestley, in Eric Sevareid, All England Listened, xxiv

187  Postscript, Sunday 14 July 1940

188  Susan Cooper, JB Priestley: Portrait of an Author, 10

189  John Baxendale, Priestley's England, 141-142, 147-148

190  Postscript, Sunday 21 July 1940

191  Winston Churchill, quoted in Nicholas Hawkes, The Story
     of JB Priestley's Postscripts, 13

192 Interview with Tom Priestley, 16 April 2008

193 Postscript, Sunday 28 July 1940

194 Postscript, Sunday 4 August 1940

195 Angus Calder, The Myth of the Blitz, 196

196 Nicholas Hawkes, The Story of JB Priestley's Postscripts, 15

197 quoted in Angus Calder, The Myth of the Blitz, 197

198 Hamilton Fyfe, Britain's War-Time Revolution,
    entry for 25 August 1940

199 JB Priestley, in Eric Sevareid, All England Listened, xvii

200 Nicholas Hawkes, The Story of JB Priestley's Postscripts, 17

201 Nicholas Hawkes, The Story of JB Priestley's Postscripts, 15

202 Postscript, Sunday 1 September 1940

203 Letter from Jane Priestley, 11 September 1940

204 Margin Released, 213-218

205 Nicholas Hawkes, The Story of JB Priestley's Postscripts, 16

206 Postscript, Sunday 8 September 1940

207 Postscript, Sunday 15 September 1940

208 Postscript, Sunday 22 September 1940

209 D Elstein, Transcript of Thames Television interview
    with JB Priestley, 4

210 British Women Go To War, 9-13

211 Robert W Reid, 'When Priestley Talks to America',
    in Radio Times, 18 October 1940

212 Postscript, Sunday 29 September 1940

213 Postscript, Sunday 6 October 1940

214 quoted in Nicholas Hawkes, The Story of
    JB Priestley's Postscripts, 16

215 Nicholas Hawkes, The Story of JB Priestley's Postscripts, 16

216 Postscript, Sunday 20 October 1940

217 quoted in Angus Calder, The Myth of the Blitz, 197

218 Postscripts, Preface, v-viii

219 Margin Released, 216

220 Margin Released, 213-214

221 Margin Released, 214

222 JB Priestley, in Eric Sevareid, All England Listened, xviii-xxi

223  Postscript, Sunday 26 January 1941
224  Winston Churchill quoted in Nicholas Hawkes,
     The Story of JB Priestley's Postscripts, 14, 23
225  Nicholas Hawkes, The Story of JB Priestley's Postscripts, 23
226  Postscript, Sunday 2 February 1941
227  Postscript, Sunday 16 February 1941
228  Postscript, Sunday 23 February 1941
229  Postscript, Sunday 2 March 1941
230  Picture Post, quoted in Nicholas Hawkes,
     The Story of JB Priestley's Postscripts, 25
231  Nicholas Hawkes, The Story of JB Priestley's Postscripts, 26
232  Nicholas Hawkes, The Story of JB Priestley's Postscripts, 25
233  Nicholas Hawkes, The Story of JB Priestley's Postscripts, 26-28
234  Postscript, Sunday 9 March 1941
235  Postscript, Sunday 16 March 1941
236  Postscript, Sunday 23 March 1941
237  Margin Released, 213-218
238  Nicholas Hawkes, The Story of JB Priestley's Postscripts, 29-30
239  Nicholas Hawkes, The Story of JB Priestley's Postscripts, 30
240  JB Priestley, in Eric Sevareid, All England Listened, xviii-xxi
241  Maconachie to Controller (Admin) 9 April 1941,
     quoted in Nicholas Hawkes, The Story of
     JB Priestley's Postscripts, 33
242  APH, His Life and Times, 17
243  JB Priestley, in Eric Sevareid, All England Listened, xxi
244  Barnes to Maconachie, 6 June 1941 R51/383,
     BBC WAC, cited in Sian Nicholas, 'Sly Demagogues
     and Wartime Radio', 263
245  Sian Nicholas, 'Sly Demagogues and Wartime Radio', 263
246  Daylight on Saturday, 199
247  Daylight on Saturday, 249
248  quoted in Time Magazine,, 21 April 1941
249  quoted in Diana Collins, Time and the Priestleys, 94
250  Out of the People, 86-87
251  John Baxendale, Priestley's England, 147-148, 161

252 Out of the People, 66-67

253 Letter to a Returning Serviceman, 3-32

254 Susan Coper, JB Priestley: Portrait of an Author, 163

255 Diana Collins, Time and the Priestleys, 98

256 Letter to Edward Davison, 16 September 1946

257 John Baxendale, Priestley's England, 175-176

258 John Baxendale, Priestley's England, 167-168, 170

259 JB Priestley and Jacquetta Hawkes,
    Journey Down a Rainbow, 51-52

260 Literature and Western Man, 443-446

261 John Baxendale, Priestley's England, 180-181

262 Diana Collins, Time and the Priestleys, 12

263 'Britain and Nuclear Bombs', in New Statesman,
    2 November 1957

264 Diana Collins, Time and the Priestleys, 14

265 Diana Collins, Time and the Priestleys, 14

266 Over the Long High Wall

267 The Times, 16 August 1984

268 D Elstein, Transcript of Thames Television interview with
    JB Priestley, 9

269 JB Priestley, in Eric Sevareid, All England Listened, xxv